THE
EVERYTHING®
ESSENTIAL RUSSIAN BOOK

Dear Reader,

With the purchase of *The Everything® Essential Russian Book*, you are beginning an exciting journey into the Russian language and culture. The beauty of this book is that it doesn't separate one from the other, but, instead, shows the strong connection between the two. By following the readings and doing the exercises in this book, you will gain important insights into the workings of the Russian language, its writing system, grammar, pronunciation, and vocabulary, as well as begin to understand the culture's values and traditions. This book can be useful both for complete novices and those who have had some Russian lessons, but need a refresher.

I hope that your experience with this book will be productive, meaningful, but, most of all, fun. As you go through the chapters, remember to practice five language skills: speaking, listening, reading, writing, and culture. If there is no one else to practice with, make sure that you practice speaking Russian by speaking to yourself and by reading out loud in Russian. Allow yourself the freedom to experiment with various linguistic terms and to compare them to the ones from your mother tongue. But above all, keep it interesting and apply your newly developed language skills to as many contexts as possible: for example, watch a Russian movie with and without subtitles; experiment with reading headlines of a newspaper, then use an online translator to figure out what remains unclear; translate the titles of Russian novels, poems, or songs; go food shopping to a local Russian food store; or get online recipes for Russian dishes and make them in your own kitchen.

As you continue learning, be kind to yourself and celebrate your victories, both small and large, noticing the progress that you are making. Don't feel disappointed if you don't get a particular rule right away or if you make a mistake in an exercise: It is a natural part of the language learning process. Stay focused, motivated, and you will persevere. I commend you for your interest in the Russian language and culture and w............................и!

Julia

Welcome to the EVERYTHING Series!

These handy, accessible books give you all you need to tackle a difficult project, gain a new hobby, or even brush up on something you learned back in school but have since forgotten. You can choose to read from cover to cover or just pick out information from our four useful boxes.

 Alerts

Urgent warnings

 Facts

Important snippets of information

 **Essentials**

Quick handy tips

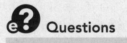 **Questions**

Answers to common questions

When you're done reading, you can finally say you know **EVERYTHING®**!

PUBLISHER Karen Cooper

MANAGING EDITOR, EVERYTHING® SERIES Lisa Laing

COPY CHIEF Casey Ebert

ASSISTANT PRODUCTION EDITOR Alex Guarco

ACQUISITIONS EDITOR Brett Palana-Shanahan

SENIOR DEVELOPMENT EDITOR Brett Palana-Shanahan

EVERYTHING® SERIES COVER DESIGNER Erin Alexander

Visit the entire Everything® series at *www.everything.com*

THE
EVERYTHING®
ESSENTIAL
RUSSIAN BOOK

All you need to learn Russian in no time

Julia Stakhnevich, PhD

Adams Media
New York   London   Toronto   Sydney   New Delhi

To Koozya, Bob, and Sam: I love you guys!

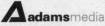

Adams Media
An Imprint of Simon & Schuster, Inc.
57 Littlefield Street
Avon, Massachusetts 02322

For information about special discounts for bulk purchases, please contact Simon & Schuster Special Sales at 1-866-506-1949 or business@simonandschuster.com.

The Simon & Schuster Speakers Bureau can bring authors to your live event. For more information or to book an event contact the Simon & Schuster Speakers Bureau at 1-866-248-3049 or visit our website at www.simonspeakers.com.

Manufactured in the United States of America

10   2020

Library of Congress Cataloging-in-Publication Data has been applied for.

ISBN 978-1-4405-8082-6
ISBN 978-1-4405-8083-3 (ebook)

Contents

Chapter 10: Happy Birthday in Russian 139

Chapter 11: Verbal Aspect and Verbs of Motion 153

Chapter 12: Daily Life and Impersonal Constructions 173

Chapter 13: Reflexive Verbs and the Instrumental Case . . 187

Introduction

When you learn a new language, you learn its pronunciation, vocabulary, and grammar. At the same time, you become more knowledgeable about the people who speak this language, about their values, traditions, and lifestyles. You gain a deeper appreciation for their cuisine, literature, music, and fine arts. You begin to understand preferred communication styles, family dynamics, and culturally acceptable ways of dealing with everyday problems. Moreover, you become more aware of the specifics of your own cultural norms and linguistic behavior. In this sense, language learning is not about rote memorization of conjugation patterns and declensions. It is about discovering new ways of looking at the world by shifting the way you think and using a different linguistic lens.

With this in mind, the goal of this book is to offer English-speaking readers an introduction to the Russian language and its culture. Learning Russian will open a door to the worldview of more than 250 million people who speak Russian as their mother tongue. The majority of them live in Russia, but there are large communities of Russian speakers in other European countries and in the United States, Canada, and Israel. Regardless of where they live, what unites them is their cultural identity, which is firmly rooted in the language and an amazing literary and artistic legacy.

As you learn Russian, you will develop an understanding of the important cultural reference points that guide Russians in their everyday lives, points that are critical for successful cross-cultural interactions and key for the effective interpretation of Russian literature, history, politics, and art. Because of the intimate and strong connection between culture and language, there is no adequate substitution to language study for anyone who is genuinely interested in learning about Russia and its people. Yes, you can read someone else's opinion in English about what it is that makes Russians Russian, but the only way to form your own opinion is to become familiar with the language. Language study allows you to dismiss secondary interpretations and go directly to the source of a culture: its language.

No matter what specific motivations you have for studying Russian, be it family roots, a desire to travel to Russia and communicate with the locals, or an interest in Russian literature, history, music, film, politics, and/or cuisine, you will be proud of your accomplishments. As a language learner you will uncover the expressive nature of the Russian language, become familiar with its creativity, and learn about the differences and similarities between the Russian and English sound systems and grammars. Last but not least, prior teaching experience shows that learning how to read and write in the Cyrillic alphabet, though a challenge at first, will eventually give you a palpable sense of achievement derived from the ability to read any and all texts in Russian.

The Everything® Essential Russian Book can serve as a one-stop study resource for the acquisition of basic skills in speaking, reading, and writing or as a steppingstone for further study. You can also use it as a handy travel guidebook as you prepare for your trip to Russia or as reference material for a language course. No matter how you use it, remember that language learning is about gaining direct access to a new culture, new ways of seeing the world, new ways of being yourself. Be brave, be open, be consistent, be creative! But most of all, enjoy it! **До**брого пут**и**!

CHAPTER 1

The Cyrillic Alphabet

Learning Russian involves learning to read the Cyrillic alphabet. You might think this would make learning the language more challenging, but it doesn't have to. In fact, you are already familiar with some of the letters and their pronunciations. In this chapter, you will apply your analytical skills to learn the Cyrillic alphabet efficiently without getting overwhelmed. Once you learn the alphabet, you will be able to sound out words and read Russian in no time.

The Roots of the Cyrillic Alphabet

You already know that Russian is not written in the Latin alphabet. Instead, it uses Cyrillic. The history of the Cyrillic alphabet spans more than a thousand years. Throughout the ages, it has been modified several times, and what we use now in Russian differs from its earlier forms. The Russian Cyrillic alphabet contains thirty-three letters, including ten letters for vowel sounds, twenty-one letters for consonant sounds, and two silent signs.

Cyrillic originated directly from the Greek alphabet without any direct impact from the Latin alphabet. However, scholars agree that the roots of the Latin alphabet also lie with the Greeks, so the Cyrillic and Latin alphabets are related by proxy. This explains why Cyrillic contains letters that are similar to Greek (e.g. Ф, П, Г) and letters that are similar to those found in Latin languages (e.g. В, К, Н).

The Cyrillic alphabet is named after St. Cyril, a monk from Byzantium. St. Cyril and St. Methodius are credited with spreading Christianity among the Slavs in southern Europe in the ninth century A.D. Everyone agrees on that much, but some scholars argue that St. Cyril didn't actually create the alphabet that bears his name.

St. Cyril himself may have developed the alphabet during his missionary trip to Bulgaria and Moravia where he and his brother worked on translating the Bible for newly converted Slavs. Other researchers suggest the alphabet was invented later in the tenth century, probably by other missionaries who followed in the footsteps of St. Cyril and St. Methodius. Another theory suggests that Slavs educated in the Greek tradition created the alphabet to share the word of God with the rest of their people.

✅ Fact

In the Soviet Union, several languages that had previously used the Arabic (Kazakh and Azerbaijani) or Latin scripts (Moldovan) were forcefully switched over to the Cyrillic alphabet. After the breakup of the Soviet empire, many of these languages returned to their previous scripts or, in the case of Azerbaijani, have switched over to Latin script.

What is clear is that the alphabet was created in order to facilitate the translation of the Bible into Old Church Slavonic, the language spoken at that time by the Slavic people of southern Europe. The creation of an original alphabet made it possible to develop a writing system that can effectively express all of the sounds of the Slavic phonetic system without relying on approximations and diacritic marks. Since then, Cyrillic has been successfully used to write Slavic languages such as Russian, Belorussian, Ukrainian, Bulgarian, Serbian, and Macedonian. Due to Russian imperial expansion, the Cyrillic alphabet was adopted in the native languages of the Russian North and Siberia.

Although the territory where Cyrillic is used today has diminished since the deconstruction of the Soviet Union, it is still used in several non-Slavic languages, including the languages of Uzbekistan and Turkmenistan. Before we begin looking closely at specific Cyrillic letters, consult Table 1-1 to get a general idea of the alphabet and see the approximations of the sound of its letters in English.

Table 1-1

▼ **РУССКИЙ АЛФАВИТ RUSSIAN ALPHABET**

Russian Capital Letter	Lower Case	English Approximation
А	а	**fa**ther
Б	б	**B**en

В	в	**V**ictor
Г	г	**g**row
Д	д	**d**inner
Е	е	**ye**sterday
Ё	ё	**Yo**rk
Ж	ж	plea**s**ure
З	з	**z**ero
И	и	s**ee**m
Й	й	to**y**
К	к	**c**oco
Л	л	**l**amp
М	м	**m**other
Н	н	**N**ick
О	о	**o**r
П	п	**P**eter
Р	р	pe**r**o (trilled as in Spanish)
С	с	**S**andra
Т	т	s**t**omp
У	у	l**oo**n
Ф	ф	**f**reckles
Х	х	the composer Ba**ch**
Ц	ц	ma**ts**
Ч	ч	**ch**eers
Ш	ш	**sh**eep
Щ	щ	fre**sh sh**ed
Ъ	ъ	hard sign – no sound
Ы	ы	similar to the vowel sound in **hill**
Ь	ь	soft sign – no sound
Э	э	S**e**ptember
Ю	ю	**u**nion
Я	я	**ya**hoo

Letter approximation, or transliteration, is an important technique of letter-by-letter transcription of a text or a word from one alphabet into another. You will learn more about the placement of vowels and consonants and the function of silent signs in later chapters. For now, just focus on matching the visual letter with its pronunciation.

The Letters You Already Know

Identifying the letters that are shaped and pronounced similarly in both Russian and English will help make learning Russian easier.

Table 1-2

▼ **SIMILAR LETTERS AND SOUNDS**

Russian Letter	English Approximation
A a	A a
K к	K k
M м	M m
O o	O o
T т	T t

Note the slight difference in the graphic forms of the lowercase letters K, M, and T.

Following are several Russian words that utilize these letters. Some of these words are new to you, but some are close to similar words in English. As you begin learning new words in Russian, remember to utilize what you already know.

Table 1-3

▼ **WORDS SPELLED WITH LETTERS THAT YOU KNOW**

Russian Word	English Translation
мама	mama
кот	cat
мак	poppy seed
так	so
как	how

там	over there
том	tome/volume
ат**а**ка	attack
атом	atom

Stress Patterns in Russian

When we say a word in either English or Russian, there is always a syllable that is pronounced with more strength, with more emphasis, or in other words, with stress. For example, in English we stress the first syllable in the word "treasure," as in "TREAsure." In Russian, in the word "атака" we stress the second "a," as in "атАка," but in the word "атом" we stress the first "a," as in "Атом." As you can see from these examples, in both English and Russian, vowel sounds change their pronunciation depending on whether they are in a stressed or unstressed position. Compare the pronunciation of "a" in English in such words as "rather" and "attuned." Similarly, the very same process, known as vowel reduction, occurs in Russian. You will learn more about vowel reduction as you continue learning about pronunciation in Russian in Chapter 2.

e✓ Fact

In English, many words can have two stresses, as in "REVolUtion." In Russian, only one stress is allowed per word.

Be aware that in regular Russian publications, stress is rarely indicated. However, to facilitate your learning of Russian, this book will denote stress in boldface, as in the word "м**а**ма" where the first syllable is stressed. We will not mark the stress in one-syllable words, as in "кто."

Russian children learn their ABCs or "**а**zbuka" from books which have clear indications of stress marks. ("**A**zbuka" comes from the old names of the first two letters in the Cyrillic alphabet: A and Б.) As children become more proficient in reading, stress marks become redundant. The same applies to you: As you increase your proficiency in Russian, you will develop a better sense of stress patterns, making stress marks unnecessary. Until then, it is recommended that you, too, write down words with stress indicators.

Looks Aren't Everything!

Now that you've eased into the Cyrillic alphabet by studying letters that have similar pronunciations in Russian and English, go back to Table 1-1 and identify six letters that look familiar to you but are pronounced differently in Russian. Compare your answers with the following list of letters from the Cyrillic alphabet that are visually similar to the letters from the Latin alphabet but represent different sounds. These letters are often more difficult to remember for English-speaking learners of Russian. Don't feel bad if it takes you a little while to remember them, but make it a point to keep studying them. Repetition is the key to learning a new language.

Table 1-4

▼ SIMILAR LETTERS WITH DIFFERENT PRONUNCIATION IN RUSSIAN

Russian Letter	English Approximation
В в	v
Е е	ye, as in yesterday
Н н	n
Р р	r, as in the Scottish dialect of English
С с	s
Х х	kh, as in loch

The following are several Russian words that utilize some of the letters that look familiar to you and the letters that were covered in Table 1-2.

Table 1-5

▼ RUSSIAN WORDS WITH LETTERS YOU KNOW

Russian Word	English Translation
вор	thief
хвост	tail
рост	height
в**е**ра	faith
нор**а**	burrow
м**а**рка	stamp

стен**а**	wall
т**е**ма	topic
х**о**хот	laughter
автом**ат**	machine

Similar Sounds, Different Letters

Several letters in the Russian Cyrillic alphabet represent sounds similar to those in English, but are written with different symbols. This is a good example of the arbitrary nature of the relationship between form and meaning in any language; similar sounds can be represented by different symbols in various languages, just as identical concepts are rendered differently. Table 1-6 includes a list of Russian letters that fall within this category.

Table 1-6

▼ **SIMILAR SOUNDS, DIFFERENT LETTERS**

Russian Letter	English Approximation
Б б	b
Г г	g, as in get
Д д	d
З з	z
Л л	l
П п	p
У у	oo, as in goose

Table 1-7

▼ **RUSSIAN WORDS WITH LETTERS YOU KNOW**

Russian Word	English Translation
бор	forest
г**о**род	town
дор**о**га	road
зуб	tooth

лодка	boat
продукт	product
ура	hooray

Additional Consonants

The letters in this group represent the remaining Cyrillic letters for consonant sounds. Some of these sounds are rarely heard in English or they are not used at all.

Table 1-8

▼ **SEVERAL UNUSUAL CONSONANTS**

Russian Word	English Approximation
Ж ж	zh, as in trea**s**ure
Ц ц	ts, as in dar**ts**
Ч ч	ch, as in **ch**air
Ш ш	sh, as in **sh**op
Щ щ	shch, as in fre**sh ch**eese

The sounds represented by the Cyrillic letters Ц and Щ are nearly nonexistent in the English sound system. The examples of their pronunciation provided here are rough approximations. The best way to imitate these sounds is to listen to Russian speakers and practice.

Table 1-9

▼ **RUSSIAN WORDS WITH UNUSUAL CONSONANTS**

Russian Word	English Translation
жук	beetle
цирк	circus
чемодан	suitcase
шум	noise
борщ	Russian beet soup, borscht

Additional Vowels

This is the group of the Cyrillic letters that represent the remaining vowel sounds.

Table 1-10

▼ **SEVERAL VOWEL SOUNDS TO REMEMBER**

Russian Word	English Approximation
Ё ё	yo, as in yoyo toy
Э э	e, as in let
Ю ю	yu, as in universe
Я я	ya, as in yard
Й й	y, as in boy
Ы ы	similar to the vowel sound in hill

In this group, there are three letters that have two segments in their graphic form: Ё, Й and Ы.

The letter "Ё" is always in the stressed position making it redundant to mark the stress in the words where it occurs. That's why "Ё" is often written as "Е" in Russian newspapers and other print media. Please remember this as you continue working with this textbook.

The letters "Й" and "Ы" usually occur at the end of words. The letter "Й" is an obligatory last letter in the endings of masculine forms of Russian adjectives, as in "красивый" - beautiful and "добрый" - kind. The letter "Ы" occurs in adjectives and as the last letter in plural forms of nouns, as in "умный" (clever) and "комнаты" (rooms). Neither letter ever occurs at the beginning of words, with the exception the use of Й when it is used to transliterate foreign geographic names that start with the sound combination of "yo," as in "York."

❗ Alert

Don't forget to write the cap in the letter "Й." Otherwise, you will end up with an absolutely different letter, "И."

The letter "Э" is often used at the beginning of words, especially to approximate foreign names that start with the Latin letter "E" as in Эрик - Eric, Эмили - Emily, Элизабет –Elizabeth, and Эмори - Emory.

Table 1-11

▼ **MORE RUSSIAN WORDS TO READ**

Russian Word	English Translation
Эрик	Eric
юр**и**ст	lawyer
ясно	clear
р**у**сский	Russian
р**ы**ба	fish

Writing Names in Cyrillic

Now that you know all of the letters of the Cyrillic alphabet and their Russian pronunciations, you are probably wondering how to write your own name in Cyrillic. Here are a few important points to remember:

- Russians spell foreign names in the way they are pronounced in Russian.
- In Russian, there is no letter to represent the "J" sound. English names that begin with J in their Russian version begin with "Дж", as in Джон – John.
- English names that begin with the "H" sound are usually rendered with the Russian Г sound, as in Генри – Henry and Ганнибал - Hannibal, but sometimes, especially in last names, the same H sound is transferred with the Russian "Х" sound, as in Холмс – Holmes.
- There is no corresponding sound in Russian for either of the sounds represented in English by "th," as in there and thick. English names that begin or contain these two sounds are transliterated with the Russian letter "Т," as in Теодор – Theodore.
- English names beginning with the letters "Ch" and "Sh" are written in Russian respectively with the Russian letters "Ч" and "Ш."
- Russian does not contain a sound similar to the English "W," as in Weston. English names that begin with this letter can be transliterated either with

the Cyrillic letter "В" or a letter combination of "Уа," as in Ватсон or Уатсон for Watson.

- The English sound "E," as in Mel, and "A," as in Sam and Stanley, are transliterated using the Russian letter "Е" or "Э" or "А," as in Мел, Сэм, and Станли. Some names might have several possible transliterations. For example, the name Stanley can be transliterated as Стэнли, Станли, and Стенли.

The following are some examples of American and English names written in Russian. Transliterate them into English.

Names	In English
Мишель Браун	
Дороти Блэйн	
Майкл Джонсон	
Эрик Родман	
Николас Винстон	
Эдди Мерфи	
Ричард Спаркс	

Chapter Review

Review the material covered in this chapter and complete the following exercises.

Chapter Quiz

Answer the following questions and check your answers in Appendix A.

1. How many letters are in the Cyrillic alphabet used in the Russian languages?

   _____

2. Why is it called Cyrillic?

   _____

3. What was the initial motivation for the creation of the Cyrillic alphabet?

   _____

4. What is the word for "letter approximation"?

_____

5. How many Cyrillic letters represent consonant sounds?

_____

6. What is the largest number of stresses allowable in Russian words?

_____

7. What is the Russian word for "alphabet book"?

_____

8. What is the basic rule of transferring foreign names into Russian letters?

_____

Reading Practice

Read the following Russian words describing weather.

▼ RUSSIAN WEATHER VOCABULARY

Russian Word	English Translation
погода	weather
холодно	cold
тепло	warm
жарко	hot
светло	light
темно	dark
душно	stuffy
влажно	humid
температура	temperature
мороз	frost
снег	snow
солнце	sun
прогноз	forecast
прогноз погоды	weather forecast

Writing Practice

These Americans are famous in Russia. Translate their names back into their original English form. Check your answers in Appendix A.

1. Джордж Вашингтон _____
2. Эмили Дикинсон _____
3. Чарли Чаплин _____
4. Марк Твейн _____
5. Коби Брайнт _____
6. Николас Кейдж _____

Translate the following names of American cities and states from Russian into English. Check your answers in Appendix A.

7. Детройт _____
8. Новый Орлеан _____
9. Синсинати _____
10. Бостон _____
11. Калифорния _____
12. Сан-Франциско _____
13. Сиэтл _____
14. Колорадо _____
15. Техас _____
16. Виксбург _____
17. Орегон _____

Based on the information from this chapter, transliterate your surname and your first name into Russian.

1. My name in Russian is _____

CHAPTER 2

Russian Pronunciation

Now that you are familiar with the Cyrillic alphabet, your next task is to master the sounds of the letters and explore how these sounds impact each other in words. This chapter explores the specific roles of Russian vowels and consonants, and silent signs are also covered. In this chapter, you will practice your reading skills with an introduction to Russian geography and learn several commonly used greetings and ways to say goodbye.

Pronunciation of Vowel Pairs

Scholars usually separate Russian vowels into two groups: those that contain a distinctive y-sound and those that do not.

Table 2-1

▼ **VOWEL PAIRS**

Regular Vowels	Vowels with an Initial Y-Sound
А	Я
Э	Е
О	Ё
У	Ю

Vowels with an initial y-sound keep their original phonetic form if they occur at the beginning of a word or after another vowel. However, after a consonant the y-sound in these letters becomes less audible.

Table 2-2

▼ PRONUNCIATION OF Я, Е, Ё, Ю

Vowel	Initial Position	After Another Vowel	After a Consonant
Я	**я**рко (bright)	ти**х**ая (quiet)	То**ля**
Е	е**да** (food)	сыр**ы**е (damp)	т**е**ма (theme)
Ё	ёлка (pine tree)	её (her)	Серёжа
Ю	**Ю**ля	понима**ю** (I understand)	Н**ю**ра

Pronunciation of O, A, E, Я

As you learned from the previous chapter, stress patterns influence the way you pronounce vowels. Typically, in a stressed position vowels are pronounced clearly, each sound retaining its individuality. In an unstressed position, vowels undergo what is often referred to as vowel reduction. This is a process that makes vowels less distinct as they lose some of their original phonetic qualities. It is important to remember that when "a" and "o" are stressed in Russian words, they are pronounced as "a" in "rather" and "o" in "snow." However, if these vowels occur in the unstressed position, their pronunciation changes.

Table 2-3

▼ O AND A

Vowel	Stressed	Unstressed Before a Stressed Symbol	Other Unstressed Positions
O	он (he)	as in snow	Москв**а** as in ox	молок**о** as the "a" in about and uh, ma-luh-KOH
A	старт (start) Мар**ина** as in father	хор**о**шая as in mother	as the "a" in about and uh, kha-ROH-shuh-yah	

The vowels E and Я also change their pronunciation depending on whether they are stressed or unstressed. Generally, when they are not stressed, they are reduced to a more neutral sound.

Table 2-4

▼ **EXAMPLES OF VOWEL REDUCTION**

Vowel	Stressed	Unstressed
E	тело (body)	перо (feather)
E	дело (deed)	метро (metro)
E	студент (student)	ребята (guys)
E	сумасшедший (crazy)	вегетарианский (vegetarian)
Я	мясо (meat)	язык (language)
Я	яблоко (apple)	американская (American)
Я	яхта (yacht)	десятилетие (decade)
Я	ясли (nursery)	синяя (dark blue)

Silent Signs and Palatalization

You may have noticed two silent sounds in the Cyrillic alphabet in Table 1-1: the soft sign ь and the hard sign ъ. Their Russian names are, respectively, мягкий знак and твёрдый знак.

The Hard Sign

In modern Russian the hard sign is rarely used, but when it is its function is to separate a prefix from the root of the word and to insert an additional y sound.

Table 2-5

▼ **THE HARD SIGN IN RUSSIAN**

With the Hard Sign	Translation	Without the Hard Sign	Translation
объявление	notice	обед	dinner
отъезд	departure	отец	father

подъ**е**зд	building entrance	пад**е**ж	grammatical case
съёмка	film shooting	сёмга	salmon
объ**е**зд	detour	об**и**да	offense

The Soft Sign and Palatalization

The soft sign ь functions as an indicator that the preceding consonant is soft, or palatalized, as in мать (mother) and спать (to sleep). In Russian, most consonants have two variants: hard and soft. Usually, English-speaking students of Russian do not have many problems imitating the pronunciation of Russian hard consonants because they are in many ways similar to English consonants. However, this is not always true with Russian soft consonants.

To get an idea of what a soft or palatalized consonant is, pronounce the following English words: beautiful, pew, view, few, mew, and situation. As you pronounce them, be mindful of how you articulate the consonants b, p, v, f, m, and t. You will notice that your pronunciation of these consonants is "softer" than when you say words such as boat, port, vote, fort, moat, and tote.

Palatalization is one of the biggest differences in the sound system between English and Russian. In English, it is rarely observed and has no semantic meaning. In Russian, it is a common feature that has a meaning-differentiation function as shown in Table 2-6.

🅴✔ Fact

To pronounce a soft consonant in Russian, press the tip of your tongue against your hard palate. The hard palate is the flat surface on the top of your mouth. To locate your hard palate, move your tongue along the top of your mouth away from the ridge behind your teeth.

Table 2-6

▼ **WORDS WITH AND WITHOUT PALATALIZATION**

Palatalized	Translation	Non-Palatalized	Translation
быть	to be	быт	everyday life
ель	pine tree	ел	ate

Спорь!	Argue!	спор	debate
влить	pour in	влит	poured in
дань	tribute	дан	given
цель	goal	цел	safe and sound

The soft sign is only one of the three indicators of palatalization. The vowel sounds Я, Е, Ё, Ю, И also signal that the consonant preceding them is soft. Finally, there is a chain reaction that you must be aware of: Palatalized consonants can make neighboring consonants soft, too.

Table 2-7

▼ **TWO ADDITIONAL METHODS OF PALATALIZATION**

Я, Е, Ё, Ю, И	Translation	Palatalization Chain Reaction	Translation
мягко	soft	листья	leaves
нет	no	если	if
мёд	honey	видимость	visibility
Анюта	nickname for Anne	всласть	to one's heart's content
никогда	never	после	after

An understanding of the distinction between hard and soft consonants is essential even for the correct pronunciation of Russian first names. Your Russian friends would be impressed if you were to try and pronounce their names the way they were meant to be, with soft and hard consonants. Without a doubt, you'll get preferential treatment if you can say "Ольга" instead of "Olga," "Юлия" instead of "Julia," and even your friend Boris will be happy to finally hear that soft "r" in his name that he has been missing for years! Following is a table with some Russian names that require soft consonants.

Table 2-8

▼ **PALATALIZATION AND RUSSIAN FIRST NAMES**

Female Names	Male Names
Ольга	Владислав
Дарья	Пётр

Татья́на	Алекса́ндр
Ксе́ния	Ви́ктор
Елизаве́та	Ники́та
Светла́на	Бори́с

Voiced and Voiceless Consonants

Both in English and in Russian, some consonants are voiceless and some are voiced. When the vocal cords are together, the air flow makes them vibrate, resulting in the production of voiced consonants; for example, English consonants D and Z and Russian consonants Ж and Г. Other consonants do not rely on the vocal cords for pronunciation; think of the English consonants T and P and Russian consonants Ф and К. In Russian and in English, voiced and voiceless consonants can be classified into pairs as in the following table.

Table 2-9

▼ **RUSSIAN VOICED AND VOICELESS CONSONANTS**

Voiced	Voiceless
В	Ф
З	С
Ж	Ш
Б	П
Г	К
Д	Т

In contrast to English, Russian voiced and voiceless consonants are not always pronounced the way they are written. At the end of words, often voiced consonants are pronounced like their voiceless counterparts. This is especially true in Standard Russian, but might vary in regional pronunciations.

Table 2-10

▼ **DEVOICING VOICED CONSONANTS**

Russian Word	Pronunciation of the Final Consonant	Translation
Рахма́нинов	[ф]	Rakhmaninov

го́род	[т]	city
клуб	[п]	club
друг	[к]	friend
враг	[к]	enemy
Петербу́рг	[к]	Petersburg
сад	[т]	garden

Unlike English, Russian allows more consonant combinations within its words. This is why you will encounter words where you will see both voiced and voiceless consonants side by side, as in встре́ча (a meeting), субти́тры (subtitles), and о́тдых (rest). Because it would be difficult to articulate both voiced and voiceless consonants side by side without a lot of effort, the language developed a conservation technique, also known as consonant assimilation.

Whenever there are adjacent voiced and voiceless consonants, the first consonant takes on the voicing quality of the second. In this manner, a voiced consonant can become voiceless, and a voiceless consonant can be transformed into a voiced consonant. This assimilation occurs not only within a word, but also within phrases. The assimilation rule does not apply to the words or phrases where the first consonant is voiceless and the second one is the voiced consonant В, as in "твой," a word that does not undergo assimilation.

Table 2-11

▼ **CONSONANT ASSIMILATION**

Russian Word/Phrase	Consonant Pronunciation	Translation
встре́ча	фст (voiced becomes voiceless)	meeting
субти́тры	пт (voiced becomes voiceless)	subtitles
о́тдых	дд (voiceless becomes voiced)	rest
про́сьба	зьб (voiceless becomes voiced)	request
в Калу́ге	ф Калуге (voiced becomes voiceless)	in Kaluga

твой	твой (no assimilation)	your
квас	квас (no assimilation)	kvas (a traditional Russian soft drink)

Pronunciation Patterns in Salutations

Now it's time to use your understanding of Russian pronunciation to learn several common greetings and ways to say goodbye in Russian.

As you learn Russian greetings, remember to apply the pronunciation rules that you have learned so far. Some Russian words might deviate from the rules. In such cases, this book will include a note on exceptions in the pronunciation of the words that you will be learning so that your Russian will sound authentic.

Russian Salutations: Cultural Notes

Russians have both informal and formal salutation and farewell expressions that correspond to the formal (вы) and informal (ты) forms of address. If you are meeting someone for the first time, or the person with whom you are speaking is older or higher on the social ladder, it is always better to err on the side of caution and use the formal forms of saying hello and goodbye. Handshakes are an accepted form of salutation among men and are becoming more and more popular among women, especially in professional situations.

A very traditional way of saying goodbye is to exchange three kisses on the cheek followed by a hug. This ritual is only used with one's closest friends and immediate family or after the consumption of large quantities of alcohol when the dividing lines have been irrevocably blurred. Whatever the situation might be, your best bet is to avoid excesses and stay more middle of the road.

🅴❗ Alert

If you greet a Russian friend with a casual "How are you?" or "What's up?" be prepared for a lengthy response. It's considered extremely rude to expect a two-word answer to these greetings. Your Russian friends will happily talk about their lives if you're genuinely interested, but they'll be offended if you ask such private questions without giving them the opportunity to engage in meaningful conversation.

Finally, remember that it is unnecessary to greet the same person several times during the day. Instead, you should say hello upon your first meeting of the day and then use eye contact or a head nod to acknowledge their presence throughout the day.

Table 2-12

▼ **GREETINGS**

Time	Formality	Greeting	Translation	Addressing
All day	Very Formal	Здр**а**вствуйте!	Hello	One or many
All day	Informal	Здр**а**вствуй!	Hello	One person
All day	Very Informal	Прив**е**т!	Hello	One or many
Morning	(In)formal	Д**о**брое **у**тро!	Good morning!	One or many
Afternoon	(In)formal	Д**о**брый день!	Good afternoon!	One or many
Evening	(In)formal	Д**о**брый в**е**чер!	Good evening!	One or many

The Russian letter "В" in Здравствуйте is not pronounced.

Table 2-13

▼ **SAYING GOODBYE**

Time	Formality	Greeting	Translation	Addressing
All day	(In)formal	До свид**а**ния!	Until we meet again!	One or many
All day	(In)formal	Всег**о** хор**о**шего!	All the best!	One or many
All day	Very Informal	Пок**а**!	Bye!	One or many
All day	(In)formal	Счастл**и**во!	All the best!	One or many
All day	Formal	До ск**о**рой встр**е**чи!	Until our next meeting!	One or many
All day	Formal	Прощ**а**йте!	Farewell!	One or many
All day	Informal	Прощ**а**й!	Farewell!	One

Night	Formal	Доброй ночи!	Have a good night!	One or many
Night	Informal	Спокойной ночи!	Good night! (before bed)	One or many

The Russian letter "Г" in Всего хорошего (in both words) is pronounced just like the Russian letter "В."

Reading Practice: Russian Geography

Now that you know how to pronounce Russian words, let's use Russian geographic names to introduce Russian spelling and pronunciation. You will know the Anglicized pronunciations of these Russian names, but the Russian pronunciation is somewhat different. For example, Russia is Россия in Russian, with the stress on the second syllable and a subsequent shift of the vowel pronunciation "O" into "A." The same rule applies to the pronunciation of the official name of the country: Российская Федерация (The Russian Federation).

Similar to some English geographic names, several Russian geographic names have meanings that can be directly translated into English. For example, Новгород (Novgorod), one of the oldest cities in Russia, can be literally translated in English as "New City." The Russian root нов- means "new," and город is "city."

The old Russian city Владимир, which also happens to be a male name, consists of the root ВЛАД-, meaning "to own" and the root МИР, which can mean either "peace" or "world," depending on the context in which it is used. Thus, Владимир could be interpreted as "he who owns the world." It comes as no surprise that the name Владимир has been a very popular name for boys, with several of Russia's leaders associating it with a prophesy or a coincidence of sorts, depending on how you look at it. Just think about Владимир Ленин or the current president of Российская Федерация, Владимир Путин.

On a more serious note, several of the Russian cities that were founded during the imperial period in Russian history were given names to commemorate a specific tsar or tsarina or a city's patron saint. For example, Санкт-Петербург, founded by Peter the Great in 1703, was named after the biblical St. Peter, who was the tsar's patron saint. Several Russian cities, Санкт-Петербург among them, include -бург, a German borrowing that means "city," as their final component, or a Russian root -град or -город, which also means "city." Finally, there is the

Russian city of Владивосток, which was founded to exert Russian imperial influence on Japan, China, and Korea. The city's name leaves no doubts about the political ambitions of the Russian empire: It is derived from two Russian roots (one of which you already know); влад- meaning "to own" and восток, which means "east."

Table 2-14

▼ **RUSSIAN GEOGRAPHIC NAMES**

Russian	English
страна	country
Россия	Russia
Российская Федерация	Russian Federation
города	cities
Москва	Moscow
Санкт-Петербург	St. Petersburg
Новгород	Novgorod
Мурманск	Murmansk
Архангельск	Arkhangelsk
Волгоград	Volgograd
Астрахань	Astrakhan
Екатеринбург	Yekaterinburg
Новосибирск	Novosibirsk
Иркутск	Irkutsk
Владивосток	Vladivostok
Магадан	Magadan
горы	mountains
Урал	the Urals
реки	rivers
Москва-река	the Moskva River
Волга	the Volga
Дон	the Don
Обь	the Ob
Лена	the Lena

Амур	the Amur
мор**я** и оз**ё**ра	seas and lakes
озеро Байк**а**л	Lake Baikal
Ч**ё**рное м**о**ре	Black Sea
Б**е**рингово м**о**ре	the Bering Sea

Chapter Review

Review the material covered in this chapter and then complete the following exercises.

Chapter Quiz

Answer the following questions and check your answers in Appendix A.

1. How many Russian vowels include an initial y-sound?

    _____

2. What is the term that describes a change in the pronunciation of Russian vowels in the unstressed position?

    _____

3. Name two silent signs from the Russian Cyrillic alphabet.

    _____

    _____

4. List three indicators of palatalization in Russian consonants.

    _____

    _____

    _____

5. When should you pronounce Russian voiced consonants as their voiceless counterparts?

    _____

6. What happens to the pronunciation of words and phrases when there are adjacent voiced and voiceless consonants?

   _____

7. What is the official Russian name of Russia?

   _____

8. Name at least three Russian cities whose names have a clear meaning in Russian.

   _____

   _____

   _____

Pronunciation Practice

Identify soft consonants in these Russian names. Check your answers in Appendix A.

Female Names

1. Марья   _____
2. Наталья   _____
3. Людмила   _____
4. Юлия   _____
5. Анастасия   _____
6. Лидия   _____
7. Валентина   _____

Male Names

8. Влад**и**мир   _____
9. Никол**ай**   _____
10. Серг**ей**   _____
11. Евг**е**ний   _____
12. Семён   _____
13. Кир**и**лл   _____
14. Макс**и**м   _____

Practicing Russian Greetings

Which greeting(s) would you use in the following situations? Write down as many appropriate answers as possible.

1. You are meeting your new colleague from Russia. It's early in the morning.

   _____

2. You are saying goodbye to a close friend late at night.

   _____

3. You are meeting an acquaintance in the middle of the day.

   _____

4. You are saying "Good night!" to your child at bedtime.

   _____

5. Your friend is joining the circus, and you might never see him again.

   _____

CHAPTER 3

Getting Around in Russia

Experienced travelers know that language skills increase the enjoyment of traveling and reduce the stress and anxiety of being in an unfamiliar environment. Knowing the correct words and phrases enhances cross-cultural understanding and prevents possible miscommunication. Familiarity with culturally acceptable ways of interacting with locals shows a degree of politeness that Russians will appreciate. This chapter introduces several key words and phrases frequently heard at border crossings, airports, railway stations, and other means of public transportation.

Cognates

The emphasis in this chapter is on acquiring new words and phrases that might be helpful to you as you travel to Russia. As you learn these words, you will discover that some Russian words are similar to their English counterparts. Like many other languages spoken in the Western world, Russian and English have been greatly influenced by ancient Greek and Latin. As a result, a considerable section of the Russian and English lexicon consists of words that have the same Greco-Roman roots. Such words are known as cognates. Compare the following English and Russian words in Table 3-1.

Table 3-1

▼ LATIN AND GREEK COGNATES IN ENGLISH AND RUSSIAN

English	Russian
democracy	демокра́тия
demonstration	демонстра́ция

revolution	революциюя
bibliography	библиогра́фия
theater	теа́тр
public	пу́блика
conflict	конфли́кт
geography	геогра́фия
consensus	консе́нсус
agency	аге́нтство

French, Arabic, and Italian also have loaned numerous words both to English and Russian. Consider such terms as метро́ – metro (from French), а́лгебра – algebra (from Arabic), and макаро́ны – macaroni (from Italian).

In addition to the cognates borrowed from other languages, there is a small group of basic terms that are shared by all Indo-European languages, including English and Russian. These terms are presumed to come from the so-called Proto-Indo-European language, an ancestral language that connects all Indo-European languages. Compare the following words in English and Russian: ночь (night), день (day), and три (three).

Although cognates have a shared ancestry that can be traced through linguistic analysis, their phonological form must accommodate the sound systems of different languages, resulting in differences in pronunciation. For example, Latin *schola* became school in English and шко́ла in Russian; Russian университе́т is connected through its Greco-Roman heritage to the English university.

Question

What is phonology?
Phonology is the system of classifying all allowable combinations of sounds in a particular language. Languages differ in their phonological systems as some languages make use of sounds that are simply not present in others.

Whereas many cognates have retained similar meanings, others have acquired independent meanings in two languages. These different semantic applications might lead to mistakes in translation when speakers assume that cognates have the same meaning in all languages. For example, "magazine" in

English has acquired a meaning of "publication, journal," whereas the Russian магазин is used in the sense of "shop, store."

As you learn more Russian words and phrases, remember that cognate recognition is an important skill that can be helpful in the development of your vocabulary in Russian; on the other hand, don't jump to conclusions when you see or hear words that look or sound similar. They just may happen to be your false friends. As Ronald Reagan once said in Russian (with a heavy American accent): Доверяй, но проверяй! (Be trustful, but always double check!)

Crossing the Border

To travel to Russia, you need to have a current паспорт and a виза (both words are cognates!). To obtain a visa, contact a Russian Consulate (Консульство Российской Федерации) directly or work with a travel agency that specializes in trips to Russia. It usually takes a couple of weeks to process a visa application, so apply well in advance. Once all of the red tape is taken care of and your travel plans are finalized, you will be all set to begin your journey.

🅴❗ Alert

It is always wise to make arrangements for transportation from the airport to your hotel in advance. Otherwise, be prepared to deal with an army of so-called gypsy cab drivers waiting to offer their services in the lobby of your terminal. Use your best judgment and don't be shy about bargaining!

If you are flying to Russia, your most likely point of entry will be Moscow or St. Petersburg. International airports in both cities do have bilingual signs, and many border officials are fluent in English. However, knowing several common words and phrases will provide some back-up to ensure a smooth border-crossing experience.

Вот мой паспорт.
Here's my passport.

Я буду в России неделю / две недели / месяц.
I will be in Russia for a week / two weeks / a month.

Я – турист/туристка.
I am a tourist (male/female).

Я мог**у** позвон**и**ть моем**у** к**о**нсулу?
Can I phone my consulate?

Мне н**у**жно заполн**и**ть **э**тот бланк?
Do I have to fill out this form?

У вас есть **э**тот бланк на англ**и**йском?
Do you have this form in English?

Note that the letter "Й" in the phrase "на англ**и**йском" is silent.

Table 3-2

▼ **CROSSING THE BORDER: HELPFUL VOCABULARY**

Russian	English
гран**и**ца	border
погран**и**чники	border officers
там**о**жня	customs
там**о**женная инсп**е**кция	customs inspection
иммиграци**о**нная сл**у**жба	immigration service
аэроп**о**рт	airport
рейс	flight
н**о**мер р**е**йса	flight number
п**а**спорт	passport
в**и**за	visa
имя	(first) name
фам**и**лия	last name
гражд**а**нство	citizenship
проф**е**ссия	occupation
цель по**е**здки	purpose of the trip
посто**я**нное м**е**сто ж**и**тельства	permanent residence
в**о**зраст	age
д**а**та рожд**е**ния	date of birth
м**е**сто рожд**е**ния	place of birth
цвет глаз / вол**о**с	color of eyes / hair
п**о**дпись	signature

In Russian, Национальность refers to one's ethnicity. To indicate someone's nationality, Russians use the word Гражданство, which can be translated into English as either "nationality" or "citizenship."

Expressions of Politeness

Whether you are a fluent speaker or have just begun learning Russian, don't underestimate the value of using polite language and gestures. A "thank you" said with a warm smile might just bridge that language barrier and perhaps make you new friends. This section introduces a list of basic polite expressions. Although they are not all-inclusive, these expressions will be appropriate in most situations.

Alert

The Russian language has more than its share of curses. You might hear them in traffic jams as drivers desperately lose their cool or see them in writing in urban graffiti. Hardcore obscenities are called мат. Although interesting from an anthropological standpoint, language learners are advised to avoid using them.

Russian has formal and informal forms of address, with the former usually reserved for interactions with strangers and figures of authority and the latter for conversations among peers and immediate family. It is better to tread lightly and use formal forms of address with all figures of authority (police, doctors, immigration officers, and customs officials) as well as with people with whom you are newly acquainted. In this chapter, all statements are made using the formal address. You will learn more about Russian formal and informal forms of address in Chapter 6.

Table 3-3

▼ EXPRESSIONS OF POLITENESS

Russian	English
Извините.	Excuse me.
Простите.	I am sorry.

Разрешите мне пройти.	May I pass through?
Спасибо.	Thank you.
Большое/огромное спасибо.	Thank you very much.
Благодарю вас.	Thank you.
Пожалуйста.	You are welcome.
Не за что.	Don't mention it.
Не стоит благодарности.	You are welcome (literally: It's not worthy of gratitude).

Извините and простите are interchangeable, unlike "I'm sorry" and "Excuse me."

Taking Public Transportation: Asking for Directions

Although car rentals and private drivers are available in many big cities, taking public transportation will allow you to experience daily life as it is for many locals. It is also a great opportunity to practice your language skills. In Moscow, St. Petersburg, and other metropolitan areas, you will have a choice of subway, buses, trams, and trolleys.

Table 3-4

▼ **PUBLIC TRANSPORTATION**

Russian	English
метро	metro/subway
автобус	bus
троллейбус	trolleybus
трамвай	tram
поезд	train
такси	taxi
остановка автобуса / троллейбуса / трамвая	bus / trolleybus / tram stop
станция метро	metro station
вокзал	train station
карта города	map of the city

44

центр (**го**рода)	(city) center, downtown
гост**и**ница	hotel
от**е**ль	hotel
общеж**и**тие	dormitory
улица	street
пл**о**щадь	square, plaza
ресtop**a**н	restaurant
каф**е**	café, coffee shop
муз**е**й	museum
те**а**тр	theater
кинотe**а**тр	movie theater
апт**е**ка	pharmacy
университ**е**т	university
шк**о**ла	school
магаз**и**н	store
библиот**е**ка	library
парк	park
стади**о**н	stadium

At central locations where there are a lot of tourists, street names and maps both in Russian and English might be available. However, in other places, you might have to rely on directions from your fellow passengers and practice your speaking and listening skills. Here are some common phrases used for asking and expressing directions.

Извин**и**те, пож**а**луйста, где гост**и**ница / магаз**и**н / вокз**а**л?
Excuse me, where is the hotel / store / train station?

Извин**и**те, вы не зн**а**ете где здесь остан**о**вка авт**о**буса / трамв**а**я / тролл**е**йбуса / метр**о**?
Excuse me, do you know where a bus / tram / trolleybus / metro stop is around here?

Вы не зн**а**ете, где нах**о**дится…?
Do you know where…is?

Подскаж**и**те, пож**а**луйста, как пройт**и** к…?
Can you please tell me how to get to…?

Я не зн**а**ю.
I don't know.

Это далек**о**/бл**и**зко отсю**да**?
Is it far/close from here?

Ид**и**те пр**я**мо.
Go straight ahead.

Поверн**и**те нал**е**во / напр**а**во.
Turn to the left / right.

Это здесь / там.
It is around here / over there.

Перейд**и**те **у**лицу / дор**о**гу.
Cross the street / road.

Это в пят**и** / десят**и** мин**у**тах ходьб**ы** отсю**да**.
It's a five- / ten-minute walk from here.

Спас**и**бо за в**а**шу п**о**мощь.
Thank you for your help.

Understanding directions in a foreign language is not an easy task. Use gestures if you need to, and don't be shy to ask the person to speak slower: "Пож**а**луйста, говор**и**те пом**е**дленней," or to see if the person could repeat the directions in English: "Повтор**и**те, пож**а**луйста, по-англ**и**йски."

Common Public Announcements and Signs

Whether you are traveling with a guide or independently, it is helpful to be able to understand common public announcements and signs. Being familiar with these expressions will give you more confidence to explore whatever destinations you choose to visit in Russia. While in the metro, stops will be announced as Сл**е**дующая ст**а**нция … (The next stop is …). Bus stops are announced as Сл**е**дующая остан**о**вка.

Fact

Moscow's metro is known around the world as the most beautiful series of underground stations and connecting tunnels in the world. The Moscow metro opened its first station in 1935, and today it is the most efficient mode of transportation in this congested city of 14 million. The metro begins its daily service at 5:30 A.M. and stops running at 1 A.M.

It is also customary to warn passengers that the train is just about to leave the station by announcing that the doors of the train are closing: Осторожно, двери закрываются (Be careful, the doors are closing). Onboard, you will see signs reminding passengers not to lean on the doors of the train: Не прислоняться (Don't lean). Look where you are sitting; a lot of seats are reserved for elderly people, pregnant women, passengers with young children, and the disabled. You can tell these seats by the stenciled: Места для пенсионеров, инвалидов и пассажиров с детьми (Seats for pensioners, the disabled and passengers with children).

Other signs that you are likely to see in many Russian cities and towns are roadside signs, including: Стоп (Stop), Осторожно (Caution), Объезд (Detour), and Дороги нет (Road Closed). In many public places, such as movie theaters, the theater, airports, and train stations, you will see two signs: "Вход" for Entrance and "Выход" for Exit. In Moscow, St. Petersburg, and other Russian cities, underground passageways are used to cross busy streets or to provide a connection to underground metro stations. These passages are announced by the sign Подземный переход.

If you are looking for a public bathroom, look for a sign that says Туалет. Women's bathrooms will be indicated by the sign with the letter "Ж" for женский туалет (women's bathroom). Men's bathrooms will bear the letter "М" for мужской туалет (men's bathroom).

Accidents and emergencies can happen to anyone. If you need to locate a police station, look for the sign that says Милиция. If you need to go to a hospital, you should ask for больница (hospital) or скорая помощь (ambulance). The following is a list of common expressions that may come in handy.

Мне плохо.
I don't feel well.

У мен**я** бол**и**т жив**о**т.
I have a stomachache.

Помог**и**те мне!
Help me!

Пож**а**р!
Fire!

Мне н**у**жен врач.
I need a doctor.

В**ы**зовите ск**о**рую п**о**мощь/мил**и**цию.
Call an ambulance / the police.

Мне необход**и**мо переговор**и**ть с мо**и**м к**о**нсулом.
I need to speak with my consul.

Пож**а**луйста, подожд**и**те здесь.
Please wait here.

Running Errands

Even in this age of ATMs and online banking, you may still need to find a bank during your stay in Russia. In Russian, a bank is called "банк." Many banks offer currency exchange services and cash machines. However, there are also many independent money exchange kiosks, easily recognizable by the sign обм**е**н вал**ю**ты (currency exchange).

If you need to mail some of your souvenirs back home or check your e-mail, ask for п**о**чта, a post office, which usually combines mailing, fax, the Internet, and utilities billing services.

Making, Accepting, and Declining Invitations

Your ability to speak Russian, combined with curiosity and a willingness to experience and appreciate a culture different from your own, will open up many opportunities for you to meet, interact, and hopefully build friendships with Russian people.

⊛ Essential

The basic way to indicate your agreement is "Да" for yes, and the easiest way of expressing your disagreement is by saying "Нет" for no.

Your Russian friends may invite you to their house, a local party, a restaurant, or a café. Or, you may want to invite your new friends for a cup of coffee or a beer. Here are some expressions that you can use when making or accepting invitations, or gracefully declining them.

Мне бы хотелось пригласить вас в кафе / ресторан.
I would like to invite you to a café / restaurant.

Пожалуйста, приходите в гости.
Please come visit. (Literally: Please, come be our guests.)

Мы будем очень рады.
We will be very glad.

Спасибо, с удовольствием.
Thank you. With pleasure.

Спасибо за приглашение.
Thank you for the invitation.

Спасибо, но я занят / занята*.
Thank you, but I am busy (male / female).

Спасибо, но сейчас у меня нет времени.
Thanks, but I don't have time now.

Может быть, в другой раз / завтра / на следующей неделе.
Perhaps next time time / tomorrow / next week.

*In Russian, adjectives have distinct forms when they refer to subjects of different genders. Stress patterns might vary in different forms of the same adjective.

Chapter Review

Review the material covered in this chapter and complete the following exercises.

Chapter Quiz

Answer the following questions and check your answers in Appendix A.

1. What are the words that have shared ancestry and are common in several languages?

   _____

2. What is the Russian word for swear words?

   _____

3. How would you say "thank you" in Russian?

   _____

4. How would you say "excuse me" in Russian?

   _____

5. How would you ask someone to speak slower?

   _____

6. How would you ask someone to explain whatever they are trying to say in English?

   _____

7. How would you thank someone for the help you received?

   _____

8. How would you ask in Russian where the bathroom is?

   _____

9. What do the letters "Ж" and "М" stand for on signs in public places in Russia?

   _____

10. How would you thank someone for inviting you?

   _____

11. Which signs are used to indicate an entrance and an exit in Russian?

_____

12. Which phrase is often used on the metro to announce the next stop?

_____

13. What are the basic ways of saying 'yes' and 'no' in Russian?

_____

14. What would a Russian "caution" sign look like?

_____

15. If you hear someone screaming "Пожар!," you will know that there is a . . .

_____

Vocabulary Building Exercise

Translate the following words into Russian using your knowledge of cognates:

1. Taxi _____
2. Hotel _____
3. Inspection _____
4. Passport _____
5. School _____
6. University _____
7. Visa _____
8. Restaurant _____
9. City center, downtown _____
10. Stop _____

Translation Practice

Translate the following sentences.

1. Excuse me, where is the men's bathroom?

_____

2. Sorry, I don't know.

_____

3. Call an ambulance.

   _____

4. Please wait here.

   _____

5. Please come visit.

   _____

CHAPTER 4

Russian Cuisine: Introduction to Nouns and Adjectives

asting new foods and going to a market to buy ingredients for traditional recipes provide language learners with unique opportunities to experience Russian culture from within—especially if you use the Russian language to do them. Learning about traditional cuisine and acquiring necessary food-related vocabulary and grammar skills makes you a more proficient language learner and offers valuable insight into the workings of Russian culture. In this chapter, you'll learn the basics of Russian cooking, read about its staple dishes and beverages, and begin your exploration of Russian nouns and adjectives.

Russian Cuisine: Basic Vocabulary

Traditional Russian cooking or "русская кухня" is famous for its variety. Spanning two continents, Russia has developed a cuisine that creatively blends elements from various cultures. Its most famous dishes include borscht (beet soup), blini (thin pancakes), caviar, and vodka. Jewish, French, Ukrainian, Georgian, and Middle Asian influences are evident in many dishes. The staple foods include potatoes, wheat, cabbage, and various meats. The following is a partial list of foods and beverages common in the Russian diet.

Table 4-1

▼ FOODS AND DRINKS

Russian	English
ед**а**	food
к**а**ша	kasha (porridge, hot cereals)
суп	soup
сал**а**т	salad
гриб**ы**	mushrooms
макар**о**ны	macaroni (plural), any type of pasta
м**я**со	meat
гов**я**дина	beef
свин**и**на	pork
к**у**рица	chicken
р**ы**ба	fish
икр**а**	caviar
колбас**а**	sausage
овощи	vegetables (plural)
кап**у**ста	cabbage
карт**о**фель	potatoes
морк**о**вь	carrot
помид**о**р	tomato
огур**е**ц	cucumber or pickle
фр**у**кты	fruits (plural)
яблоко	apple
гр**у**ша	pear
апельс**и**н	orange
клубн**и**ка	strawberry
дес**е**рт	dessert
торт	cake
щокол**а**д	chocolate
конф**е**та	candy
мор**о**женое	ice cream
молок**о**	milk

хлеб	bread
м**а**сло	butter
сыр	cheese
нап**и**тки	drinks (plural)
вод**а**	water
сок	juice
к**о**фе	coffee
чай	tea
вин**о**	wine
в**о**дочка	vodka

You may already have many of these items in your kitchen. Practice saying the Russian words for these foods while shopping at your grocery store. To find authentic Russian food in your area, look up a Russian market in the phone book or online.

The Basics of Russian Nouns

Now that you have learned a number of Russian nouns, let's examine three of their basic grammatical characteristics: case, gender, and number.

Case

In Russian, nouns change their endings to indicate specific roles that they play in a sentence:

The student is reading.
Студ**е**нт чит**а**ет.

"Student" is the subject of the sentence.

The teacher is asking the student.
Преподав**а**тель спр**а**шивает студ**е**нта.

"Student" is the direct object of action performed by the teacher. Note that in English, the syntactic role of the noun "student" is shown through the word order: It appears at the beginning of the sentence when it is used as a subject, and it occurs after the verb as an object.

On the other hand, the Russian noun "студент" has two different forms to correspond to its two different syntactic roles. Such forms are called cases, or declensions. There are six different cases in the Russian language:

- **Nominative:** This case is used to indicate that the noun is the subject of a sentence. Nouns given in a dictionary or in a vocabulary list are presented in the nominative case.
- **Accusative:** This case is used to indicate that the noun is the direct object of a sentence. It is also used to denote motion toward something when used after the prepositions в and на.
- **Genitive:** The genitive case is used to show possession, quantity, and negation.
- **Prepositional:** This case is used to describe location. As its name suggests, it uses prepositions; three of the most common are о (about), в ("in" or "on"), and на ("in" or "on"). These prepositions may be used with other cases, but their meaning is different.
- **Dative:** This case indicates the indirect object of a sentence. It is commonly used to indicate the giving of a gift and is also used to demonstrate motion toward another person ("to the teacher").
- **Instrumental:** This case is used to indicate the means used to accomplish an action. It is also used to indicate a noun's relationship to other nouns (with, above, below, in front, behind, among), or a state / condition.

In addition to nouns, pronouns and adjectives also follow the case system. Adjectives also adopt the number and gender of the nouns they modify.

Grammatical Gender
One of the major grammatical differences between English and Russian is the use of gender. English nouns do not have a gender; they are neutral, or neuter.

Russian nouns have one of three grammatical genders: masculine, feminine, or neuter. It is usually possible to tell the gender of a Russian noun by examining its last letter.

Table 4-2

▼ **GRAMMATICAL GENDER OF RUSSIAN NOUNS**

Masculine	Neuter	Feminine
consonant, Й, Ь	О, Е (Ё)	А, Я, Ь
суп	м**я**со	кап**у**ста
чай	мор**о**женое	вод**а**
карт**о**фель		морк**о**вь

Nouns ending in -ь have to be memorized! Some of them are masculine, and some are feminine.

There are several exceptions to the rules expressed in Table 4-3:

- Several nouns that refer to males end in -я or -а: п**а**па (dad), д**я**дя (uncle), and д**е**душка (grandfather).
- Several masculine first names have short names that end in -я or -а: К**о**ля is short for Никол**а**й (Nicholas) and С**а**ша is short for Алекс**а**ндр (Alexander).
- Nouns ending in -мя are neuter: **и**мя - first name, пл**е**мя - tribe, вр**е**мя - time.
- Nouns borrowed from other languages might or might not follow the traditional pattern: мен**ю** - menu (neuter), к**о**фе - coffee (masculine), метр**о** - metro (neuter), каф**е** - café (neuter).

Russian adjectives also have grammatical gender; however, their gender changes according to the noun they modify. This means that each Russian adjective usually has masculine, feminine, and neuter versions.

Number

Most Russian nouns have a singular and plural form. The number is indicated by the ending of the noun. In English, to express a plural form, the great majority of nouns take the -s ending, as in one dog—many dogs.

In Russian, there are several forms of the plural ending. In order to determine which ending you should use, remember that Russian nouns can be categorized based on their stem as either nouns with a hard stem or nouns with a soft stem. Hardness or softness of the stem is based on the phonetics quality of palatalization, which you learned about in Chapter 2. Some nouns take what is called a "zero ending."

Table 4-3

▼ **SINGULAR AND PLURAL FORMS OF NOUNS IN THE NOMINATIVE CASE**

Hard Stemmed Nouns		
Masculine: Singular/ Plural	Feminine: Singular/Plural	Neuter: Singular/Plural
Zero ending / -Ы or -И	-А / -Ы or -И	-О / -А
суп-суп**ы**	конф**е**та-конф**е**ты	вин**о**-в**и**на
универм**а**г-универм**а**ги	гр**у**ша-гр**у**ши	
Soft Stemmed Nouns		
Masculine: Singular/ Plural	Feminine: Singular/Plural	Neuter: Singular/Plural
-Й or –Ь / -И	-Я or –Ь /-И	-Е / -Я
муз**е**й-муз**е**и	там**о**жня-там**о**жни	вар**е**нье-вар**е**нья

In some nouns, the stress pattern might change in the plural form.
Masculine nouns in the nominative case that have a zero ending end in a consonant.

How do you choose between the ending of -Ы or -И? Make your selection based on the spelling rule: choose "И" after the consonants К, Г, Х, Ж, Ч, Ш, and Щ. This spelling rule is known as Spelling Rule 1. It is used in many other situations when you have to choose between the vowels И and Ы.

Several Russian nouns have irregular plural forms that must be memorized:

- Some nouns have a fleeting vowel, as in огур**е**ц-огурцы (cucumber - cucumbers). Also, от**е**ц-отц**ы** (father - fathers), ц**е**рковь-ц**е**ркви (church - churches), нап**и**ток-нап**и**тки (drink - drinks), and америк**а**нец - америк**а**нцы (American male - Americans).
- Some nouns do not have a plural form and are only used in singular, as in м**я**со, мор**о**женое, молок**о**, and м**а**сло. Some of these words also do not have a plural form in English, for example, milk and butter. However, be

careful: some nouns that are uncountable in English are countable in Russian and vice versa.

Knowing the gender, number, and case of a noun is essential in determining what form a modifying adjective needs to take.

Russian Meals

The most important meal of the day is served in the afternoon, sometime between 1 р.м. and 3 р.м. It is called "об**е**д," and it includes soup, an entrée, and possibly tea with dessert. Breakfast, or in Russian "з**а**втрак," consists of tea or coffee with a slice of bread served with cheese or salami, or a bowl of hot kasha with milk. Блин**ы** (pancakes) are often reserved for Sunday brunch or a holiday breakfast. Thin and light, блин**ы** are different from American pancakes and, depending on one's preference, can be eaten with different types of вар**е**нье (jam) or икр**а** (caviar).

Between з**а**втрак and об**е**д, many people like to have a small snack, often referred to as "п**о**лдник." The British tradition of tea is not known as British in Russia, but it is popular with many Russians. In fact, tea drinking, or in Russian "чаеп**и**тие," is considered a national pastime.

e✔ Fact

"Чай" (tea) was not well known in Russia until the nineteenth century when the construction of railroads allowed for an uninterrupted supply from China and India. As prices for tea decreased, its popularity soared, and black tea became a staple of the Russian diet. Russians brew strong tea, called зав**а**рка, in a small teapot. The tea is diluted with hot water in individual cups. Sugar and milk are added to taste.

Between 7 р.м. and 8 р.м. families gather for a hearty dinner, which might be similar to об**е**д in the dishes served. The following language formulas are frequently used to encourage guests and family members to enjoy their meal and to thank hosts:

При**я**тного аппет**и**та! Bon appetit!

К**у**шайте на здор**о**вье! Enjoy your meal! (Literally: Eat to your health!)

Очень вк**у**сно!	Delicious!
Спас**и**бо за вк**у**сный з**а**втрак / об**е**д / **у**жин!	Thank you for a delicious breakfast / lunch / dinner!

You can practice these phrases at your own dinner table with friends or family. Try cooking a traditional Russian meal for all to enjoy.

Traditional Russian Dishes and Beverages

The philosophy behind Russian cuisine is that a meal should provide an opportunity not only to satisfy one's hunger, but also to engage in pleasant conversation with others. Evening meals with family or friends are considered an important social activity. Except for breakfast, Russian meals incorporate appetizers or "зак**у**ски"—small dishes served all at once as an accompaniment to a pre-meal shot of vodka or a glass of wine.

Зак**у**ски provide a way to simultaneously tempt one's palate before the real meal arrives and to get a conversation going. Pickled vegetables and mushrooms together with a selection of cheeses and cold meats are often served as зак**у**ски.

The next dish is usually суп (soup); щи, a cabbage beef soup, or борщ, a soup made out of beets and other vegetables, are common. Soups are served hot with a small serving of смет**а**на (sour cream) and chopped parsley. After the soup comes the main dish. One of the most popular main dishes is пельм**е**ни, Russian dumplings, which are usually stuffed with a mixture of beef and pork and seasoned with соль (salt) and п**е**рец (pepper).

ⓔ❗ Alert

In Russian, there are two words for potatoes: карт**о**фель (masculine) and карт**о**шка (feminine). The two forms are interchangeable, and the second one is less formal. Both words are usually used in the singular.

Although today Russian stores carry a wide selection of pre-made frozen пельм**е**ни, many families prefer to make their own in keeping with old family traditions. A mundane activity on the surface, for many Russians it has become a family ritual symbolizing unity and cooperation. Another popular dish is гриб**ы** с карт**о**шкой, fried mushrooms with potatoes.

Russians are known for their love of хлеб (bread). It is offered with every meal, and there are usually at least two types to choose from: white wheat and dark rye. Many Russians believe that a meal without bread is not a nourishing meal.

The significance of bread in Russian culture is such that sharing bread and salt has become a common metaphor for friendship and trust. Bread symbolizes all the good of the world, and salt stands for the tears shed due to earthly turmoil. This is why in traditional Russian culture, hosts offer bread and salt to distinguished guests upon their arrival. Related to bread is квас, a mildly alcoholic beverage made by the natural fermentation of rye or wheat bread. It is sometimes flavored with fruits and berries, and because its alcoholic content is extremely low (no more than 1.5 percent), is enjoyed by people of all ages.

Eating Out

You will find a wide selection of restaurants in big Russian cities, from very affordable mom-and-pop stands to trendy sushi bars and French bistros. American-style fast food is everywhere, but gets a lot of competition from local chains such as Ёлки-Палки which sells блины, пироги, and other traditional Russian dishes. For lunch, office workers and students often go to a кафетерий or столовая (cafeteria). In the afternoon, stop for a coffee at a trendy кафе (café) and remember to order Turkish coffee and Russian ice cream, an unbeatable combination for any lover of caffeine and sweets.

As dark descends upon the town, it's time to check out a more upscale venue: a traditional Russian ресторан (restaurant) where you will be treated to a dinner with live music played in the background. Don't be surprised to see couples dancing between different courses! Relax and savor the atmosphere, but remember that the night is young, and you still have time to visit one of the big city's салса-бар (salsa bars) or ирландский паб (an Irish pub) or have a couple of beers in a пивная (a Russian bar). If you are happy with the service, remember to leave чаевые (a tip, literally "tea money"). The following is a list of words and phrases that might be helpful as you navigate your way through a menu in Russian.

Table 4-4

▼ ORDERING FOOD IN A RESTAURANT

Russian	English
рестора́н	restaurant
ба́р	bar
кафете́рий	cafeteria
столо́вая	cafeteria
меню́	menu
спи́сок вин	wine list
официа́нт	waiter
официа́нтка	waitress
заказа́ть обе́д	to order dinner
кокте́йль	cocktail (masculine)
заку́ски	starters
горя́чие блю́да	main dishes
пе́рвые блю́да	first dishes
вегетариа́нские блю́да	vegetarian dishes
спе́ции	spices
десе́рт	dessert
счёт	bill
заплати́ть по счету́	to pay the bill
чаевы́е	tip (noun)

It's possible to sample many different dishes in Russia, and you don't have to limit yourself to Russian specialties. Caucasian, Central Asian, East Asian, and South Asian restaurants are common, especially in urban areas. It's also not hard to find European restaurants.

Introduction to Russian Adjectives

In Russian, adjectives serve the same syntactic role as in the English language: to describe qualities of objects. The following adjectives are often used to describe different food tastes:

Table 4-5

▼ **FOOD-RELATED ADJECTIVES**

Russian	English	Russian	English
вк**у**сный	tasty	невк**у**сный	not tasty
хор**о**ший	good	плох**о**й	bad
н**о**вый	new	ст**а**рый	old
г**о**рький	bitter	сл**а**дкий	sweet
сол**ё**ный	salty	пр**е**сный	fresh (water), or bland (taste)
св**е**жий	fresh	несв**е**жий	not fresh
гор**я**чий	hot	хол**о**дный	cold
м**я**гкий	soft	тв**ё**рдый	hard

It is important to remember that Russian adjectives agree with the nouns that they denote in gender, number, and case, for example, св**е**жий хлеб (masculine) – св**е**жая клубн**и**ка (feminine) – св**е**жее молок**о** (neuter). Russian adjectives are grouped according to the palatalization of their stem into hard-stemmed adjectives and soft-stemmed adjectives.

Table 4-6

▼ **ADJECTIVES IN THE NOMINATIVE CASE**

Hard Stem			
Masculine	Feminine	Neuter	Plural
-ЫЙ / -ИЙ (stress on the stem) –ОЙ (stress on the ending)	-АЯ	-ОЕ	-ЫЕ (stress on the stem) / -ИЕ (stress on the ending)
Soft Stem			
Masculine	Feminine	Neuter	Plural
-ИЙ	-ЯЯ	-ЕЕ	-ИЕ
гор**я**чий суп	горячая каша	горячее блюдо	горячие макароны

Use Spelling Rule 1 to choose between И and Ы.

Chapter Review

Review the material in this chapter and complete the following exercises.

Chapter Quiz

Answer the following questions and check your answers in Appendix A.

1. List at least three products that are considered typical of the Russian diet.

   _____

2. How can you tell the syntactic roles of Russian nouns?

   _____

3. How many cases does Russian have?

   _____

4. What is the function of the nominative case?

   _____

5. What genders are assigned to Russian inanimate nouns?

   _____

6. What are the typical endings of Russian feminine nouns?

   _____

7. Name all typical daily Russian meals in Russian.

   _____

8. Explain what "закуски" are.

   _____

9. Name several typical Russian dishes.

   _____

10. Wish someone *Bon appetit!* in Russian.

   _____

11. Compliment a dish by saying that it is very delicious.

   _____

12. What does sharing bread and salt symbolize in Russian culture?

_____

13. In which grammatical categories do Russian adjectives agree with Russian nouns?

_____

14. Why is it important to know whether a particular adjective has a hard or a soft stem?

_____

Grammar Drill

Denote the grammatical gender of the following nouns. Check your memory to make sure that you remember the meaning of these words by writing down their meanings in English.

1. обед _____
2. варенье _____
3. икра _____
4. сок _____
5. хлеб _____
6. клубника _____
7. картофель _____
8. колбаса _____
9. мясо _____
10. вино _____
11. ресторан _____
12. меню _____
13. счёт _____
14. десерт _____

Translation Drill

Translate the following phrases into Russian, taking into consideration what you have learned in this chapter about the grammatical agreement between Russian nouns and adjectives.

1. good wine _____
2. new menu _____
3. salty sausage _____
4. bitter chocolate _____
5. tasty dinner _____
6. soft bread _____
7. salty cucumbers (pickles) _____
8. fresh tomatoes _____
9. good soup _____
10. bad Russian dumplings _____

CHAPTER 5

Russian Names and Family

R eading Dostoyevsky or Tolstoy is a wonderful way to explore Russian heritage, but readers who are unfamiliar with the Russian language often find it difficult to decode important cultural information embedded in the names of the characters. Examining the structure of Russian names will allow you to pick up on cultural nuances and will introduce you to the dynamics of Russian family life. In this chapter, you will learn new vocabulary dealing with family relations, discover the basics of Russian verbs, and learn about Russian personal pronouns.

Russian Family Life

The Russian family has undergone major social changes over the last hundred years. Historically, Russia is a society that values extended family, but it has become a country where a rate of divorce approximates or exceeds that of the United States.

Despite these dramatic changes, the traditional value of respect toward the elderly is still alive. Grandparents, or in Russian бабушки и дедушки (grandmothers and grandfathers), occupy a revered place in the Russian family.

Following is a vocabulary list with words to describe family relations. Note the conceptual difference between English and Russian ways of referring to in-laws. English uses generic terms that apply to both sides of the family, e.g. mother-in-law, while Russian has specific terms that help to identify who is who on what side of the family, e.g. тёща – the mother-in-law on wife's side, and свекровь – the mother-in-law on the husband's side. The concept of "son- or daughter-in-law" is expressed in Russian through terms that bear no similarities to that of "son or daughter." Compare the following pairs: сын – son, зять – son-in-law; дочь – daughter, невестка – daughter-in-law.

Table 5-1

▼ **FAMILY RELATIONS**

Russian	English
семь**я**	family
мать / м**а**ма (informal)	mother
от**е**ц / п**а**па (informal)	father
сын	son
дочь / д**о**чка (informal)	daughter
сестр**а**	sister
брат	brother
двою**ю**родная сестра	cousin (female)
двою**ю**родный брат	cousin (male)
б**а**бушка	grandmother
д**е**душка	grandfather
внук	grandson
вн**у**чка	granddaughter
т**ё**тя	aunt
д**я**дя	uncle
плем**я**нник	nephew
плем**я**нница	niece
отчим	stepfather
п**а**дчерица	stepdaughter
п**а**сынок	stepson
сирот**а**	orphan (male/female)
муж	husband
жен**а**	wife
свекр**о**вь	mother-in-law (husband's mother)
св**ё**кр	father-in-law (husband's father)
нев**е**стка	daughter-in-law
т**ё**ща	mother-in-law (wife's mother)
тесть	father-in-law (wife's father)
зять	son-in-law
неве**ста**	bride

жен**их**	groom
вдов**а**	widow
вдов**ец**	widower

The form "мать" is used only in formal paperwork. In nearly all other situations, the form "мама" is more appropriate. Be careful with similarly sounding words "невеста" (bride) and "невестка" (daughter-in-law).

Russian Names

Russians have three names: a first or given name (**и**мя), patronymic (**о**тчество), and the surname (фам**и**лия). For instance:

Миха**и**л (first name) Серг**е**евич (patronymic) Горбач**ёв** (last name)
Анна (first name) Андр**е**евна (patronymic) Ахм**а**това (last name)

These three names constitute an individual's legal name, the one that appears on all official papers, including passport, birth certificate, and court proceedings.

First Names

Имя, in English a first name, is the given name selected for the baby by the parents. As in English, many Russian names have full and short or diminutive forms. Compare the following names: Алекс**а**ндра (feminine) – Алекс**а**ндр (masculine), Мар**и**я (feminine) – Григ**о**рий (masculine), Н**и**на (feminine) – **И**горь (masculine). The general rule is that first names referring to males usually end in a consonant, a soft sign, or -Й. First names referring to females usually end in -А or -Я. There are very few exceptions to this rule: Дан**и**ла and Ник**и**та end in -a, but they are male names. All Russian short names, regardless of whether they are masculine or feminine, end in -Я or -А.

Following are two tables with popular Russian first names for men and women. Both full and short names are included. Note that some Russian names have a literal meaning: В**е**ра (Faith), Сл**а**ва (Glory).

Table 5-2

▼ MASCULINE FIRST NAMES

Russian Name	Short Name(s)	English Equivalent
Алекса́ндр	Са́ша, Шу́ра	Alexander
Алексе́й	Алёша, Лёша	Alexei
Андре́й	Андрю́ша	Andrew
Валенти́н	Ва́ля	Valentin
Васи́лий	Ва́ся	Basil
Вита́лий		Vitaly
Влади́мир	Влад, Воло́дя	Vladimir
Гео́ргий	Го́ша, Жо́ра	George
Григо́рий	Гри́ша	Gregory
Дани́ла	Да́ня	Daniel
Дми́трий	Ди́ма, Ми́тя	Dmitry
Ива́н	Ва́ня	Ivan
Евге́ний	Же́ня	Eugene
Ники́та	Ни́ка	Nikita
Никола́й	Ко́ля	Nicholas
Матве́й	Матю́ша	Matthew
Михаи́л	Ми́ша	Mikhail/Michael
Оле́г	Оле́жка	Oleg
Па́вел	Па́влик, Па́ша	Paul
Пётр	Пе́тя, Петру́ша	Peter
Фёдор	Фе́дя	Fyodor/Theodor
Серге́й	Серёжа	Sergei
Станисла́в	Стас	Stanislav

Remember that although the names Дани́ла and Ники́та end in –a, they are male names.

Table 5-3

▼ **FEMININE FIRST NAMES**

Russian Name	Short Name(s)	English Equivalent
Алекс**а**ндра	С**а**ша, Ш**у**ра	Alexandra
Анна	**А**ня, Ан**ю**та, Н**ю**ра	Anna
Алла	**А**ля	Alla
Анастас**и**я	Н**а**стя	Anastasia
Валент**и**на	В**а**ля	Valentina
В**е**ра		Vera (Faith)
Д**а**рья	Д**а**ша	Daria
Евг**е**ни**я**	Ж**е**ня	Eugenia
Екатер**и**на	К**а**тя	Catherine
Елизав**е**та	Л**и**за	Elizabeth
Ир**и**на	**И**ра	Irina
Кс**е**ния	Кс**ю**ша	Xenia
Люб**о**вь	Л**ю**ба	Lyubov (Love)
Людм**и**ла	Л**ю**да	Ludmila
Мар**и**на		Marina
Мар**и**я	М**а**ша, Мар**у**ся	Maria
Над**е**жда	Н**а**дя	Nadia (Hope)
Нат**а**лья	Нат**а**ша	Natalia
Н**и**на		Nina
Ольга	**О**ля	Olga
Светл**а**на	Св**е**та	Svetlana
Тать**я**на	Т**а**ня	Tatiana
Юлия	**Ю**ля	Julia

Patronymics

Отчество, or a patronymic, is derived from the father's first name. The literal translation of the patronymic is "the son of" or "the daughter of." It is always put after the individual's full first name. To form a patronymic, add a gender-specific suffix to the first name. For example, **Ю**лия Петр**о**вна is a woman whose first name is **Ю**лия and whose patronymic name is Петр**о**вна, which means her father's name is П**ё**тр.

Table 5-4

▼ FORMING A PATRONYMIC

Father's Name	Son's Patronymic	Daughter's Patronymic
Father's Name	+ -ович / -евич	+ -овна / -евна
Борис	Борисович	Борисовна
Александр	Александрович	Александровна
Николай	Николаевич	Николаевна
Григорий	Григорьевич	Григорьевна
Валентин	Валентинович	Валентиновна

Patronymics are never used with short names or nicknames. They are used to address or refer to adults in formal and professional situations. They show respect and sometimes a certain degree of social distance. For example, students will address their teacher with a combination of her full first name and patronymic, or in Russian **имя-отчество**. All official documents used internally in Russia also require a patronymic.

Last Names

Фамилия, or "last name" in English, usually has both masculine and feminine variants, as in Сидоров – Сидорова and Волчонков – Волчонкова. The basic rule to remember is that if the male form of the last name ends in a consonant, the female form ends in -a, or if the male form of the last name ends in -ий, the female form ends in -ая. Foreign surnames do not follow this pattern and retain the same form for both genders: Шевченко (Ukrainian), Рено (French), and Смит (English).

Table 5-5

▼ COMMON RUSSIAN LAST NAMES

Male Form	Female Form
Ending in a consonant or -Й	Ending in -A or -Я
Иванов	Иванова
Кузнецов	Кузнецова
Вронский	Вронская
Кипренский	Кипренская

Personal Pronouns:
Subject and Direct Object Forms

Now that you have learned about Russian names, let's figure out how to ask people what their names are. First we must go over some of the basics of Russian personal pronouns.

Personal pronouns are pronouns that can be used in place of a noun, for example, "boy" (noun) or "he" (personal pronoun). In both English and Russian, personal pronouns change their form to indicate their role in the sentence, such as that of a subject or a direct object.

She calls for / is calling him.	Он**а** зовёт ег**о**.
He calls for / is calling her.	Он зовёт её.

You can see that the forms of the personal pronouns "he" and "she" are different in these sentences in both languages. This is because in the first sentence, the pronoun "she" is used as the subject, whereas in the second it is a direct object, and vice versa for the pronoun "he." In the previous chapter, you learned that Russian nouns have a case system, also known as declensions. This case system also applies to pronouns. The following tables show the subject and direct object forms of Russian personal pronouns. These tables introduce you to the nominative and accusative cases of Russian personal pronouns.

Table 5-6

▼ **SUBJECT PERSONAL PRONOUNS: NOMINATIVE CASE**

	Singular	English	Plural	English
1st person	я	I	мы	we
2nd person	ты/вы (familiar/ formal)	you	вы	you
3rd person	он/он**а**/он**о**	he/she/it	он**и**	they

In Russian, the first person singular is never capitalized unless it is the first word in the sentence.

Table 5-7

▼ DIRECT OBJECT PERSONAL PRONOUNS: ACCUSATIVE CASE

	Singular	English	Plural	English
1st person	мен**я**	me	нас	us
2nd person	теб**я**/вас	you	вас	you
3rd person	ег**о**/её/ег**о**	him/her/it	их	them

The form "его" is pronounced [yivo]. The form её is pronounced [yeyo].

 Alert

The personal pronoun вы can refer either to formal you (second person singular) or to "you all" (second person plural). You can deduce the meaning through context.

Russian has two forms of the second person singular: familiar you, "ты," and formal you, "вы." Use the familiar "ты" when addressing someone you know very well, such as a relative, a child, or a pet. Remember that this form can only be used when addressing one person or animal. Use the formal you, "вы," to address a person whom you do not know well, an elderly person, or a person of authority. The rule of thumb is to use "вы" whenever you are in a formal situation or you would like to show respect.

Introduction to Russian Verbs: What Is Your Name?

The structure used in Russian to ask someone about his or her name is different than in English. There are two important elements in this structure: the use of the direct object personal pronoun, and the use of the verb "звать," or in English "call," which you'll learn here.

Fact

The form of the verb you will find in the dictionary is called the infinitive. "Звать" is an example of the infinitive in Russian. Examples in English are write, read, and play. In English, the infinitive is often used with the particle "to," as in "to call." In Russian, most infinitive forms end in –ть.

74

The literal translation of the Russian structure corresponding to the English "What is your name?" is "How do they call you?" or in Russian, "Как теб**я** зов**у**т?" A standard response is "Мен**я** зов**у**т + Name." When you are reporting on the name of another person or persons, you can also use the construction "This is / These are . . . ," which is translated into Russian with only one word, "**Э**то . . . " If you are not sure who the person in front of you is, you can also ask the question "Кто **э**то?", meaning "Who is this/that?"

Essential

Note that in the present tense of the Russian verb, "to be" is often omitted, as in "Кто **э**то?" / "**Э**то М**а**ша." or "Who is this?" / "This is Masha." In sentences where both the subject and the predicate are nouns, a dash is used to indicate the omission of the verb "to be" as in "Мар**и**я – жен**а** и м**а**ма," or "Maria is a wife and a mother."

The following are some examples of questions and answers you might hear as people discuss their names.

Как теб**я** зов**у**т?
What is your name? (familiar)

Мен**я** зов**у**т Сл**а**ва.
My name is Slava.

Как вас зов**у**т?
What is your name? (formal)

Мен**я** зов**у**т Андр**е**й Мих**а**йлович С**у**риков.
My name is Andrei Mikhailovich Surikov.

Как ег**о** зов**у**т?
What is his name?

Ег**о** зов**у**т / **Э**то Фёдор.
His name is / This is Fyodor.

Как её зов**у**т?
What is her name?

Её зов**у**т / **Э**то Светл**а**на Никол**а**евна Тихом**и**рова.
Her name is / This is Svetlana Nikolayevna Tikhomirova.

Как вас зов**у**т?

What are your names?

Нас зов**у**т Мар**и**я и Вит**а**лий.

Our names are Maria and Vitaly.

Как их зов**у**т?

What are their names?

Их зов**у**т / **Э**то Нат**а**ша и **А**ня.

Their names are / They are Natasha and Anya.

Verbs in Russian change their form depending on the person who accomplishes the action the verbs denote. Compare in English: I call / she calls / they call, and in Russian: я зов**у** / он**а** зов**ёт** / он**и** зов**у**т. Russian verbs have six distinctive forms, or conjugations, to go with six grammatical persons:

- 1st person singular (I / я)
- 2nd person singular (you / ты/вы)
- 3rd person singular (he/she/it / он/он**а**/он**о**)
- 1st person plural (we / мы)
- 2nd person plural (you all / вы)
- 3rd person plural (they / они)

The conjugation for the formal you is the same as that for the second person plural. In the Russian structure "Как теб**я**/вас/ег**о**/её/их зов**у**т?" we are using the third person plural form of the Russian verb "звать." You will learn more about Russian verbs and their conjugations in the next chapters. Meanwhile, to practice the use of the structures that you have learned in this chapter, read aloud the following dialogue between a teacher and her students on the first day of school.

◉ Alert

The Russian conjunction "а" is used to connect sentences that contain slightly contrasting ideas and is translated either as "and" or "but," depending on the context. The conjunction "и" can only be translated as "and." It connects ideas of equal status that do not contrast with one another.

Teacher:	Добрый день, дети! Меня зовут Валентина Петровна. А как вас зовут?
	Good afternoon, children! My name is Valentina Petrovna. And what are your names?
Student 1:	Меня зовут Люда.
	My name is Lyuda.
Student 2:	Меня зовут Даша.
	My name is Dasha.
Teacher:	А как тебя зовут?
	And what is your name?
Student 3:	Меня зовут Вася.
	My name is Vasya.
Teacher (pointing at a boy who has been silent so far):	А как его зовут?
	And what is his name?
Student 2:	Это Коля Серов.
	That's Kolya Serov.

This example highlights the traditional ways of introducing yourself and others. Notice that the teacher introduced herself with her given name and her patronymic, the three students introduced themselves with their short names, and the fourth student was introduced by another student who used his short name and surname.

Chapter Review

Review the material covered in this chapter and complete the following exercises.

Chapter Quiz

Answer the following questions and check your answers in Appendix A.

1. Who are considered the guardians of traditional values in Russian families?

   _____

2. If you were to rely on English to pronounce the Russian word for grandmother, what mistake are you likely to make?

   _____

3. Name one of the differences in the conceptualization of family relations in English and Russian as evidenced in family-related vocabulary.

_____

4. List all of the forms used in Russian to refer to mother and father.

_____

5. How many names does a Russian person have?

_____

6. Are there any Russian full first names that can be used both for men and women?

_____

7. Give at least one example of a Russian full first name that is masculine, but ends in a typically feminine ending.

_____

8. What is the literal translation of a patronymic?

_____

9. What suffixes are used to form a patronymic?

_____

10. As a foreign visitor to Russia, are you expected to introduce yourself with a patronymic name?

_____

11. What is one major difference between English and Russian last names?

_____

12. What is the culturally acceptable way to address a Russian doctor or teacher?

_____

13. What form of the second person singular would you use when talking with your best Russian friend? With the grandfather of your best Russian friend? With your professor at the university?

_____

14. In most cases, how can you tell the infinitive form of a Russian verb?

_____

15. Give at least one example of a sentence in Russian where the verb "to be" is omitted.

_____

Name Recognition and Vocabulary Drill

The following list of names reflects three generations of two different families. Remember that many Russian women take their husband's last name. Figure out who is related to whom and in what capacity. Write down your answers in English and then translate terms indicating family relations in Russian.

1. Мария Петровна Сергеева _____
2. Пётр Николаевич Сергеев _____
3. Владимир Сергеевич Никаноров _____
4. Ксения Борисовна Сергеева _____
5. Николай Дмитриевич Сергеев _____
6. Станислав Сергеевич Никаноров _____
7. Борис Алексеевич Никаноров _____
8. Александр Петрович Сергеев _____
9. Сергей Матвеевич Никаноров _____
10. Наталья Петровна Сергеева _____

Grammar Drill

Translate the following phrases into Russian, applying what you have learned in this chapter about Russian personal pronouns and Russian verbs.

1. My name is Ivan.

_____

2. What is his name?

_____

3. His name is Vladimir.

   _____

4. Who is this?

   _____

5. This is Marina. She is a mother and a wife.

   _____

6. What are their names?

   _____

7. Their names are Alexander and Maria.

   _____

CHAPTER 6

Descriptions and Possessions

The goal of this chapter is to introduce the expressions and grammar you need to express possession and describe objects and people. We will focus on possessive pronouns, adjectives, and nouns referring to professions and common household objects. You will learn how to describe your family, talk about their professions, and make and accept compliments. You will also find out how to use culturally appropriate terms to address people of different ages and genders, even if you don't know their names. You will explore differences and similarities in making statements, posing questions, and constructing negative sentences.

Possessive Pronouns

Possessive pronouns express who or what possesses the nouns they modify. Compare the following expressions in English and in Russian: мой папа (my father), моя мама (my mother), моё вино (my wine), мои родственники (my relatives). As you can see from these examples, the possessive pronoun "мой" agrees in gender and number with the noun that it modifies.

🅔 Alert

Keep in mind that grammatical agreement in Russian includes gender, number, and case. Adjectives change form depending on the gender of the noun they modify. They also change depending on whether the noun is singular or plural. You will learn more about cases of nouns, adjectives, and pronouns in the following chapters.

Table 6-1 shows Russian possessive pronouns and their forms in the nominative case. Although there are many forms to remember, note that third person possessives его, её, and их have only one form. However, don't confuse these possessive pronouns with the accusative case of the personal pronouns *he, she, it,* and *they* that were covered in Chapter 5.

Table 6-1

▼ **POSSESSIVE PRONOUNS: NOMINATIVE CASE**

English Personal Pronoun	Russian Personal Pronoun	Masc.	Fem.	Neuter	Plural
I	я	мой	моя	моё	мои
you	ты	твой	твоя	твоё	твои
he	он	его	его	его	его
she	она	её	её	её	её
it	оно	его	его	его	его
we	мы	наш	наша	наше	наши
you	вы	ваш	ваша	ваше	ваши
they	они	их	их	их	их

The possessive ваш can refer either to formal you (second person singular polite) or to you all (second person plural).

Describing Your Family

Following is a list of adjectives that people often use to describe family members. Russian adjectives have several forms because they agree in gender, number, and case with the nouns they modify. The form you will encounter in the dictionary is masculine, singular, and in the nominative case.

Table 6-2

▼ **PRONOUNS, ADJECTIVES, AND NOUNS: DESCRIBING FAMILY MEMBERS**

Russian Adjective	Example	English Translation
молодой	молодая мама	young mother

ст**а**рый	ст**а**рый д**е**душка	old grandfather
крас**и**вый	крас**и**вая жен**а**	beautiful wife
хор**о**ший	хор**о**ший муж	good husband
симпат**и**чный	симпат**и**чный брат	good-looking brother
умный	**у**мная сестр**а**	smart sister
тал**а**нтливый	тал**а**нтливый сын	talented son
ст**а**рший	ст**а**ршие д**е**ти	elder children
мл**а**дший	мл**а**дший брат	younger brother
люб**и**мый	люб**и**мая тётя	favorite aunt

Nouns: Professions

When describing your relatives, you might also want to mention their professions. Following is a list of Russian terms for various professions and occupations. Note that some names of professions have distinctive masculine and feminine forms, while others remain invariable, and it doesn't matter whether they are applied to men or women.

Table 6-3

▼ PROFESSIONS

Masculine	Feminine	English Translation
уч**и**тель	уч**и**тельница	teacher
преподав**а**тель	преподав**а**тельница*	instructor (university/ college)
пис**а**тель	пис**а**тельница*	writer
худ**о**жник	худ**о**жница*	painter
по**э**т	поэт**е**сса*	poet
п**о**вар	повар**и**ха*	cook
студ**е**нт	студ**е**нтка	student
спортсм**е**н	спортсм**е**нка	athlete
пев**е**ц	пев**и**ца	singer
актёр	актр**и**са	actor/actress
арт**и**ст	арт**и**стка	performer

официа́нт	официа́нтка	waiter/waitress
продаве́ц	продавщи́ца	salesman/saleswoman
стю́ард	стюарде́сса	flight attendant
вое́нный	вое́нная	military serviceman
рабо́чий	рабо́чая	manual worker
врач, до́ктор		doctor
инжене́р		engineer
строи́тель		builder
води́тель		driver
фармаце́вт, апте́карь		pharmacist
ветерина́р		veterinarian
профе́ссор		professor
бухга́лтер		accountant
ме́неджер		manager
дире́ктор		director
учёный		scientist
президе́нт		president
офице́р		officer
солда́т		soldier
пило́т		pilot

An asterisk indicates professions for which some women prefer to use the masculine form when referring to their own occupation as a way to express their equal status.

Making Compliments

When people describe their family to their friends, it is customary to compliment newly introduced family members by commenting on their youthful appearance, beauty, or other positive qualities. Here is how you can do this in Russian:

Кака́я у вас/ у тебя́ у́мная / краси́вая сестра́!
What a smart / beautiful sister you've got! (informal, plural/singular)

У вас так**о**й симпат**и**чный / тал**а**нтливый брат!
What a cute / talented brother you've got! (formal)

Ваш муж так**о**й **у**мный!
Your husband is so smart!

If you are introducing your family members to someone else, you can do so with the construction **Э**то . . . , which was first introduced in Chapter 5. To compliment someone's relatives, use the construction У вас так**о**й . . . , which literally means "By you, there is . . . "

Read the following dialogue to learn more about how to introduce family members and make compliments. The dialogue is between two friends, **И**горь and Евг**е**ний, who are students at Moscow State University. **И**горь is showing a picture of his family to Евг**е**ний.

Игорь:	Евг**е**ний, **э**то мо**я** м**а**ма. (Yevgeny, this is my mother.)
Евг**е**ний:	У теб**я** так**а**я молод**а**я м**а**ма! Как её зов**у**т? (Your mother is so young! What is her name?)
Игорь:	Её зов**у**т Н**и**на Алекс**а**ндровна. Он**а** – врач. (Her name is Nina Alexandrovna. She's a doctor)
Евг**е**ний:	А **э**то кто? (And who is this?)
Игорь:	**Э**то мо**я** нев**е**ста, Н**а**стя. Он**а** - студ**е**нтка. (This is my fiancée, Nastya. She is a student.)
Евг**е**ний:	У теб**я** так**а**я крас**и**вая нев**е**ста! А **э**то кто? (You have such a pretty fiancée! And who is this?)
Игорь:	**Э**то мой п**а**па. Он – проф**е**ссор. (This is my father. He is a professor.)

If you would like to compliment someone directly, learn the following words and expressions:

Table 6-4

▼ **MAKING FACE-TO-FACE COMPLIMENTS**

Russian	English
ж**е**нщина	woman
д**е**вушка	young girl
мужч**и**на	man

молодой человек	young man
человек	person
мальчик	boy
девочка	girl
дети	children
Вы / Ты – такой умный!	You are so smart!
Вы / Ты – такая талантливая женщина!	You are such a talented woman!

Treat такой as an adjective. It can be translated as "such" or "so." Remember to make sure it agrees with the noun it modifies.

The general structure for making compliments is as follows: pronoun, adjective, noun. If you are going to use такой for emphasis, it should be placed before the main adjective(s).

Note that if you don't know the person's name, it is acceptable to address him or her with nouns and adjectives indicating their gender and age, such as молодой человек (only for men), мужчина, девочка. However, be careful with the use of женщина—many Russian women prefer to be called девушка well into their golden years! It is advisable to rely exclusively on the formal pronoun вы as a way to address all people you don't know. Children are the exception; use the familiar ты to address children you do not know.

ⓔ✪ Essential

During Soviet times, it was common to use the terms товарищ / товарищи (comrade/s) or гражданин / гражданка / граждане (citizen: masculine, feminine, plural) to address others. Today, these terms are outdated. The terms господин / госпожа / господа (mister, miss, generic plural) are slowly being resurrected, but they are more commonly used in formal settings than in everyday interactions.

The Russian "девушка" and "молодой человек" are also equivalents to the English "girlfriend" and "boyfriend." A boyfriend can be also referred to as "друг" (friend). Today some young Russians use the English terms "boyfriend" and "girlfriend" in place of their Russian equivalents.

Statements, Questions, and Negative Sentences

As opposed to English, in order to form a question in Russian, you don't have to change the order of words.

Это твой сын.	This is your son.
Это твой сын?	Is this your son?
Это его внучка.	This is his granddaughter.
Это его внучка?	Is this his granddaughter?
Это её муж.	This is her husband.
Это её муж?	Is this her husband?

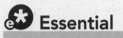 **Essential**

Remember the word for "yes" in Russian is да, and the word for "no" is нет. To form a negative statement or question, add the particle не in front of the word that you are negating, as in Это не моя жена. (This/That is not my wife.)

Use different intonation to indicate the difference between a statement and a question. Generally, statements are pronounced with a falling pitch, while questions have a rising pitch with a stress on the word that is the focus of the question. Add an appropriate question word at the beginning of the sentence to form questions that require more than a yes-no answer:

Table 6-5

▼ QUESTION WORDS

Russian	English
Кто	Who
Кто там?	Who is there?
Что	What
Что там?	What is there?
Какой	Which / What kind
Какой это город, Москва или Санкт-Петербург?	Which city is this, Moscow or St. Petersburg?
Как	How
Как дела?	How are things going? / How are you?

The "I Have" Construction

Earlier in this chapter, you learned to compliment other people's relatives by using the У вас так**ой** . . . construction. In this section, we will examine a similar construction that allows us to express possessions:

У мен**я** есть м**а**ма и п**а**па.	I have a mother and a father.
У теб**я** есть брат и сестр**а**.	You have a brother and a sister.

The literal translation of this construction is "By me/you, there is . . . " The construction includes the verb есть ("to be"), which can be translated as "to have" in this context. The first part of the construction is a preposition "у" (by) plus the appropriate personal pronoun in the genitive case followed by есть and a noun in the nominative case.

Table 6-6

▼ **PERSONAL PRONOUNS: GENITIVE CASE**

Singular	English	Plural	English
First person			
мен**я**	me	нас	us
Second person			
теб**я**/вас	you((in)formal)	вас	you
Third person			
ег**о**/её/ ег**о**	him/her/it	их	them

Remember: The form "его" is pronounced [yivо]. The form её is pronounced [yeyо]

Note that the third person singular and plural forms of pronouns acquire an additional initial letter "н" when preceded by the preposition "у": у нег**о**, у неё, у нас, у них. Also, remember that you already know another way to express possession through the use of possessive pronouns, which you learned in Chapter 5. Following is a list of sentences with examples of how to express possessions using either the есть formula or possessive pronouns.

У мен**я** есть кот и соб**а**ка.	I have a cat and a dog.
Это мо**и** кот и соб**а**ка.	These are my cat and dog.
У мен**я** есть маш**и**на.	I have a car.
Это мо**я** маш**и**на.	This is my car.

У тебя есть хлеб, молоко и сыр.	You have bread, milk, and cheese.
Это мой хлеб, молоко и сыр.	This is my bread, milk, and cheese.

Common Possessions

To increase your vocabulary, study the following words and expressions that will help you describe what you and others have:

Table 6-7

▼ **EVERYDAY OBJECTS AND POSSESSIONS**

Russian	English
машина	car
мотоцикл	motorcycle
велосипед	bicycle
дом	house
квартира	apartment
дача	country house (dacha)
телевизор	TV set
компьютер	computer
телефон	telephone
мобильный телефон	cell phone
собака	dog
кот	cat (male)
попугай	parrot

Other Uses for есть

You can also use the есть construction to talk about "деньги" (money) and "время" (time) as illustrated in the following dialogue:

Пётр: У тебя есть время?	Do you have time?
Виктор: Да. Чем я могу тебе помочь?	Yes. How can I help you?
Виктор: Да, конечно.	Yes, certainly.
Пётр: Огромное спасибо.	Thank you so much.

Expressing the Lack of Possession

If you would like to provide a short negative answer to a question about a possession, simply reply "нет" (no) to the question, as in

У теб**я** есть чай? – Нет. Do you have tea? – No.

Giving a full-sentence negative answer requires knowledge of the genitive case of nouns, which will be covered later.

Describing Possessions

Memorize the following adjectives to describe your possessions and to praise or criticize things that belong to others. Note that in Russian you can almost always form an adjective with the opposite meaning by simply adding the particle "не" to the adjective.

Table 6-8

Russian	English	Russian	English
уд**о**бный	comfortable	неуд**о**бный	uncomfortable
крас**и**вый	beautiful	некрас**и**вый	not beautiful, unattractive
стр**а**шный	scary	нестр**а**шный	not scary
больш**о**й	big	небольш**о**й	not big
м**а**ленький	small	нем**а**ленький	not small
дорог**о**й	expensive	недорог**о**й	inexpensive
деш**ё**вый	cheap	недеш**ё**вый	not cheap
хор**о**ший	good	нехор**о**ший	not good
плох**о**й	bad	неплох**о**й	not bad
интер**е**сный	interesting	неинтер**е**сный	not interesting

The adjective "неплох**о**й" is usually used in the sense of "satisfactory" or "average." It is a modest way of praising something or somebody. Use the word "**о**чень" (very) to intensify your statements.

ⓔ✱ Essential

Use the words "там"(over there) and "здесь"(here) to generally indicate the location of the object that you are referring to. For example: Где твой дом? - Мой дом — там. (Where is your house? - My house is over there.)

Coordinating Conjunctions

In Chapter 5, you learned about two Russian conjunctions, "**а**" (and/but) and "**и**" (and). These conjunctions are called coordinating conjunctions because they connect words and/or sentences of equal importance: "и" connects a series of parallel ideas that cannot be contrasted, whereas "а" links ideas of slight contrast. Another very common coordinating conjunction is "но" (but), which is used to connect contrasting ideas. See the following sentences for examples of how to use these three conjunctions appropriately.

Саша – очень хороший муж и отец.
Sasha is a very good husband and father.

Борис Петрович – не преподаватель, а инженер.
Boris Petrovich is not a teacher but an engineer.

Это Лена, моя младшая сестра. А это Нина, моя старшая сестра.
This is Lena, my younger sister. And this is Nina, my elder sister.

Это моя машина. Она – маленькая, но очень хорошая.
This is my car. It is small but very good.

Chapter Review

Review the material covered in this chapter and complete the following exercises.

Chapter Quiz
Answer the following questions and check your answers in Appendix A.

1. Explain the notion of grammatical agreement as it applies to Russian nouns, pronouns, and adjectives.

   _____

2. List all Russian possessive pronouns that do not follow the general rules of grammatical agreement and keep their form invariable.

   _____

3. Identify one Russian personal and possessive pronoun that can refer to one person or several people.

   _____

4. In which form will you find Russian adjectives in the dictionary?

   _____

5. How would you compliment a smart and pretty sister of your good friend, Ivan?

   _____

6. What is the most foolproof way to address strangers in Russian?

   _____

7. What are current substitutes for the Soviet тов**а**рищ / граждан**и**н / гражд**а**нка / гр**а**ждане?

   _____

8. Which verb should you use to express possession in Russian?

   _____

9. How can you tell a statement from a question in Russian?

   _____

10. How can you make a positive sentence into a negative one?

    _____

11. How would you give a negative answer about having something? How would you give a positive answer?

    _____

12. Do all terms for professions have distinct masculine and feminine forms?

_____

13. List three common coordinating conjunctions in Russian.

_____

14. Explain the meaning of the Russian adjective "неплох**о**й."

_____

Grammar and Vocabulary Drill

Translate the following expressions to practice describing family members. Pay specific attention to possessive pronouns and grammatical agreement between nouns, adjectives, and pronouns.

1. Your pretty sister

_____

2. His good-looking son

_____

3. My talented daughter

_____

4. His mother-in-law and father-in-law

_____

5. Her old grandfather

_____

6. Your (formal) smart husband

_____

7. You are so cute! (addressing a woman)

_____

8. You are so handsome! (addressing a man)

_____

9. What a nice husband you've got! (formal)

_____

10. What a talented and beautiful daughter you've got!

_____

11. This is my younger sister. Her name is Lena. She is a student.

_____

12. Who is this? – This is my wife, Vera. She is a talented scientist and a good teacher.

_____

CHAPTER 7

Introduction to Russian Verbs and Numerals

This chapter introduces the very basics of Russian verbs. It establishes their major conjugation groups in the present tense and offers examples of both regular and irregular verbs. Once you understand the basics, apply your new knowledge of Russian verbs to learn how to discuss your hobbies and ask others about their favorite seasonal pastimes. Finally, do your math in Russian and find out Russian names for the days of the week and months.

Verb Groups I and II

Russian verbs are listed in the dictionary in their infinitive forms. Verbs in their infinitive forms have two parts, a stem and a suffix. Infinitive verbs usually end in -ть.

Essential

In Russian, each verb has two stems: the infinitive stem derived by chopping of the –ть ending from the infinitive form of the verb and the present tense stem found by cutting off the conjugation ending from any of the conjugation forms of the verb in the present tense.

Infinitive verbs are not meant to show the tense, person, or number of the verb. All of that must be accomplished through conjugation. In this chapter, we will focus on conjugating verbs in the present tense.

Russian verbs are usually classified into two large groups, each following a distinctive pattern in their conjugations. The groups are known as Group I, or the E Group, and Group II, or the И Group. The letters е and и are the so-called thematic vowels. Group I verb stems take on the letter Е in their conjugations, and Group II verb stems end with the letter И.

The secret to forming correct conjugations of Russian verbs in the present tense is to remember that conjugation endings are added to the present tense stem of the verb, not to its infinitive stem. Whenever these stems are different (which happens often), you must memorize the forms of both stems.

The following charts provide conjugations for the verb читать (to read), which falls within Group I, and the verb говорить, which belongs to Group II. If you memorize the endings of these two verbs, you will be able to conjugate most Russian verbs. Remember that verbs taking -ю and -ют endings are known as Group I or Group II Model 1 verbs. Verbs that have the endings -у and -ут or -ат are known as Group I or Group II Model 2 verbs.

Table 7-1

▼ **GROUP I: ЧИТАТЬ – THE PRESENT TENSE STEM ЧИТА-**

Person	Singular	Plural
I	читаю - ю/у	читаем - ем
II	читаешь - ешь	читаете - ете
III	читает - ет	читают - ют/ут

Note that the endings "-у" and "-уT" are less common.

Verbs that follow the Group I pattern include verbs with the present tense stem ending in vowels. The following are examples of Group I Model 1 verbs. Note that infinitive stems and present tense stems for these verbs are identical.

понимать	to understand
работать	to work
играть	to play
отдыхать	to rest, to be on vacation
плавать	to swim
делать	to do
думать	to think
гулять	to walk, to take a stroll
уметь	to know how to do something
считать	to count

Now let's examine the conjugation pattern for Group II verbs.

Table 7-2

▼ **GROUP II: ГОВОРИТЬ – THE PRESENT TENSE STEM ГОВОР-**

I	говор**ю** - ю/у	говор**им** - им
II	говор**ишь** - ишь	говор**ите** - ите
III	говор**ит** - ит	говор**ят** - ят/ат

Note that the endings "-у" and "-аТ" are less common.

Verbs that follow the Group II pattern include verbs with the present tense stem ending in a consonant with the -ить and sometimes -еть endings in the infinitive form, for example:

смотр**е**ть   to watch
плат**ить**   to pay

Beware that in some verbs stress patterns change in different conjugations. For example, take the verb смотр**е**ть: я смотр**ю**, ты см**о**тришь, он см**о**трит, мы см**о**трим, вы см**о**трите, они см**о**трят. In these cases, you must memorize the stress patterns in addition to the conjugation endings.

⊖ Alert

Keep in mind the differences between the pronouns ты and вы: the form ты чит**а**ешь is used to address family members, relatives, friends, children, and pets, whereas the вы чит**а**ете form is reserved for formal address or to refer to several people.

Stem Variations in the Present Tense

Remember that some variation is possible within Group I and II regular verbs. For example, although the verb пис**а**ть (to write) belongs to Group I Model 2, its present tense stem is different from its infinitive stem, resulting in the consonant variation in the present tense in all persons:

Table 7-3

▼ ПИСАТЬ (GROUP I, MODEL 2) – THE PRESENT TENSE STEM ПИШ-

Person	Singular	Plural
I	пиш**у**	пи**и**шем
II	пи**и**шешь	пи**и**шете
III	пи**и**шет	пи**и**шут

Note the stress shift in the present tense.

Finally, in the verb люб**и**ть (to like, love) that belongs to Group II, an additional consonant –л is added to form its present tense stem, resulting in the following conjugation in the present tense:

Table 7-4

▼ ЛЮБИТЬ (GROUP II, MODEL 1) – THE PRESENT TENSE STEM ЛЮБЛ-

Person	Singular	Plural
I	люб**лю**	лю**б**им
II	лю**б**ишь	лю**б**ите
III	лю**б**ит	лю**б**ят

*Note the shift in the stress pattern of this verb. Use this verb to form infinitive constructions, as in "я люблю раб**о**тать."*

Based on variations in their present tense stems, Russian verbs are classified in additional subclasses. You will learn more about this in the following chapters.

Russian Present Tense: The Specifics

Now that you know the basics of the conjugations of Russian verbs in the present tense, let's examine the differences and similarities between how this tense is used in Russian and English.

In English, there are several grammatical tenses that describe present actions, including the simple present (I write), the present continuous (I am writing), and the present perfect (I have been writing). In Russian, there is only one present tense, and all of these sentences are translated as "я пиш**у**." The Russian present tense denotes actions that are happening at this moment, continuous actions,

actions that have begun in the past and are continuing now, and habitual or repetitive actions.

Question

What does the word "tense" mean?

Tense is a grammatical concept that expresses the time when an action takes place. There are three basic tenses: present, past, and future. In English, there are many additional tenses formed using auxiliary verbs and participles. Russian has only three grammatical tenses but uses other ways to indicate an attitude toward action in time.

Reflexive Verbs

Russian has reflexive verbs, just like English. Reflexive verbs express actions that reflect back on the performer. For example, "I washed myself" (reflexive) as opposed to "I washed my dog" (non-reflexive). In Russian, reflexivity is expressed through the addition of the particle -ся as in смотреть (to look, watch) – смотреться (to look at oneself / to appear to others (colloquial)). The reflective particle is added at the very end of the verb. Note that some verbs that are reflexive in English are not reflexive in Russian, and vice versa. Russian reflexive verbs follow the same conjugation rules as their non-reflexive counterparts. Following is a conjugation table for the verb кататься (to ride or roll / skate oneself), a verb that is used in several idiomatic expressions that you will learn in the following section of this chapter.

Table 7-5

▼ **КАТАТЬСЯ (GROUP I, MODEL 1) – THE PRESENT TENSE STEM КАТА-(СЯ)**

Person	Singular	Plural
I	катаюсь -юсь/усь	катаемся -емся
II	катаешься -ешься	катаетесь -етесь
III	катается -ется	катаются -ются/-утся

Note that the particle –ся changes to –сь in the first person singular and second person plural.

Another reflexive verb to remember is заниматься (to occupy oneself) (Group I, Model 1) – the present tense stem is занима-(ся).

Recreational Activities and Seasons

Sports, arts, and reading are popular recreational activities in Russia. Russians are proud of their accomplishments in international competitions in chess, tennis, and gymnastics, and many people choose these sports as hobbies. Hockey and soccer remain the most popular team sports and activities for boys all over the country. One famous Soviet song goes, "В хоккей играют настоящие мужчины . . . " (Real men play hockey), and this somewhat macho attitude toward this sport is still typical today. Volleyball and basketball are equally popular among men and women and are often played with teams consisting of members of both genders.

Figure skating and skiing continue to be popular winter activities for many Russians, some of whom choose to pursue these sports on the professional level, reaching the very top in international competitions. The following is a list of expressions with the verbs играть, читать, and слушать that describe some popular hobbies and recreational activities.

Играть в шахматы / футбол / баскетбол / волейбол / хоккей / теннис / бейсбол / американский футбол
to play chess / soccer / basketball / volleyball / hockey / tennis / baseball / football

Играть на пианино / скрипке / саксофоне / гитаре
to play piano / violin / saxophone / guitar

Читать книги / журналы / газеты
to read books / magazines / newspapers

Рисовать акварелью
to paint watercolors

Слушать музыку
to listen to music

Кататься на коньках / лыжах / велосипеде / мотоцикле
to skate / to ski / to bike / to ride a motorcycle

Пл**а**вать в басс**е**йне
to swim in a swimming pool

Заним**а**ться сп**о**ртом
to do sports

Танцев**а**ть в кл**у**бе
to dance at a club

Read the following dialogue between two friends, К**о**ля and Бор**и**с, who are discussing their favorite things to do.

К**о**ля: Что ты л**ю**бишь д**е**лать в своб**о**дное вр**е**мя?
What do you like to do in your free time?

Бор**и**с: Я любл**ю** кат**а**ться на л**ы**жах и игр**а**ть в футб**о**л. А ты?
I like to ski and play soccer. And you?

К**о**ля: А я любл**ю** игр**а**ть в хокк**е**й и чит**а**ть кн**и**ги.
And I like to play hockey and read books.

Бор**и**с: А чем л**ю**бит заним**а**ться тво**я** сестр**а** А**н**я в своб**о**дное вр**е**мя?
And what does your sister Anya like to do in her free time?

К**о**ля: **А**ня л**ю**бит танцев**а**ть и рисов**а**ть. А ещё, он**а** игр**а**ет в баскетб**о**л и л**ю**бит кат**а**ться на конькáх.
She likes to dance and draw. And also, she plays basketball and likes to skate.

Бор**и**с: Я т**о**же любл**ю** танцев**а**ть и игр**а**ть в баскетб**о**л.
I also like to dance and play basketball.

Hobbies and Seasons

Many hobbies are seasonal. The following is a vocabulary list with words that will help you describe the hobbies you like to pursue in different seasons of the year. Note that the instrumental case is required to express the season when you enjoy a particular activity.

Table 7-6

▼ SEASONS: ВРЕМЕНА ГОДА

Russian (Nominative Case)	English	Russian (Instrumental)	English
время года	season		
зима	winter	зимой	in the winter
весна	spring	весной	in the spring
лето	summer	летом	in the summer
осень (feminine)	fall	осенью	in the fall

Here is a dialogue between Саша and Наташа about their hobbies during different times of the year.

Саша: Наташа, что ты любишь делать летом?
Natasha, what do you like to do in the summer?

Наташа: Летом я люблю играть в баскетбол.
In the summer, I like to play basketball.

Саша: А зимой?
And in the winter?

Наташа: А зимой, мой муж и я любим кататься на лыжах в парке. Саша, а ты любишь кататься на лыжах?
And in the winter, my husband and I like to ski in the park. Sasha, do you like to ski?

Саша: Нет, но я люблю кататься на коньках.
No, but I like to ice skate.

Additional Idiomatic Phrases

Just like English, Russian is full of metaphoric and idiomatic expressions: these are phrases that use images to produce colorful associations between the things being described and our experiences. The following are several examples of such expressions with the verbs that you have learned in this chapter:

играть на нервах
to irritate someone, literally "to play on someone's nerves" ·

занима́ться ерундо́й

to waste time by doing something inconsequential, literally "to engage in nonsense"

чита́ть ле́кцию

to lecture someone, literally "to read a lecture"

Лю́бишь ката́ться – люби́ и са́ночки вози́ть.

If you are enjoying something, be ready to deal with all aspects of it; literally "If you like to ride in the sled, then you should like dragging it along, too."

Cardinal and Ordinal Numerals

Do you like to count, or in Russian, Вы лю́бите счита́ть? If you are mathematically inclined, study this section to learn cardinal and ordinal numbers in Russian from one to 100. Note that some numerals are similar to the ones in English. Compare два (two), три (three), and шесть (six). These similarities can be explained through the common Indo-European ancestry of the English and Russian languages.

Table 7-7

▼ CARDINAL AND ORDINAL NUMBERS

Numeral	Cardinal	Ordinal
0	ноль	
1	оди́н	пе́рвый
2	два	второ́й
3	три	тре́тий
4	четы́ре	четвёртый
5	пять	пя́тый
6	шесть	шесто́й
7	семь	седьмо́й
8	во́семь	восьмо́й
9	де́вять	девя́тый
10	де́сять	деся́тый
11	оди́ннадцать	оди́ннадцатый
12	двена́дцать	двена́дцатый

13	трин**а**дцать	трин**а**дцатый
14	чет**ы**рнадцать	чет**ы**рнадцатый
15	пятн**а**дцать	пятн**а**дцатый
16	шестн**а**дцать	шестн**а**дцатый
17	семн**а**дцать	семн**а**дцатый
18	восемн**а**дцать	восемн**а**дцатый
19	девятн**а**дцать	девятн**а**дцатый
20	дв**а**дцать	двадц**а**тый
21	дв**а**дцать од**и**н	двадцать п**е**рвый
22	дв**а**дцать два	двадцать втор**о**й
30	тр**и**дцать	тридц**а**тый
31	тр**и**дцать од**и**н	тр**и**дцать п**е**рвый
40	с**о**рок	сороков**о**й
50	пятьдес**я**т	пятидес**я**тый
60	шестьдес**я**т	шестидес**я**тый
70	с**е**мьдесят	семидес**я**тый
80	в**о**семьдесят	восьмидес**я**тый
90	девян**о**сто	девян**о**стый
100	сто	с**о**тый

The pattern of forming complex ordinal numerals from twenty-one on consists of putting an appropriate cardinal number together with an ordinal number (one through nine).

The following dialogue illustrates how to ask someone for their telephone number. Remember that in Russian, telephone numbers can be given using simple numbers (zero through ten). Make logical pauses to indicate the sequences of numbers when reading out a telephone number. If you have to call Russia, the country code is семь (seven) and the city code for Moscow is чет**ы**ре д**е**вять пять (495).

Ольга: У вас как**о**й н**о**мер телеф**о**на?
What is your telephone number?

Д**а**рья: Два три пять – чет**ы**ре од**и**н – в**о**семь три.
Two three five – four one – eight three.

Writing a Date in Russian

In Russian, the day is written before the month, just like in other European countries, which means 3/12 is the 3rd of December, not March 12.

The following is a vocabulary list with the seven days of the week in Russian. The Russian week begins with Monday, not Sunday. Typically, people have Saturday and Sunday as their days off, or выходные дни.

Table 7-8

▼ **RUSSIAN DAYS OF THE WEEK: ДНИ НЕДЕЛИ**

Russian	English
неделя	week
день (masculine)	day
сегодня	today
завтра	tomorrow
вчера	yesterday
понедельник	Monday
вторник	Tuesday
среда	Wednesday
четверг	Thursday
пятница	Friday
суббота	Saturday
воскресенье	Sunday

Note the pronunciation of the word сегодня – the letter "г" is pronounced as the consonant "в."

Read the following models to learn how to ask about the day of the month and the day of the week for today, tomorrow, and yesterday.

Сегодня какой день недели? – Четверг.
What day of the week is it today? – Thursday.

Завтра какой будет день недели? – Пятница.
What day of the week will it be tomorrow? – Friday.

Вчера какой был день недели? – Среда.
What day of the week was yesterday? – Wednesday.

Какое сегодня число? – Сегодня пятое мая.
What date is it today? – Today is May 5.

Как**о**е числ**о** б**у**дет з**а**втра? – З**а**втра б**у**дет шест**о**е м**а**я.
What will the date be tomorrow? Tomorrow will be May 6.

Как**о**е числ**о** б**ы**ло вчер**а**? – Вчер**а** б**ы**ло четвёртое м**а**я.
What date was yesterday? – Yesterday was May 4.

Note that in Russian word order is much more flexible than in English. Russian uses endings to indicate the syntactic roles that words play in the sentence, while English relies more on word order.

Russian Months

Study the following list to learn the Russian names for months. You will notice that many of them are very similar to the ones used in English. Be aware that you will have to know the genitive case forms to express the date in Russian. Compare: May – май (nominative case), the 1st of May – п**е**рвое м**а**я (genitive case). The genitive case is used to express the same notion that is conveyed in English through the preposition "of," and it is discussed in detail in Chapter 14. Observe the stress shift in several genitive forms.

Table 7-9

▼ **MONTHS OF THE YEAR: МЕСЯЦЫ ГОДА**

Nominative Case Form	Genitive Case Form	English
янв**а**рь	январ**я**	January
февр**а**ль	феврал**я**	February
март	м**а**рта	March
апр**е**ль	апр**е**ля	April
май	м**а**я	May
и**ю**нь	и**ю**ня	June
и**ю**ль	и**ю**ля	July
август	**а**вгуста	August
сент**я**брь	сентябр**я**	September
окт**я**брь	октябр**я**	October
но**я**брь	ноябр**я**	November
дек**а**брь	декабр**я**	December

None of the months are capitalized. They are all masculine.

To indicate the date, or "число," numerals must be used as neuter forms of adjectives. Consider the following examples.

Восьм**о**е м**а**рта	the 8th of March
Дев**я**тое м**а**я	the 9th of May
Тр**и**дцать п**е**рвое декабр**я**	the 31st of December

Chapter Review

Review the material covered in this chapter and complete the following exercises.

Chapter Quiz

Answer the following questions and check your answers in Appendix A.

1. How many conjugation groups are in the Russian language?

   _____

2. In addition to remembering the endings for the two conjugation groups of Russian verbs, what else do you need to remember to form the correct present tense?

   _____

3. How can you tell a Russian reflexive verb from a non-reflexive verb?

   _____

4. How many grammatical tenses does the Russian language have?

   _____

5. Is it appropriate to address an adult that you have never met before using the ты говор**и**шь form?

   _____

6. Which form of the pronoun/verb would you use to address a group of young children?

   _____

7. How can you tell who the implied subject in the sentence is even when the grammatical subject is omitted?

   _____

Conjugate the following verbs:

8. ду́мать _____

9. занима́ться _____

10. смотре́ть _____

11. люби́ть _____

Answer the following questions in Russian using the expressions in parentheses:

12. Что ты лю́бишь де́лать в свобо́дное вре́мя ле́том? (to swim in the pool)

_____

13. Что ты лю́бишь де́лать в свобо́дное вре́мя зимо́й? (to skate and ski)

_____

14. Что ты лю́бишь де́лать в свобо́дное вре́мя зимо́й? (to read books, play piano, and do sports)

_____

Writing Dates

Write the following dates in Russian:

1. Monday, November 1st _____

2. Sunday, May 17th _____

3. Thursday, September 4th _____

4. Saturday, February 7th _____

5. Tuesday, March 9th _____

6. Wednesday, October 11th _____

7. Friday, January 22nd _____

8. My birthday is _____

CHAPTER 8

Making Connections: Nouns, Verbs, and Pronouns

This chapter introduces the basic uses of all six cases in Russian. It then focuses on the specifics of the prepositional case, discussing ways to express location and objects of thought or speech. Special attention is given to prepositions, idiomatic expressions, and demonstrative pronouns. Verb conjugations and vocabulary to describe people's language abilities are also provided. The cultural focus in this chapter is on typical Russian housing in urban settings.

Declensions and the Case System

Russian nouns change their endings to reflect their role in the sentence. As you learned in Chapter 4, Russian nouns have six cases to express all of the roles they can possibly assume in any grammatically correct sentence. These noun endings are called declensions. There are three major declension patterns for Russian nouns, also known as the first, second, and third declensions.

🅔❗ Alert

Russian pronouns and adjectives also follow the case system. They have their own declension patterns. Russian adjectives must agree with the nouns they modify not only in case but also in number and gender.

It is possible to predict which declension pattern any noun would follow by considering the final letter in the nominative case and its grammatical gender.

- **First declension:** Masculine nouns ending in a consonant, a soft sign, or "й" (e.g. хлеб - bread, тесть - father-in-law on the wife's side, музей - museum) and neuter nouns ending in -о/-е (e.g. молоко - milk, здание - building) follow the first declension pattern.
- **Second declension:** Feminine and masculine nouns ending in -а/-я (e.g. вода - water, неделя - week, папа - dad, дядя - uncle) belong to the second declension.
- **Third declension:** Feminine nouns ending in a soft sign (морковь - carrot) follow the third declension pattern.

🅔❗ Alert

Although masculine nouns ending in -а/-я are not common, many masculine short names end in -а/-я: Валя (Валентин) Дима (Дмитрий), Витя (Виктор). Several nouns denoting male relatives also end in -а/-я. See Chapter 4 for review.

Review the complete model of Russian declensions in the following table for the singular and plural forms of the nouns стол (masculine, table), вода (feminine, water), and тетрадь (feminine, notebook).

Table 8-1

▼ SIMPLIFIED TABLE OF DECLENSION PATTERNS

Case	First	Second	Third	Plural
Nominative	стол	вода	тетрадь	столы/воды/тетради
Accusative	стол	воду	тетрадь	столы/воды/тетради
Genitive	стола	воды	тетради	столов/вод/тетрадей
Prepositional	столе	воде	тетради	столах/водах/тетрадях

Dative	стол**у**	вод**е**	тетр**а**ди	стол**а**м/ в**о**дам/ тетр**а**дям
Instrumental	стол**о**м	вод**о**й	тетр**а**дью	стол**а**ми/ в**о**дами/ тетр**а**дями

Now that you have an idea of how each case is formed, let's briefly review their main functions:

- **Nominative Case:** This is the case used for the subject of a sentence or clause.
- **Accusative Case:** This is the case used for direct objects. Several prepositions also require that nouns take the accusative case.
- **Genitive Case:** This is the case used to show possession. Several prepositions also require that nouns take the genitive case.
- **Prepositional Case:** This is the case used to express location. It is always accompanied by a preposition.
- **Dative Case:** This is the case used with indirect objects. Several prepositions also require that nouns take the dative case.
- **Instrumental Case:** This is the case that shows the means, manner, or agent of the action. Several prepositions also require that nouns take the instrumental case.

You already learned about the nominative case in Chapter 4. This chapter focuses on the prepositional case, and you will master the other cases in the following chapters.

Prepositional Case

The main function of the prepositional case is to express location of an object or a person. Compare the following examples:

Уч**и**тельница раб**о**тает в шк**о**ле.	The teacher works at a school.
В шк**о**ле раб**о**тает мой муж.	My husband works at a school.
Тетр**а**дь леж**и**т на стол**е**.	The notebook is on the table.
На стол**е** леж**и**т тетр**а**дь.	There is a notebook on the table.

These examples illustrate the basic use of the prepositional case and show that Russian sentences are structured so that the new information is usually put at the end of the sentence. When answering who, what, or where questions, Russian allows shortened answers just like English.

Что лежит на столе? – Тетрадь.
What is on the table? – A notebook.

Где лежит тетрадь? – На столе.
Where is the notebook? – On the table.

Где работает твой брат? – На заводе.
Where does your brother work? – At a factory.

Кто работает на заводе? – Мой брат.
Who works at the factory? – My brother.

The prepositional case is expressed through specific endings:

- Most nouns that follow the first and second declension patterns take the ending -e, as in класс – в классе (classroom – in the classroom), окно – в окне (window – in the window), школа – в школе (school – in the school).
- Masculine nouns from the first declension pattern that end in -ий, -ия, and -ие and feminine nouns that follow the third declension pattern take the ending -и, as in санаторий – в санатории (sanatorium – in a sanatorium).
- Several nouns that belong to the first declension pattern take the ending -y, which is always stressed, as in сад – в саду (garden – in the garden), лес – в лесу (forest – in the forest), пол – на полу (floor – on the floor).

ⓔ✱ Essential

The endings of the prepositional case are added to the stem of the noun, as in тетрадь – в тетради (notebook – in the notebook), школа – в школе (school – in the school).

In addition to the endings, the prepositional case is always formed using prepositions. Use the prepositions в (in, at) or на (on, at, in) to express location. There is one basic difference in meaning between these two prepositions: в usually expresses the location of the object inside of something, and на shows that the location of the object is on the surface of something. Compare:

стол – в стол**е**	table – in the table (drawers)
стол – на стол**е**	table – on the table (top)

Generally, when referring to the location in a city, town, or county, the preposition в is used, as in Москв**а** – в Москв**е** (Moscow – in Moscow), Нью-Йорк - в Нью-Й**о**рке (New York – in New York), Росс**ия** – в Росс**ии** (Russian – in Russia). In many other cases, the choice between the two prepositions must be memorized:

Table 8-2

▼ **PROPER USE OF PREPOSITIONS WITH NOUNS IN THE PREPOSITIONAL CASE**

Preposition В	English	Preposition На	English
инстит**у**т - в инстит**у**те	at the institute	**о**стров - на **о**строве	on an island
университ**е**т - в университ**е**те	at the university	пл**о**щадь - на пл**о**щади	in the square
шк**о**ла - в шк**о**ле	at school	стади**о**н - на стади**о**не	at a stadium
кин**о** -в кин**о**	at the cinema	зав**о**д - на зав**о**де	at a plant
те**а**тр - в те**а**тре	at the theater	ст**а**нция - на ст**а**нции	at a station
гост**и**ница - в гост**и**нице	at a hotel	конц**е**рт - на конц**е**рте	at a concert
рестор**а**н - в рестор**а**не	at a restaurant	ур**о**к - на ур**о**ке	in class
дом - в д**о**ме	at the house	**у**лица - на **у**лице	on a street
санат**о**рий - в санат**о**рии	at the sanatorium	в**е**черинка - на в**е**черинке	at a party

Alert

In addition to expressing location, the prepositional case is used to express the object of thought or speech, as in:

Я говорю о Маше.
I am talking about Masha.

Он думает о его невесте.
He is thinking about his bride.

Мы думаем об экскурсии.
We are thinking of the excursion.

Николай Петрович говорит о заводе, где он работает.
Nikolai Petrovich is talking about the factory where he works.

Света думает о доме.
Sveta is thinking about home.

Note that the prepositional case expressing the object of thought or speech requires the use of the prepositions о / об (about): об is reserved for the nouns beginning with the vowels а, и, о, у, э; otherwise, the preposition о is used.

In a Russian Apartment

In Russian cities, the great majority of people live in large apartment buildings. Although Soviet-built housing is still prevalent, the number of new, more spacious apartments is growing. When talking about an apartment, or квартира, Russians usually do not think in terms of number of bedrooms. Instead, a total number of rooms is mentioned, for example, однокомнатная квартира is a one-room apartment (a studio with a separate kitchen, bathroom, and hallway) and двухко́мнатная кварти́ра is a two-room apartment (with a separate kitchen, bathroom, and hallway). Note that kitchens, hallways, and bathrooms are not included in the total number of rooms. Because many apartments are small, rooms often serve several functions.

Another interesting feature of a typical Russian apartment is that a bathroom is often divided into two completely separate units. One, known as ва́нная, will have a sink and a bathtub, and the other, the туале́т, will only have a toilet. The doors to both bathroom sections are generally kept closed: Knock on the door or check if the light is on to see if you can use them.

🅔 Essential

Don't be surprised if your Russian hosts ask you to take your shoes off after entering their apartment. Just think about all the bad weather, and you will understand the reasons behind this tradition. You will not be expected to walk around shoeless, as your hosts will offer you a pair of slippers, or та́почки.

The following is a list of house-related vocabulary.

Table 8-3

▼ AT HOME

Russian	English
кварти́ра – на / в кварти́ре	at / in the apartment
дом – в до́ме; до́ма	in the house; at home
пол – на полу́	on the floor
стена́ – на стене́	on the wall
потоло́к – на потолке́	on the ceiling
дверь – на две́ри	on the door
окно́ – на окне́	on the window
ко́мната – в ко́мнате	in the room
прихо́жая – в прихо́жей	in the hallway
столо́вая – в столо́вой	in the dining room
больша́я ко́мната / гости́ная	living room
спа́льня – в спа́льне	in the bedroom

к**у**хня – на/в к**у**хне	in the kitchen
в**а**нная (к**о**мната) – в в**а**нной	in the bathroom
гар**а**ж – в гараж**е**	in the garage
м**е**бель (fem.) - на м**е**бели	on the furniture
див**а**н – на див**а**не	on the couch
стол – на / в стол**е**	on/in the table
стул – на ст**у**ле	on/in the chair
кр**е**сло – в кр**е**сле	on/in the armchair
кров**а**ть (fem.) – на кров**а**ти	on the bed
шкаф – в /на шкаф**у**	in the wardrobe
кн**и**жный шкаф – в кн**и**жном шкаф**у**	in the bookcase
п**о**лка – на п**о**лке	on the shelf
т**у**мбочка	stand
л**а**мпа	lamp
карт**и**на	picture
ковёр	carpet
плит**а**	stove
холод**и**льник	refrigerator
стир**а**льная маш**и**на	washing machine
з**е**ркало	mirror
телев**и**зор	TV set
магнитоф**о**н	stereo
кн**и**га	book
журн**а**л	magazine

Helpful Verbs to Remember

Following are several verbs that you will find helpful when talking about locations. Review the regular conjugation patterns in Chapter 7.

The verb "жить" ("to live") belongs to Group I Model 2. Its present tense stem contains an additional consonant -в (жить - жив-) that appears in all forms of the present tense:

Table 8-4

▼ **ЖИТЬ (GROUP I, MODEL 2) – THE PRESENT TENSE STEM ЖИВ-**

Person	Singular	Plural
I	жив**у**	жив**ём**
II	жив**ёшь**	жив**ёте**
III	жив**ёт**	жив**ут**

The verbs леж**а**ть (to lie down) (Group II, Model 2) and сто**я**ть (to stand) (Group II, Model 1) are frequently used in Russian not only to refer to the physical actions of people and animals, but also to describe locations of inanimate objects. Read the following description of an apartment to see how these verbs can be used in context.

Это мо**я** кварт**и**ра. Он**а** м**а**ленькая, но уд**о**бная. В ней есть стол**о**вая, сп**а**льня, м**а**ленькая к**у**хня, больш**а**я прих**о**жая и в**а**нная. В стол**о**вой сто**и**т стол, ст**у**лья и два кр**е**сла. А ещё там есть телев**и**зор и магнитоф**о**н. На к**у**хне есть плит**а**, холод**и**льник и п**о**лки. Шкаф сто**и**т в прих**о**жей, а кров**а**ть, кон**е**чно, в сп**а**льне. Ковёр леж**и**т на пол**у** в стол**о**вой, а кн**и**ги сто**я**т на п**о**лках в сп**а**льне. На т**у**мбочке в сп**а**льне леж**а**т журн**а**лы. В в**а**нной есть з**е**ркало и стир**а**льная маш**и**на.

This is my apartment. It is small but comfortable. In it, there is a dining room, a bedroom, a small kitchen, a big hallway, and a bathroom. In the dining room, there is a table, chairs, and two armchairs. And also there is a TV set and a stereo. In the kitchen, there is a stove, a refrigerator, and shelves. A wardrobe is in the hallway, and the bed is, of course, in the bedroom. A carpet is on the floor in the dining room, and books are on the shelves in the bedroom. Magazines are on the stand in the bedroom. In the bathroom, there is a mirror and a washing machine.

Note that the construction using есть that you learned in Chapter 6 can be also used to express location. In this sense, it is translated as "there is / there are." Although it is incorrect to use the adverb of place там (there) in the sentences where location is expressed through the prepositional case, it is acceptable to do so in constructions with есть.

Demonstrative Pronouns

Russian has a system of demonstrative pronouns that change their form to reflect the gender, number, and the case of the noun they modify. The most frequently used demonstrative pronoun is этот. It can be translated as this/that. If the speaker is trying to express a contrast between two objects or the conversation is about something that is out of reach and/or sight, the pronoun тот is used. Use the following table to study forms of demonstrative pronouns:

Table 8-5

▼ **DEMONSTRATIVE PRONOUNS**

Case	Masculine	Feminine	Neuter	Plural
Nominative	этот	эта	это	эти
Accusative	этот/этого	эту	это	эти/этих
Genitive	этого	этой	этого	этих
Prepositional	этом	этой	этом	этих
Dative	этому	этой	этому	этим
Instrumental	этим	этой	этим	этими

Note that for masculine pronouns and nouns denoting people and animals, the forms for the genitive and accusative cases overlap, both in singular and plural. On the other hand, for masculine and neuter pronouns and nouns denoting inanimate objects, the forms for the nominative and accusative cases are the same, in singular and plural.

Adjectives and Adverbs of Nationality

You already know some adjectives of nationality, for example, русский. In English, the same adjectives are used to describe nationality and to describe a corresponding language, as in English (a citizen of England) – to speak English. In Russian, on the other hand, an adverb is required to describe someone's language abilities, for example "Мария Петровна говорит по-русски и по-английски" (Maria Petrovna speaks Russian and English).

The list in Table 8-6 contains the names of countries with appropriate adjectives and adverbs of nationality. Remember that Russian nouns have grammatical gender. This is why all nouns for nationalities have two forms: a feminine and a masculine form. Make sure that you know the difference between adjectives of nationality and corresponding nouns: in most cases, the forms of nouns and adjectives will be different, but in some cases they will completely overlap. Compare американский (American, adjective) – американец / американка (American, noun: masculine and feminine forms) and русский (Russian, adjective) – русский / русская (Russian, noun: masculine and feminine forms).

Neither nouns nor adjectives of nationality are capitalized in Russian. Finally, take notice that there are two forms of the noun/adjective "Russian": российский and русский. The first one refers to Russian nationality and things that belong to the Russian Federation, whereas the second one refers to Russian ethnicity, one of many ethnicities in the Russian Federation.

Table 8-6

▼ **COUNTRIES, NATIONALITIES, AND LANGUAGE CAPABILITIES**

Country	Adjective	Noun	Adverb
Соединённые Штаты Америки (США) / Америка	американский	американец / американка	по-английски
Канада	канадский	канадец / канадка	по-английски / по-французски
Мексика	мексиканский	мексиканец / мексиканка	по-испански
Российская Федерация / Россия	российский / русский	россиянин / россиянка (русский/ русская)	по-русски
Англия	английский	англичанин / англичанка	по-английски
Франция	французский	француз / француженка	по-французски
Испания	испанский	испанец / испанка	по-испански

Ит**а**лия	италь**я**нский	италь**я**нец / италь**я**нка	по-итал**ья**нски
Герм**а**ния	н**е**мецкий	н**е**мец / н**е**мка	по-нем**е**цки
Гр**е**ция	гр**е**ческий	грек / греч**а**нка	по-гр**е**чески
Эфи**о**пия	эфи**о**пский	эфи**о**п / эфи**о**пка	по-эфи**о**пски
Ег**и**пет	ег**и**петский	египт**я**нин / египт**я**нка	по-ар**а**бски
Австр**а**лия	австрал**и**йский	австрал**и**ец / австрал**и**йка	по-англ**и**йски
Кит**а**й	кит**а**йский	кит**а**ец / кита**я**нка	по-кит**а**йски
Яп**о**ния	яп**о**нский	яп**о**нец / яп**о**нка	по-яп**о**нски

Note that plural forms of nouns denoting people of both genders belonging to the same nationality are formed from the masculine singular form, as in кит**а**ец – кит**а**йцы or египт**я**нин – египт**я**не. Masculine nouns that end in -ец omit the e vowel in their plural forms, as in:

америк**а**нец – америк**а**нцы
кан**а**дец – кан**а**дцы
мексик**а**нец – мексик**а**нцы

Read the following model dialogue to learn how to ask someone about the languages they speak.

Д**а**рья: Вы говор**и**те по-англ**и**йски?
Do you speak English?

Светл**а**на: Да, говор**ю**. А ещё я говор**ю** по-р**у**сски и по-франц**у**зски.
Yes, I do. I also speak Russian and French.

Russian adverbs that refer to language abilities are not capitalized. Also, Russians often skip the actual grammatical subject in a conversation if it is already clear from the context. For example, in the previous dialogue, Светл**а**на omits the pronoun "I." This is possible because Russian verbs clearly identify the noun that they refer to. If in doubt, check the form of the verb; it will help you figure out the grammatical subject of the sentence.

Use adverbs to add an evaluative comment to your description of someone's language abilities, as in чуть-чуть / плохо / неплохо / хорошо / свободно говорить по-русски (to speak Russian a little / badly / okay / well / fluently).

Chapter Review

Review the material covered in this chapter and complete the following exercises.

Chapter Quiz

Answer the following questions and check your answers in Appendix A.

1. What is meant by the term "declension"?

    _____

2. How can you tell which of the three major declension patterns a noun will follow?

    _____

3. What is the main function of the prepositional case?

    _____

4. Which are typical endings of the prepositional case?

    _____

5. When the prepositional case is used to express the object of thought or speech, which prepositions are used?

    _____

6. When Russians report the number of rooms in an apartment, do they include kitchen, bathroom, and hallway in the total number of rooms?

    _____

Prepositional Case

Transform the following nouns from the nominative to the prepositional case, then translate the phrases expressing location into English:

1. дом – в _____
2. завод – на _____
3. театр – в _____
4. университет – в _____
5. ресторан – в _____
6. Россия – в _____
7. Санкт-Петербург – в _____

Adjectives and Nouns of Nationality

A. Match the adjectives of nationality with the most appropriate nouns from the following list. Some of the nouns in the list have cognates in English. Try to combine adjectives with the nouns with which they are typically associated. Make sure that adjectives and nouns agree in gender and number.

Nouns: чай, квас, футбол, самурай, вино, пирамиды, парламент, пиво, принцесса

1. американский _____
2. японский _____
3. китайский _____
4. французское _____
5. немецкое _____
6. английский _____
7. испанская _____
8. мексиканские _____
9. русский _____

B. Form proper sentences with the words provided. Remember that Russian nouns and adjectives agree in gender and number and that Russian verbs are conjugated.

10. Катя Иванова (русский)

_____

11. Хуан Карлос и Маркос Гарсия (испанец)

_____

12. Франсуа Лерош (говорить по-французски свободно)

_____

13. Генрих Манн (немецкий писатель)

_____

14. Марина Цветаева (русский поэт)

_____

CHAPTER 9

Transitive Verbs

This chapter introduces the notion of transitivity and discusses how it is expressed in Russian. Special attention is given to stem variation and irregularities in verbs. This chapter also focuses on the form and function of the accusative case in the Russian language. The cultural spotlight in this chapter is on shopping for clothes. You will study the vocabulary used to communicate with shop assistants and words and phrases helpful in describing clothing, colors, materials, and patterns.

The Verbal Category of Transitivity

As in English, Russian verbs can be divided into two large groups: verbs that take a direct object (transitive), and verbs that do not take a direct object (intransitive). Compare the following sentences in English:

I read a book.   I swim in the sea.

The verb "to read" is transitive because it can take a direct object ("a book"). On the other hand, the verb "to swim" is intransitive because it can never take a direct object.

You already know several transitive verbs in Russian, including the verbs читать (to read), смотреть (to watch), писать (to write), and любить (to like/love). Following is a list of additional transitive verbs that belong to Group I Model 1:

слушать	to listen
спрашивать	to ask
получать	to get
показывать	to show
покупать	to buy
встречать	to meet

The verb учить (to teach) belongs to Group II Model 2. To review major conjugation patterns of Russian verbs in the present tense, refer to Chapter 7.

Stem Variations and Conjugation Irregularities

In addition to verbs that consistently follow regular conjugation patterns, there are several transitive verbs that exhibit slight variation in their stems. In Chapter 7, you examined the verb писать (to write) and learned that it is prone to consonant variation in the present tense in all persons, as in я пишу – ты пишешь – он пишет, etc. The verbs брать (to take), звать (to call), and ждать (to wait) are conjugated in a similar fashion. Review the following tables to practice their conjugations.

Table 9-1

▼ БРАТЬ (GROUP I MODEL 2)

Person	Singular	Plural
I	беру	берём
II	берёшь	берёте
III	берёт	берут

Table 9-2

▼ ЗВАТЬ (GROUP I MODEL 2)

Person	Singular	Plural
I	зову	зовём
II	зовёшь	зовёте
III	зовёт	зовут

Table 9-3

▼ ЖДАТЬ (GROUP I MODEL 2)

Person	Singular	Plural
I	жду	ждём
II	ждёшь	ждёте
III	ждёт	ждут

These three verbs follow a variation of the Group I conjugation pattern, taking on the consonant ё in all the endings that typically take the consonant e.

Finally, let's take a look at the transitive verb хот**е**ть. This is a highly irregular verb that follows both conjugation patterns. In addition to its irregularities in the endings, pay close attention to the consonant variation in its stem (т-ч) and a shifting stress pattern.

Table 9-4

▼ **ХОТЕТЬ (IRREGULAR)**

Person	Singular	Plural
I	хоч**у**	хот**и**м
II	х**о**чешь	хот**и**те
III	х**о**чет	хот**я**т

This verb is similar to the verb люб**и**ть (to like/love) in that it can be used in infinitive constructions, such as я хоч**у** есть/пить/гул**я**ть/кат**а**ться на конько́х (I want to eat/drink/go for a walk/ice skate).

The Accusative Case

As mentioned previously, the Russian language relies on the case system to express different syntactic roles that nouns can perform in a sentence. The accusative case is used to indicate that a noun is a direct object in a sentence:

Я чит**а**ю кн**и**гу.	I am reading a book.
Он**и** сл**у**шают м**у**зыку.	They are listening to music.
К**а**тя покуп**а**ет кварт**и**ру в Москв**е**.	Katya is buying an apartment in Moscow.

Just like other cases in Russian, the accusative case is expressed through specific endings. Nouns that stand for people and animals, also known as animate nouns, and nouns that stand for objects and places, also known as inanimate nouns, have different accusative forms. Read the following explanation to learn the specific endings for each group of nouns:

• Animate nouns that belong to the first declension pattern take the ending –a or –я, as in друг – жд**а**ть др**у**га (friend – to wait for a friend), тесть

– ждать тестя (father-in-law – to wait for a father-in-law). It depends on whether the preceding consonant is hard (друг) or soft (тесть).

- The accusative case form for inanimate nouns that belong to the first declension pattern is identical to the nominative case form of these nouns, as in фильм – смотреть фильм (film – to see a film), письмо – писать письмо (letter – to write a letter).

- The nouns from the second declension pattern take the ending –y or –ю, regardless of whether they are animate or inanimate, as in музыка – слушать музыку (music – listen to the music), дядя - спрашивать дядю (uncle – to ask the uncle). Most—but not all—of these nouns are feminine.

- The accusative forms for both animate and inanimate nouns that follow the third declension pattern coincide with their nominative forms, as in шаль – покупать шаль (shawl – to buy a shawl).

- The accusative forms for inanimate nouns in plural are identical to the nominative plural forms of these nouns, as in книги – читать книги (books – to read books), фильмы – смотреть фильмы (films – to see films), шали – покупать шали (shawls – to buy shawls).

- The accusative forms for animate nouns in the plural are identical to the genitive plural, which you will study in the following chapters.

Revisit Chapter 5 to review the accusative forms of Russian personal pronouns. The following is a list of verb and noun combinations that are frequently used in everyday conversations. All of the nouns are used in the accusative case.

Читать книгу / газету / журнал
To read a book / newspaper / magazine

Смотреть фильм / шоу / концерт / спектакль / оперу / балет
To see a film / show / concert / play / opera / ballet

Писать письмо / книгу / заявление / жалобу
To write a letter / book / statement / complaint

Любить мужа / жену / детей / маму / папу / брата / сестру / бабушку / дедушку
To love a husband / wife / children / mother / father / brother / sister / grandmother / grandfather

Слушать музыку / радио / учителя
To listen to music / the radio / a teacher

Спрашивать учителя / преподавателя / врача
To ask the teacher / university instructor / doctor

Получать деньги / зарплату
To receive money / a salary

Показывать фильм / одежду / дом / квартиру
To show a film / clothes / a house / an apartment

Покупать продукты / одежду / мебель / машину / квартиру / дом
To buy food products / clothes / furniture / a car / an apartment / a house

Possessive Pronouns: The Nominative, Accusative, and Prepositional Cases

Russian possessive pronouns also change to agree with the nouns they modify. Following is a table with the forms of possessive pronouns in the nominative, accusative, and prepositional cases.

Table 9-5

▼ POSSESSIVE PRONOUNS: ACCUSATIVE CASE

Personal Pronouns	Masculine	Feminine	Neuter	Plural
я	мой (inanimate) / моего (animate)	мою	моё	мои (inanimate) / моих (animate)
ты	твой (inanimate) / твоего (animate)	твою	твоё	твои (inanimate) / твоих (animate)
он	его	его	его	его
она	её	её	её	её
оно	его	его	его	его

мы	наш (inanimate) / нашего (animate)	нашу	наше	наши (inanimate) / наших (animate)
вы	ваш (inanimate) / вашего (animate)	вашу	ваше	ваши (inanimate) / ваших (animate)
они	их	их	их	их

The pronouns моего and его are pronounced with the "в" sound, instead of the "г" sound. Make sure you remember that the third person possessive pronouns его, её, and их keep the same form in all cases.

Shopping for Clothes

Buying clothes in a foreign country can be an interesting experience. Not only will you have to deal with potentially different fashion sensibilities, you will have to adapt to a new system of sizes and learn a culturally appropriate way of communicating with salespeople and other shoppers. During Soviet times when goods were few and far between, Russia was known for long lines of frustrated shoppers ready to buy just about anything. Fortunately, this has changed dramatically. Today, major Russian cities are jam-packed with fashionable stores and boutiques, all filled with expensive, trendy merchandise.

A Russian proverb says "По одежде встречают, а по уму провожают." In English, it can be loosely interpreted as "People are met according to their dress, but sent off according to their intellect." Today the desire to follow the latest fashions is common, especially among young people who are willing to spend a considerable portion of their salary on brand name products. In general, looking fashionable is a way for people to show off themselves and their prosperity.

Russian Clothing

Sometimes young Russians spend more money on "keeping up appearances" than any other aspects of their lives. Women especially are prone to spend a lot of money on the way they look, often choosing feminine and sexy clothes as opposed to more relaxed styles. Don't be surprised to see a lot of people of both genders wearing furs in the winter. People for the Ethical Treatment of Animals has not yet made an impact on clothing choices in Russia. Long and cold Russian winters make a thick warm coat and a pair of well-insulated boots a necessity for everyone.

⊕ Alert

Russians use European sizes, both for clothing and shoes. Shop assistants might be able to help you "convert" your size; however, it might be easier to try on several sizes to see which one fits you best. You may also find it helpful to look up a conversion chart before you leave or keep a cheat sheet in your wallet.

Although Russians usually do not wear traditional national dress, for many people the Russian ушанка (a fur hat with ear flaps, worn either tied up on top of the hat or down protecting the ears), валенки (felt boots, worn outside with rubber galoshes to protect them from getting wet), and платок (a Russian wool headscarf often decorated with images of colorful flowers) constitute important elements of a traditional folk costume. See the following list to learn more vocabulary for clothing items and popular types of shoes.

Table 9-6

▼ SHOPPING FOR CLOTHES

Russian	English
одежда	clothes
платье	dress
рубашка	shirt
блуза	blouse
брюки	pants
джинсы	jeans
юбка	skirt
костюм	suit
кофта	sweater, sweatshirt
свитер	sweater

пиджак	sports jacket (both for men and women)
галстук	tie
платок	kerchief, headscarf
шаль (fem.)	shawl
шапка	hat
шарф	scarf
пальто	coat
куртка	jacket or coat
шуба	fur coat
туфли (pl.)	women's shoes, pumps
ботинки (pl.)	boots
перчатки (pl.)	gloves

Russian Stores

Like Macy's in Manhattan, there are several Russian stores that are known nationwide, including ГУМ or Государственный универсальный магазин (State Universal Store), ЦУМ or Центральный универсальный магазин (Central Universal Store), and Детский мир (Children's World). All three are department stores located in the very heart of Moscow and have a long history.

⊖! Alert

Rules of capitalization are different in Russian. Usually only the first word in a title is capitalized, as opposed to English, where most of the words in a title are capitalized. The preceding and following store names provide examples of this Russian language quirk.

ГУМ is perhaps more famous than others because it is located in Red Square and is housed in a gorgeous early-twentieth-century art nouveau building. Its layout concept is similar to that of a Parisian arcade. Today, more and more new chains are appearing in Russian cities, including stores such as Метро and Седьмой континент. These stores often sell clothes, household goods, and food products.

ⓔ✔ Fact

Many Russian clothing stores, or in Russian магазины одежды, that cater to women bear female names, such as Людмила or Наташа. Sometimes, the store's sign might have a subtitle, as in Людмила – магазин женской одежды. Other stores are named after the products that they carry, as in Молоко (Milk – dairy products), Хлеб (Bread), Радио товары (Radio Products).

Remember that abbreviations act as regular nouns, for example, ГУМ (a store GUM) – в ГУМе (at the store GUM). ГУМ stands for магазин, which is a masculine noun belonging to the first declension pattern. This is why in the prepositional case, ГУМ acquires the ending –e, as in the following dialogue:

Вера: Где ты покупаешь твою одежду?
(Where do you buy your clothes?)

Валя: В ГУМе. У них такая хорошая модная одежда. Это моё любимое синее шерстяное пальто. А это мой бежевый хлопчатобумажный свитер.
(At GUM. They have such good, fashionable clothes. Here's my favorite blue wool coat. And this is my beige cotton sweater.)

Shopping Phrases

Following are several expressions that are helpful to know in order to communicate with salespeople in stores as you are buying clothes:

Чем я могу вам помочь?
How can I help you?

Я хочу купить. . .
I'd like to buy. . .

Позвольте мне показать вам эту вещь.
Allow me to show you this item.

Сколько это стоит?
How much does it cost?

Это (стоит) дорого/дёшево.
This (costs/is) expensive/cheap.

Это вам (**о**чень) к лиц**у**.
This suits you (very much).

Это вам (**о**чень) идёт.
This looks good on you.

Где в**а**ша к**а**сса?
Where is the checkout desk?

Я мог**у э**то пом**е**рить?
Can I try this on?

Где у вас в магаз**и**не прим**е**рочная?
Where do you have a fitting room in the store?

Мне **э**то мал**о**/велик**о**.
This is too small/big for me.

Как**о**й **э**то разм**е**р?
What size is this?

Colors, Materials, and Patterns

When buying clothes, it is important to be able to describe colors, patterns, and materials. Following is a list of adjectives for basic colors, popular patterns, and materials used for clothing. All adjectives are given in singular masculine, just as they would be in a dictionary. Remember that you must change the adjective's form so that it matches the grammatical gender, case, and number of the noun that it modifies. Adjectives are usually placed before nouns, with adjectives for colors in the initial position, as in б**е**лая шёлковая бл**у**за (white silk blouse), unless there is a qualifying adjective that describes the quality of the item, as in крас**и**вая б**е**лая шёлковая бл**у**за (pretty white silk blouse). Other qualifying adjectives that are helpful to know include хор**о**ший (good), уд**о**бный (comfortable), н**о**вый (new), м**о**дный (fashionable or trendy), дорог**о**й (expensive), дешёвый (cheap), люб**и**мый (favorite), and ст**а**рый (old).

Table 9-7

▼ **COLORS, PATTERNS, AND MATERIALS FOR CLOTHES**

Russian	English
бéлый	white
чёрный	black
крáсный	red
рóзовый	pink
зелёный	green
голубóй	light blue
сѝний	dark blue
сéрый	grey
жёлтый	yellow
орáнжевый	orange
корѝчневый	brown
бéжевый	beige
кóжаный	leather (adj.)
меховóй	fur (adj.)
шерстянóй	wool (adj.)
шёлковый	silk (adj.)
хлопчатобумáжный	cotton (adj.)
клéтчатый	checkered
в горóшек	polka dotted
в полóску	striped
в цветóчек	flower pattern

In Russian, adjectives are usually placed before nouns. However, expressions such as "в горóшек" are placed after the nouns that they refer to.

As you already know, adjectives are also declined. Following are two tables that summarize adjectival endings for nominative, accusative, and prepositional forms. Remember that all Russian adjectives can be roughly divided into hard-stemmed (stems ending with hard consonants) and soft-stemmed (stems ending with a soft consonant). The endings for the accusative forms in the masculine, neuter, and plural forms are different depending on whether the noun defined is inanimate or animate.

Table 9-8

▼ **HARD-STEMMED ADJECTIVE ENDINGS: NOMINATIVE, ACCUSATIVE, PREPOSITIONAL CASES**

Case	Masculine	Feminine	Neuter	Plural
Nominative	-ый/-ий/-ой	-ая	-ое	-ые/-ие
Accusative	-ый/-ий/-ой (inanimate) -ого/-его (animate)	-ую	-ое	-ые/-ие (inanimate) -ых/-их (animate)
Prepositional	-ом/-ем	-ой/-ей	-ом/-ем	-ых/-их

Table 9-9

▼ **SOFT-STEMMED ADJECTIVE ENDINGS: NOMINATIVE, ACCUSATIVE, PREPOSITIONAL CASES**

Case	Masculine	Feminine	Neuter	Plural
Nominative	-ий	-яя	-ее	-ие
Accusative	-ий (inanimate)/ -его (animate)	-юю	-ее	ие (inanimate) -их (animate)
Prepositional	-ем	-ей	-ем	-их

Chapter Review

Review the material covered in this chapter and complete the following exercises.

Chapter Quiz

Answer the following questions and check your answers in Appendix A.

1. What is the major difference between transitive and intransitive verbs?

2. Name the irregularities in the conjugation of the Russian verb хотеть.

3. What is the major function of the accusative case?

_____

4. In addition to different declension patterns, what other variable is important to remember when you decide on the accusative form?

_____

5. Give examples of clothing items that are considered by many to be staples of Russian national folk dress.

_____

6. List two examples of Russian verbs that allow infinitive constructions.

_____

7. What grammatical concepts determine the ending that a noun and an adjective would take in the accusative case?

_____

Grammar and Vocabulary Practice

A. Translate the following verb-noun expressions into Russian to practice forming accusative forms:

1. to buy a sweater   _____
2. to wait for a friend   _____
3. to listen to music   _____
4. to read a book   _____
5. to love Moscow   _____
6. to buy a shirt   _____
7. to show a film   _____
8. to take a book   _____
9. to ask the mother   _____
10. to show a fur coat   _____

B. Translate the following sentences from Russian into English or from English into Russian. Make sure that you remember how to conjugate verbs and decline nouns, adjectives, and possessive pronouns:

11. Я чита**ю** мо**ю** газ**е**ту.

_____

12. Вы сл**у**шаете их м**у**зыку.

_____

13. Он**а** покуп**а**ет ег**о** од**е**жду в Г**У**Ме.

_____

14. Мы л**ю**бим в**а**шу м**у**зыку.

_____

15. Он покуп**а**ет прод**у**кты.

_____

16. I am buying a beautiful red suit.

_____

17. He is meeting his good friend.

_____

Reading Practice

Read the following store names and write down in English what kind(s) of products these stores carry:

1. Д**е**тский мир   _____
2. Нат**а**ша   _____
3. Молок**о**   _____
4. ГУМ   _____
5. **О**птика   _____
6. Апт**е**ка   _____
7. Р**а**дио тов**а**ры   _____
8. Электр**о**ника   _____
9. Кн**и**ги   _____

CHAPTER 10

Happy Birthday in Russian

In this chapter, you will become familiar with the major function of the Russian dative case and learn dative forms for nouns, personal pronouns, and adjectives. Furthermore, you will become more aware of the connection between nouns and verbs by learning new verbal constructions that require nouns in the dative case. You will read about Russian birthday parties and gift-giving customs. Finally, you will be able to practice some new vocabulary and learn the basics of the Russian past tense.

Nouns and Pronouns in the Dative Case

The main function of the dative case is to indicate indirect objects, as in the following examples:

Кому ты пишешь письмо? — Я пишу письмо моей маме.
To whom are you writing a letter? — I am writing a letter to my mother.

Кому она читает книгу? — Она читает книгу её сыну.
To whom is she reading a book? — She is reading a book to her son.

Кому ваша жена покупает подарок? — Моя жена покупает подарок нашей внучке.
For whom is your wife buying a present? — My wife is buying a present for our granddaughter.

In the previous sentences, the words моей маме (to my mother), её сыну (to her son), and нашей внучке (for our granddaughter) are indirect objects, and thus they are used in the dative case. Contrary to English, Russian indirect objects are identified by the dative case and do not always require the use of prepositions.

ⓔ✷ Essential

Indirect objects are nouns that are indirectly impacted by verbs. When in doubt, remember that indirect objects answer the questions to whom, for whom (кому in Russian), to what, or for what (чему in Russian), immediately followed by a verb, as in to whom something is given.

The dative case shares some similarities with the nominative, accusative, and prepositional cases that you have already studied. The dative case is also expressed through a specific ending added to the stem of a noun:

- The nouns from the first declension pattern take the ending -у if they are hard-stemmed or their stem ends with the letters ж, ш, ч, or щ, as in профессор – профессору (professor – to the professor), врач – врачу (doctor – to the doctor), окно – окну (window – to the window).
- The nouns from the first declension pattern take the ending -ю if they are soft-stemmed, as in писатель – писателю (writer – to the writer), словарь – словарю (dictionary – to the dictionary).
- The endings of the dative case for the nouns that follow the second and third declension patterns are identical to the endings that these nouns take in the prepositional case, as in женщина – женщине (woman – to the woman), аудитория – аудитории (lecture hall – to the lecture hall), тетрадь – тетради (notebook – to the notebook).
- Plural nouns in the dative case assume the ending -ам if they have a hard stem and the ending -ям if they have a soft stem, as in классы – классам (classrooms – in the classrooms), тетради – тетрадям (notebooks – in the notebooks).

The dative case forms for personal pronouns are grouped together with the nominative forms, which were presented initially: я — мне, ты — тебе, он — ему (masculine), она — ей (feminine), оно — ему (neuter), мы — нам, вы — вам, они — им. When learning these forms, remember that the third-person singular masculine and neuter forms are identical.

Adjectives in the Dative Case

Russian adjectives are declined, just like nouns. Hard-stemmed and soft-stemmed adjectives follow different declension patterns. The following tables summarize adjective endings for the nominative and dative cases for hard-stemmed and soft-stemmed adjectives.

Table 10-1

▼ **HARD-STEMMED ADJECTIVE ENDINGS: DATIVE CASE**

Case	Masculine	Feminine	Neuter	Plural
Nominative	-ый/-ий/-ой	-ая	-ое	-ые/-ие
Dative	-ому/-ему	-ой/-ей	-ому/-ему	-ым/-им
Nominative	красивый	красивая	красивое	красивые
Dative	красивому	красивой	красивому	красивым

Table 10-2

▼ **SOFT-STEMMED ADJECTIVE ENDINGS: DATIVE CASE**

Case	Masculine	Feminine	Neuter	Plural
Nominative	-ий	-яя	-ее	-ие
Dative	-ему	-ей	-ему	-им
Nominative	лишний	лишняя	лишнее	лишние
Dative	лишнему	лишней	лишнему	лишним

Remember to apply Spelling Rule 1 when choosing the appropriate ending for adjectives: after Ж, Ш, Щ, Ч, К, Г, and Х always write И, not Ы. For example, холодный – горячий (cold – hot). This rule only applies to the adjectives with stressed stems. Compare: горячий – большой (hot – big).

Verbs in the Dative Case

There are several verbs that are commonly used with the indirect object, which requires the use of the dative case. These verbs include the following:

давать   to give (Group I Model 1; present tense stem да-)

подарить   to give as a present (Group II Model 1)

покуп**а**ть	to buy (Group I Model 1)
расск**а**зывать	to tell a story (Group I Model 1)
пок**а**зывать	to show (Group I Model 1)
помог**а**ть	to help (Group I Model 1)
предлаг**а**ть	to offer, suggest (Group I Model 1)
сов**е**товать	to advise (Group I Model 1)

The present tense stem of the verb сов**е**товать is сов**е**т-, which results in the following conjugation pattern:

Table 10-3

▼ **СОВЕТОВАТЬ – THE PRESENT TENSE STEM СОВЕТ-**

Person	Singular	Plural
I	сов**е**тую	сов**е**туем
II	сов**е**туешь	сов**е**туете
III	сов**е**тует	сов**е**туют

In addition, the verb нр**а**виться (to appeal) also requires the use of the dative case, as presented in the following examples:

Мне нр**а**вится **э**тот парк.
I like this park. (Literally: This park is appealing to me.)

Валент**и**не нр**а**вятся исп**а**нские ф**и**льмы.
Valentina likes Spanish films. (Literally: Spanish films are appealing to Valentina.)

Let's look carefully at the structure of these sentences. The subjects of these sentences are парк and фильмы. How do we know this? Let's examine the forms of the verb нр**а**виться. In the first example it is conjugated to agree with the word парк, and in the second example it is conjugated to agree with the word ф**и**льмы. In these sentences, the subjects are the things that are being liked and the person to whom they appeal is in the dative case.

⊛ Essential

Structurally, these verbs are very different; люб**и**ть is followed by a noun in the accusative case (direct object), and нр**а**виться is preceded by a noun or pronoun in the dative case (indirect object) and is followed by a noun in the nominative case (the nominal subject of the sentence, the thing that is appealing).

In previous chapters, you learned the verb люб**и**ть, which has a similar meaning to the verb нр**а**виться. However, the difference is that the verb люб**и**ть has a more general meaning and denotes a strong feeling of love, whereas the verb нр**а**виться usually refers to specific, isolated things or incidents and has a more subdued quality. Compare the following statements: Я любл**ю** кин**о** (I love cinema) and Мне нр**а**вится **э**тот фильм (I like this movie).

At a Russian Birthday

Birthday celebrations are popular social occasions. In Russia, it is traditional for the person who is celebrating his or her birthday to organize a party, prepare food, and supply the drinks. The guests are responsible for presents and toasts. At children's parties, the parents of the birthday child are responsible for arranging entertainment, which may include a clown, games, and contests. Adults usually have a nice dinner with some singing and dancing afterward.

✔ Fact

"Dative" is derived from the Latin verb stem "da," meaning "to give." This is an appropriate name for the case that is used to indicate the giving of something, be it a gift, an answer, or some advice.

There is no traditional Russian version of the song "Happy Birthday." Often, the song is sung in English or sometimes it is substituted by a Russian song about birthdays from a classic children's cartoon. In addition to presents, guests often bring flowers, sweets, and cards. The person who is receiving presents is expected to be grateful and cheerful, because of the old saying: Дар**ё**ному кон**ю** в з**у**бы не см**о**трят (Don't look a gift horse in the mouth). The following list contains useful words and expressions related to birthday celebrations:

под**а**рить (Group II Model 1) под**а**рок
to give a present to somebody (a noun in the dative case)

куп**и**ть цвет**ы** / конф**е**ты / торт
to buy flowers, candies, a cake for somebody (a noun in the dative case)

день рожд**е**ния
birthday (literally: day of birth)

С днём рождения!
Happy Birthday! (a greeting to use in person or in writing on the birthday card)

поздравлять с днём рождения (Group I Model I)
to wish happy birthday

приглашать гостей (Group I Model I)
to invite guests

играть в прятки / в шахматы / в шарады (Group I Model I)
to play hide and seek / to play chess / to play charades

печь пирог / торт
to bake a cake

готовить праздничный ужин
to prepare/cook a festive dinner

танцевать
to dance

разговаривать
to talk

петь
to sing

смеяться
to laugh

Be careful with the following verbs that exhibit irregularities in their conjugations:

Table 10-4

▼ **ПЕЧЬ (GROUP I MODEL 2)**

Person	Singular	Plural
I	пеку	печём
II	печёшь	печёте
III	печёт	пекут

Table 10-5

▼ ГОТОВИТЬ (GROUP I MODEL 1)

Person	Singular	Plural
I	готовлю	готовим
II	готовишь	готовите
III	готовит	готовят

Table 10-6

▼ ТАНЦЕВАТЬ (GROUP I MODEL 1)

Person	Singular	Plural
I	танцую	танцуем
II	танцуешь	танцуете
III	танцует	танцуют

Table 10-7

▼ ПЕТЬ (GROUP I MODEL 1)

Person	Singular	Plural
I	пою	поём
II	поёшь	поёте
III	поёт	поют

Table 10-8

▼ СМЕЯТЬСЯ (GROUP I MODEL 1)

Person	Singular	Plural
I	смеюсь	смеёмся
II	смеёшься	смеётесь
III	смеётся	смеются

Read the following dialogue between two friends who came to celebrate another friend's birthday:

Володя: Привет, Лариса! Как дела дома?
Hello, Larisa! How things are at home?

Лариса: Всё нормально, спасибо. А как ваши дела? Как жена, дети?

Everything is fine, thank you. And how are you doing? How are the wife and children?

Володя: Тоже всё хорошо. А что ты купила Ане в подарок на день рождения?

All good as well. What did you buy for Anya as a birthday gift?

Лариса: Мы купили две книги и путешествие на неделю в Африку. Но пока это секрет.

We bought two books and a one-week trip to Africa. But it's a secret for now.

Володя: Здорово. Я знаю, что Аня любит путешествовать и ей нравится читать книги, когда она в пути.

Great. I know that Anya likes to travel and that she likes reading books when she is traveling.

Аня: Лариса Петровна, Володя! Проходите, пожалуйста! Как хорошо, что вы здесь у нас.

Larisa Petrovna, Volodya! Please, come in! How nice it is that you are here with us.

Лариса and Володя: Аня, поздравляем тебя с днём рождения! Ура! Желаем тебе всего прекрасного, хорошего настроения, побольше улыбок, счастья и исполнения всех твоих желаний!

Anya, happy birthday! Hooray! We wish you all the best, a good mood, more smiles, happiness, and may all of your wishes come true.

Аня: Огромное спасибо! Пожалуйста, проходите в большую комнату и садитесь с нами за стол.

Thank you so much! Please, come into the living room and join us at the table.

Two Irregular Verbs to Remember

There are several verbs that are sometimes referred to as isolated because they combine elements of both major patterns of conjugation. These verbs include хотеть (to want) and бежать (to run).

Table 10-9

▼ ХОТЕТЬ

Person	Singular	Plural
I	хоч**у**	хот**им**
II	х**о**чешь	хот**ите**
III	х**о**чет	хот**ят**

Table 10-10

▼ БЕЖАТЬ

Person	Singular	Plural
I	бег**у**	беж**им**
II	беж**ишь**	беж**ите**
III	беж**ит**	бег**ут**

Read the examples below to see how these two irregular verbs can be used in context:

Он**а** х**о**чет к**о**шку себ**е** в под**а**рок.
She wants a cat for a present.

Он**и** бег**у**т дом**о**й.
They are running home.

Мы беж**а**ли в магаз**и**н чт**о**бы куп**и**ть торт.
We were running to the store to buy a cake.

Introduction to the Russian Past Tense

As you know, there are several past tenses in English. Compare the following sentences:

I went home yesterday.
By the time he arrived, I had gone home.
As I was going home, I saw him in the crowd in front of our office.

In Russian, there is only one past tense. The forms of the past tense are formed from the stem of the verb by adding the suffix –л and appropriate endings:

- Singular verbal forms that denote masculine persons and objects take on the suffix -л plus the zero ending, meaning they do not take on an additional ending. [-л]
- Singular verbal forms that refer to feminine persons and objects take on the suffix -л plus the ending -а. [-ла]
- Singular verbal forms that denote neutral objects take on the suffix -л plus the ending -о. [-ло]
- All plural forms irrespective of gender take on the suffix -л followed by the ending -и. [-ли]

See the following table to better understand the formation of the past tense verbal forms:

Table 10-11

▼ **FORMATION OF PAST TENSE FORMS**

Infinitive	Stem	Masculine	Feminine	Neuter	Plural
Читать	Чита-	Я, ты, он читал	Я, ты, она читала	Оно читало	Мы, вы, они читали
Писать	Писа-	Я, ты, он писал	Я, ты, она писала	Оно писало	Мы, вы, они писали
Говорить	Говори-	Я, ты, он говорил	Я, ты, она говорила	Оно говорило	Мы, вы, они говорили

Alert

Remember that the pronoun вы always goes with either the plural verbal form, as in Девочки, вы читали эту книгу? (Girls, have you read this book?) or the formal form, as in Екатерина Владимировна, вы готовили ужин? (Yekaterina Vladimirovna, have you been preparing dinner?).

Remember that the Russian past tense is a simple tense that does not require the use of any auxiliary verbs. Compare the following statements and questions in English and Russian:

Ты пис**а**л письм**о**?	Were you writing a letter?
Нет, не пис**а**л.	No, I didn't.

The Past Tense and the Verb быть

The previous chapters mentioned that in the present tense, the Russian verb быть (to be) is always omitted. In the past tense, the verb быть (to be) is not omitted. Its past tense forms include the following:

- masculine singular – я, ты, он был
- feminine singular – я, ты, он**а** был**а**
- neutral singular – он**о** б**ы**ло
- plural – мы, вы, он**и** б**ы**ли

In the feminine forms of the otherwise one-syllable verbs, the stress shifts onto the final -a ending, as in the following examples:

быть: Я был в магаз**и**не, а Л**ю**ба был**а** д**о**ма.
I was at the store, and Lyuba was at home

брать: Я брал ур**о**ки м**у**зыки, а он**а** брал**а** ур**о**ки ф**и**зики.
I was taking music lessons, and she was taking physics classes.

In the negative forms of the verb быть, the stress is on the negative particle не (with the exception of the singular feminine form), as in н**е** был, не был**а**, н**е** было, н**е** были. For example:

Ты вчер**а** был в гост**я**х у Лар**и**сы? – Нет, я н**е** был.
Were you at Larisa's yesterday? – No, I wasn't.

У не**ё** был день рожд**е**ния. Б**ы**ло мн**о**го гост**е**й, но н**е** было т**о**рта.
She had a birthday yesterday. There were many guests, but there was no cake.

Chapter Review

Review the material covered in this chapter and complete the following exercises.

Chapter Quiz

Answer the following questions and check your answers in Appendix A.

1. What is the main function of the dative case in the Russian language?

   _____

2. What is the connection between the dative case and such Russian verbs as покуп**а**ть, сов**е**товать, дать?

   _____

3. What are the similarities and differences between the Russian verbs люб**и**ть and нр**а**виться?

   _____

4. When you need to add an indirect object to a sentence in Russian, should you use prepositions?

   _____

5. What is the meaning of the following saying: Дарёному кон**ю** в з**у**бы не см**о**трят?

   _____

6. What is the suffix that you need to add to the stem of a verb to form any past tense form?

   _____

7. How many modes of the past tenses are there in the Russian language?

   _____

8. Which Russian verb is usually omitted in the present tense, but is present in the past tense?

   _____

Translation Exercises

A. Translate the following verb-noun expressions into Russian to practice forming dative forms.

1. to help Nina   _____
2. to give advice to a friend   _____
3. to suggest a plan to Helen   _____
4. to buy a gift for my mother   _____
5. to tell a story to your family   _____
6. to write a letter to Vladimir   _____
7. to give Misha a plate   _____
8. to help Vera   _____

B. Translate the following sentences from English into Russian. Make sure that you remember how to create questions and negative statements in Russian.

9. I like this small house.   _____
10. She likes beautiful clothes.   _____
11. He likes these magazines and newspapers. _____
12. Do you like these books?   _____
13. They don't like this university.   _____

C. Translate the following expressions into Russian and conjugate the verbs in the present tense:

14. to want a present

_____

15. to cook dinner

_____

D. Translate the following sentences into Russian using what you know about the past tense:

16. I haven't been at home, but she was there.

_____

17. She was cooking dinner, and I was at the university.

_____

18. We wanted to write a letter to the senator.

_____

19. They were waiting for teachers in the classrooms.

_____

20. You (formal) spoke the truth to Natasha.

_____

E. Translate the following sentences into English and then translate them into Russian using the past tense.

21. Я хочу поздравить тебя с днём рождения!

_____

22. Он не понимает, что ты ему говоришь.

_____

23. Павел, вы думаете, что это хорошая книга?

_____

24. Марина любит читать газеты и журналы.

_____

25. Тебе нравится русский язык?

_____

CHAPTER 11

Verbal Aspect and Verbs of Motion

T his chapter provides a basic overview of how verbal aspect functions in the Russian language. English does not have aspects, but the concept is familiar. Verbal aspect in Russian demonstrates when the action of a verb occurred—either in the present or the past. This chapter focuses on recognizing the differences between the usage and formation of imperfective and perfective verbs. You will learn useful prefixes, suffixes, adverbs, temporal expressions, and basic verbs of motion. At the end of the chapter, you will apply your knowledge of verbs of motion to the accusative and dative cases.

Verbal Aspect in Russian

In addition to tenses, Russian verbs have two aspects: imperfective and perfective. The major function of the aspect is to show the speaker's attitude toward an action in time. Russian uses the imperfective aspect to describe actions in process and the perfective aspect to express actions that have been accomplished.

🔔 Alert

Most of the verbs that you have learned so far are imperfective. As your proficiency in Russian increases, you will acquire more verbs of both kinds and will be able to use them appropriately.

Imperfective Russian verbs can be used in the present tense, as in:

Я чит**а**ю **э**ту кн**и**гу.
I read / I am reading this book.

Я рис**у**ю маш**и**ну в тетр**а**ди.
I draw / I am drawing a car in the notebook.

In the following sentences, observe the change of meaning when perfective verbs are used:

Я прочит**а**л **э**ту кн**и**гу.
I (have) read this book.

Я нарисов**а**л маш**и**ну в тетр**а**ди.
I have drawn / drew a car in the notebook.

As you can see from the examples, a different verbal meaning is expressed by adding extra parts directly to the verb, the prefixes про- and на-. This way of forming perfective verbs is called prefixation. Often imperfective and perfective verbs form pairs that have a similar lexical meaning when translated into English, for example, чит**а**ть – прочит**а**ть (to read, literally "to read" – "to have read"), рисов**а**ть – нарисов**а**ть (to draw, literally "to draw" – "to have drawn").

ⓔ❓ Question

Does English have the category of aspect?
No, English does not use the category of aspect in the same way as Russian. Actions are expressed as ongoing or as completed through complex verbal forms. In English, these take the form of the continuous and perfect tenses. Compare the following sentences: I am reading (continuous) – I have read (perfect), or I am drawing (continuous) – I have drawn (perfect).

Choosing Sides: Perfective or Imperfective?

Whenever you use a verb in Russian, you need to decide whether to use a perfective or an imperfective verb. The following are general guidelines to help you make the most appropriate selection. In general, remember that imperfective verbs describe actions as processes that have no temporal borders, whereas perfective verbs are concerned with actions limited in time.

Imperfective verbs are used to describe ongoing actions or repetitive actions. Use imperfective verbs in the following situations:

- To describe continuous actions that have not been completed: Я читаю книгу. (I am reading a book.)
- To underscore the length of an action: Вчера я долго читала эту книгу. (Yesterday I read this book for a long time.)
- To describe habitual and/or repetitive actions: В детстве я читала японские сказки. (In childhood, I used to read Japanese fairy tales.)
- To describe the state of being of an object: На столе лежала книга. (A book was lying on the table.)
- To describe a quality, ability, or characteristic of a person: Мой брат хорошо плавает. (My brother swims well.)

Perfective verbs generally describe one-time actions. With perfective verbs, the focus is on the completion of the verb, not the process used to complete it. Use perfective verbs in the following situations:

- To describe one-time actions, as in Вчера я купила машину. (Yesterday, I bought a car.) Here is a partial list of perfective verbs that are frequently used to describe one-time actions: вспомнить (to remember), встретить (to meet), купить (to buy), ответить (to answer), открыть (to open), показать (to show), положить (to put), получить (to receive), понять (to understand), послать (to send), сказать (to say), and спросить (to ask).
- To describe regular completed actions, as in Я написала письмо. (I have written a letter.) Here is a partial list of frequently used verbs to describe completed actions: выпить (to drink), вымыть (to wash), выучить (to learn), написать (to write), нарисовать (to draw), сделать (to do), позавтракать (to have breakfast), прочитать (to read).
- To denote quick, unexpected actions in conjunction with the adverb "вдруг" (suddenly), as in Вдруг он крикнул. (Suddenly he screamed.) Other verbs often used to express quick unexpected actions include: увидеть (to see), услышать (to hear), прыгнуть (to jump), крикнуть (to scream), свиснуть (to whistle), вздрогнуть (to shudder).

Many Russian verbs have both a perfective and an imperfective form, and both forms are used regularly.

Forming Perfective Verbs

Many perfective verbs are formed from imperfective verbs by adding an appropriate prefix. Unfortunately (or fortunately, depending on how you feel about the syntactical complexity of Russian), it is quite difficult to predict which prefix should be used with a particular verb, requiring students of Russian to practice their memorization skills.

The good news is that after you have learned a good deal of verbs, you will develop a better sense of the language (similar to that of a native speaker), which will help you make appropriate grammatical choices. Be patient and refer to the following list to learn some of the more frequently used prefixes and the perfective verbs they create. The first verb in each pair is imperfective and the second is perfective.

The prefix с-:

д**е**лать – сд**е**лать	to do
танцев**а**ть – станцев**а**ть	to dance
фотограф**и**ровать – сфотограф**и**ровать	to photograph

The prefix на-:

пис**а**ть – напис**а**ть	to write
рисов**а**ть – нарисов**а**ть	to draw
уч**и**ть – науч**и**ть	to teach
уч**и**ться – науч**и**ться	to learn

The prefix у-:

в**и**деть – ув**и**деть	to see
сл**ы**шать – усл**ы**шать	to hear

The prefix про-:

чит**а**ть – прочит**а**ть	to read

The prefix под- (подо-):

ждать – подожд**а**ть	to wait

The prefix вы-:

мыть – в**ы**мыть	to wash
пить – в**ы**пить	to drink

The prefix вы- is always stressed, as in пить – в**ы**пить (to drink).

The prefix при-:

гот**о**вить – пригот**о**вить	to prepare
гот**о**виться – пригот**о**виться	to prepare oneself, to study

The prefix за-:

плат**и**ть – заплат**и**ть	to pay
плак**а**ть – заплак**а**ть	to cry
кур**и**ть – закур**и**ть	to smoke

The prefix по-:

есть – по**е**сть	to eat
з**а**втракать – поз**а**втракать	to have breakfast
об**е**дать – поо**б**едать	to have lunch/dinner
ужинать – по**у**жинать	to have dinner
сл**у**шать – посл**у**шать	to listen
звать – позв**а**ть	to call
прос**и**ть – попрос**и**ть	to ask
д**у**мать – под**у**мать	to think
игр**а**ть – поигр**а**ть	to play
раб**о**тать – пораб**о**тать	to work
люб**и**ть – полюб**и**ть	to love

The prefix за-:

говор**и**ть – заговор**и**ть	to talk
крич**а**ть – закрич**а**ть	to scream
молч**а**ть – замолч**а**ть	to be/go silent
петь – зап**е**ть	to sing
сме**я**ться – засме**я**ться	to laugh

Some pairs of perfective and imperfective verbs differ by one or two root vowels and/or a suffix. Again, the first verb in each pair is imperfective and the second is perfective:

отвеч**а**ть – отв**е**тить	to answer
пок**а**зывать – показ**а**ть	to show
расск**а**зывать – рассказ**а**ть	to tell
спр**а**шивать – спрос**и**ть	to ask

вставать – встать	get up
открывать – открыть	to open
закрывать – закрыть	to close

Some pairs of perfective and imperfective verbs have completely different stems and must be memorized. As in the previous examples, the first verb in each pair is imperfective and the second is perfective:

отдыхать – отдохнуть	to rest
понимать – понять	to understand
покупать – купить	to buy
говорить – сказать	to speak, say

Several Russian verbs that denote states of being, as opposed to actions, have no perfective forms. Some of these verbs include лежать (to lie), сидеть (to sit), учиться (to study at school), иметь (to own), жить (to live), and существовать (to exist).

Adding Prefixes and Suffixes

You already know that some Russian verbs rely on prefixes to modify their meaning. For example, читать (to read, imperfective) and прочитать (to read, perfective), рисовать (to draw, imperfective) and нарисовать (to draw, perfective). This way of forming perfective verbs is known as prefixation.

A more general term that is often applied to this word-formation strategy is suffixation. Suffixation includes the addition of grammatical and lexical word parts to the beginning and end of words to change their grammatical affiliations and/or to modify their lexical meanings.

❓ Question

What is the difference between a prefix and a suffix?
A prefix is a word part that is added in front of the root, whereas a suffix is added to the end of the root. It is good to remember that usually Russian words can have only one prefix, but they might incorporate multiple suffixes. For example, the word "подписавшийся" (the one who signed the document) includes a prefix "под-", root "пис-" and several suffixes.

In brief, Russian uses two verbal aspects (perfective and imperfective) to show the speaker's attitude toward action in time.

As an example of how suffixation works in Russian verbs, let's look at the verb писать (to write, imperfective) together with a chain of closely related verbs.

With the help of the grammatical prefix "на-", we can form its perfective counterpart: написать (to write, perfective). Using various lexical prefixes, we can produce a series of perfective verbs based on the verb писать, yet each distinctly different in their meaning. These perfective verbs in turn form imperfective pairs, also known as secondary imperfectives. Secondary imperfectives are produced with the help of the imperfective grammatical suffixes "-ыва-/-ива-":

Table 11-1

▼ **PREFIXATION: THE VERB "ПИСАТЬ" (TO WRITE)**

Perfective	Perfective Meaning	Secondary Imperfective
написать	to have written	
переписать	to copy	переписывать
подписать	to sign	подписывать
записать	to write down	записывать
вписать	to write in	вписывать
выписать	to write out	выписывать
описать	to describe	описывать
дописать	to finish writing	дописывать
приписать	to add in writing	приписывать

Take note of the regularly changing stress patterns in secondary imperfectives.

Russian verbs that have prefixes form imperfectives either by dropping their prefix, as in написать – писать (to write), or by adding an imperfective suffix while retaining their lexical prefix, as in подписать – подписывать (to sign). The following is a table of verbs and lexical prefixes that are frequently used in everyday speech in Russian:

Table 11-2

▼ **LEXICAL PREFIXES AND VERBS**

Prefix	Meaning	Verb(s)
в-/во-	in, into, to: inward movement	вписать (to write in), внести (to carry in), войти (to enter)
вы-	out: outward movement	выписать (to write out), вынести (to carry out), выиграть (to win)
до-	completion of the action	дописать (to finish writing), дорисовать (to finish drawing), донести (to deliver), доиграть (to finish playing)
за-	action along the way	забежать (to run in), занести (to drop off), зайти (to drop in)
недо-	incomplete action	недоделать (to do incompletely), недоесть (not to finish eating), недоспать (not to finish sleeping)
от-/ото-	action away from	отойти (to walk off), отнести (to carry away/off)
пере-	action over, across or change in the direction	переписать (to write over), перенести (to carry over), передумать (to rethink)
при-	action close by or adding to	приписать (to add in writing), принести (to bring), придумать (to come up with)

Lexical Prefixes for Adjectives and Nouns

Nouns and adjectives also use lexical prefixes. See the following list to learn some key prefixes that will help you expand your Russian vocabulary:

- Prefix "не" (negative, similar to the English un-, im-, ir-, dis,-less): неосторожный (careless), неосторожность (carelessness) from осторожный (careful); независимый (independent), независимость (independence) from зависимый (dependent).
- Prefix " без-" (negative, similar to the English im-, in-, un-): безопасный (safe), безопасность (safety) from опасный (dangerous).
- Prefix "под-" (under): подземный (underground, adjective), подземелье (underground, noun) from земля (ground).
- Prefix "за-" (beyond): заграница (foreign land) – заграничный (foreign) from граница (border).
- Prefix "со" (together, similar to English co-): собеседник (conversation partner) from беседа (conversation), сотрудник (co-worker) from труд (work, labor).
- Prefix "меж-/между" (between, similar to English inter-): международный (international) from народный (people, adjective), народ (people, noun), межпланетный (interplanetary) from планета (planet).
- Prefix "до" (before, similar to English pre-): довоенный (pre-war, adjective) from война (war, noun).
- Prefix "после" (after, similar to English post-): послевоенный (post-war, adjective) from война (war, noun).
- Prefix "анти-" (English anti-): антинаучный (unscientific) from научный (scientific) – наука (science), антигуманитарный (inhumane) from гуманитарный (humane).
- Prefix "ультра-" (English ultra-): ультраправый (ultra-right, adjective) from правый (right), ультрамодный (ultra-trendy) from модный (trendy) – мода (fashion).

The last two prefixes, анти- and ультра-, are Latin-based prefixes that exist in both Russian and English. Although it is helpful to recognize them and look for similarities across the languages, remember that they might be applied to different words in each language.

Useful Adverbs and Temporal Expressions

Adverbs are words that describe verbs, adjectives, or other adverbs. Although there are many types of adverbs, most of them indicate either manner, quality, quantity, time, place, or intensity of the action, as in:

Я мало читаю.	I read a little.
Он много знает.	He knows a lot.
Мы долго говорили.	We spoke for a long time.
Вы хорошо говорите по-русски.	You speak Russian well.
Я плохо понимаю по-испански.	I understand Spanish badly.

Russian adverbs do not change their form. The following is a list of common adverbs and expressions to describe quality, quantity, speed, and frequency:

хорошо	good, well
плохо	badly
нормально	fine, OK
мало	a little
много	a lot
немного	not much
быстро	quickly
медленно	slowly
вдруг	suddenly
немедленно	at once
уже	already
обычно	usually
всегда	always
часто	often
каждый день	every day
каждое утро	every morning
каждый вечер	every evening
целый/весь день	whole/all day
целое/всё утро	whole/all morning
иногда	sometimes
редко	rarely
никогда	never

Notice that most Russian adverbs end in –o. Similarly, in English most adverbs end in -ly.

Three Verbs of Motion to Remember

As the name suggests, the verbs of motion express movement. Examples of verbs of motion in English include the verbs "to go," "to walk," "to drive," and "to fly." The following are conjugation tables of several useful Russian verbs of motion: гул**я**ть (to go for a walk, to stroll), идт**и** (to walk, to go, to be going), and **е**хать (to go, to drive, to ride).

Table 11-3

▼ ГУЛЯТЬ (TO GO FOR A WALK, TO STROLL)

Present Tense		
Person	Singular	Plural
I	гул**я**ю	гул**я**ем
II	гул**я**ешь	гул**я**ете
III	гул**я**ет	гул**я**ют

Past Tense: гулял/а/о, гуляли

Table 11-4

▼ ИДТИ (TO WALK, TO GO, TO BE GOING)

Present Tense		
Person	Singular	Plural
I	ид**у**	идём
II	идёшь	идёте
III	идёт	ид**у**т

Past Tense: шёл/шла/шло, шли

Table 11-5

▼ **ЕХАТЬ (TO GO, TO MOVE, TO DRIVE, TO RIDE)**

Present Tense

Person	Singular	Plural
I	**е**ду	**е**дем
II	**е**дешь	**е**дете
III	**е**дет	**е**дут

Past Tense: **ехал/а/о, ехали**

Although the verbs гул**я**ть, идт**и**, and **е**хать in some cases can be translated with the same English verb "to go," they have distinctive semantic differences in Russian.

- The verb гул**я**ть is associated with leisure and strolling.
- The verb идт**и** denotes either walking on foot, as in "Я ид**у** дом**о**й" (I am going home) or can refer to the movement of particular means of transport, as in "П**о**езд идёт" (The train is coming).
- Finally, the verb ехать refers to movement by transport, as in "Он**и** д**о**лго **е**хали на п**о**езде." The type of transportation is expressed through an appropriate noun in the prepositional case with the preposition "на," which is the equivalent of the English word "by": **е**хать на п**о**езде, на метр**о**, на авт**о**бусе, на трамв**а**е, на такс**и** (to go, ride by train, metro, bus, tram, taxi).

Read the following dialogue between two friends, М**а**ша and В**и**тя, at the bus station. Pay special attention to how the verbs of motion are used, and practice your understanding of Russian perfective and imperfective verbs.

М**а**ша: Прив**е**т, В**и**тя! Как дел**а**?
Hello, Vitya! How's it going?

В**и**тя: Спас**и**бо, М**а**ша, всё хорош**о**. Куд**а** ты идёшь?
Thanks, Masha! Everything is fine. Where are you going?

М**а**ша: В прод**у**ктовый магаз**и**н. Мо**я** м**а**ма попрос**и**ла мен**я** куп**и**ть прод**у**кты и цвет**ы**. З**а**втра у моег**о** п**а**пы день рожд**е**ния и мо**я** м**а**ма гот**о**вит пр**а**здничный об**е**д.

To the grocery store. My mom asked me to buy some food and flowers. Tomorrow is my dad's birthday and my mom is making a celebratory dinner.

В**и**тя: А, пон**я**тно. А я **е**ду в инстит**у**т. Сег**о**дня у нас экз**а**мены по ист**о**рии.
Oh, okay (gotcha). I am going to the institute. Today we have a history exam.

М**а**ша: Ты в**ы**учил весь матери**а**л?
Have you learned all of the material?

В**и**тя: По-м**о**ему, да. Вчер**а** я гот**о**вился ц**е**лый день.
I think so. Yesterday I studied all day long.

М**а**ша: Молод**е**ц! Я ув**е**рена, что ты прекр**а**сно пригот**о**вился к экз**а**мену. А вот и мой авт**о**бус идёт. Я обяз**а**тельно позвон**ю** теб**е** сег**о**дня в**е**чером, л**а**дно?
Well done! I am sure that you have beautifully prepared for the exam. Here's my bus. I will definitely call you tonight, okay?

В**и**тя: Хорош**о**. Пок**а**!
All right. Bye!

ⓔ❓ Question

How can you praise someone in Russian?
In informal situations when addressing someone of equal or lesser status, it is customary to praise someone by using the word "молодец" (literally "ace," or "fine fellow"). Although grammatically it is a masculine noun, it can be applied in reference to both men and women. In English, this expression of praise is usually translated as "Well done!" or "Good job!" If you need to praise a group of people, use the plural form "Молодцы!"

Unidirectional and Multidirectional Verbs of Motion

Russian differentiates between the verbs that describe motion in one direction and the verbs that describe motion in more than one direction. Compare the following sentences:

Я ид**у** в шк**о**лу.
I am going to school. (Meaning: I am on the way to school.)

Я хож**у** в шк**о**лу.

I go to school. (Meaning: I attend school and come back home when school is over.)

The verbs идт**и** and **е**хать are unidirectional. The multidirectional verb that corresponds to the verb идт**и** is ход**и**ть, and the multidirectional verb that corresponds to the verb **е**хать is **е**здить. In other words, these four verbs form the following pairs: идт**и** – ход**и**ть and **е**хать – **е**здить. You already know how to conjugate the verbs идт**и** and **е**хать. Following are the conjugations for the verbs ход**и**ть and **е**здить.

Table 11-6

▼ **ХОДИТЬ (TO GO ON FOOT AND TO COME BACK; TO GO BACK AND FORTH: MULTIDIRECTIONAL)**

Present Tense		
Person	Singular	Plural
I	хож**у**	х**о**дим
II	х**о**дишь	х**о**дите
III	х**о**дит	х**о**дят

*Past Tense: ход**и**л/а/о, ход**и**ли*

Table 11-7

▼ **ЕЗДИТЬ (TO MAKE ROUND TRIPS BY VEHICLE: MULTIDIRECTIONAL)**

Present Tense		
Person	Singular	Plural
I	**е**зжу	**е**здим
II	**е**здишь	**е**здите
III	**е**здит	**е**здят

*Past Tense: **е**здил/а/о, **е**здили*

The verbs ход**и**ть and **е**здить can be used in the following contexts:

- The verb ход**и**ть implies a round trip to a particular location and back, as in Я хож**у** в шк**о**лу к**а**ждый день. – I go to school (and come back) every day.

- The verb "ход**и**ть" is typically limited to describing only movement on foot. In order to express multidirectional movement that covers longer distances (and thus requires transportation) use the verb "**е**здить." Similar to the construction used with the verb "**е**хать," the exact type of transportation is specified by an appropriate noun in the prepositional case together with the preposition "на," as in "**е**здить на маш**и**не, на авт**о**бусе, на метр**о**, на велосип**е**де" – to go by car, by bus, by metro, or by bike. However, sometimes the manner of transportation is omitted altogether, as in "Он**а** **е**здит на раб**о**ту к**а**ждый день," i.e., she goes (by some means of transportation) to work every day.

- A special note should be made about expressing the process of making round trips in the past. In addition to ход**и**ть and **е**здить, you can also use the verb to be (быть) in its past tense forms to indicate going places, as in "Вчер**а** я был**а** д**о**ма, а ты где был?" – Yesterday I was at home, and where were you?

Perfective Verbs of Motion

Imperfective multidirectional verbs of motion (ход**и**ть and **е**здить) do not have perfective counterparts. The unidirectional verbs of motion (идт**и** and **е**хать) have corresponding perfective verbs of motion, which are formed with the help of the prefix по-, as in идт**и** – пойт**и** (to go, to walk), **е**хать – по**е**хать (to go, to ride, to drive). Both пойт**и** and по**е**хать indicate the initial stage of movement or trip, as in to start walking, to set off, to begin the journey. Compare these examples:

Он пошёл дом**о**й.

He has gone/left for home. (Meaning: The beginning of the trip has been initiated by foot.)

Он**а** шла дом**о**й.

She was walking/walked home. (Meaning: The process of walking is being described.)

Мы по**е**хали на маш**и**не.

We set off (on our trip) by car. (Meaning: The beginning of the trip was initiated by car.)

Мы **е**хали на маш**и**не.

We were riding in a car. (Meaning: The process of riding is being described.)

Verbs of Motion and the Dative and Accusative Cases

In the previous chapters, you learned the basics uses of the dative and accusative cases. The dative and accusative cases are also used with the verbs of motion. Compare the following examples:

Я ид**у** к муз**е**ю (dative).

I am going to/toward the museum (direction toward).

Я ид**у** в муз**е**й (accusative).

I am going to/into the museum (direction inside).

Куд**а** идёт **э**тот трамв**а**й? – Он идёт к вокз**а**лу (dative).

Where does this tram go? – It goes to the railway station (direction toward).

Куд**а** идёт **э**тот п**о**езд? – Он идёт в Москв**у** (accusative).

Where does this train go? – It goes to Moscow (direction into).

Ты к**у**да **е**дешь? – Я **е**ду на п**о**чту (accusative). А ты? – Я **е**ду в те**а**тр (accusative).

Where are you going? – I'm going to the post office. And you? – I'm going to the theater (direction inside).

Авт**о**бус идёт к муз**е**ю (dative)? Нет, он идёт к кинотe**а**тру (dative).

Does this bus go toward the museum? – No, it goes toward the movie theater (direction toward).

The dative case with the preposition "к" is used to indicate the movement toward a place or a person with a goal of being near, as in "идт**и** к д**о**му, муз**е**ю, шк**о**ле, бр**а**ту, врач**у**" (to go toward the house, to the museum, to the school, to the brother, to the doctor). The accusative case is used with the prepositions "в" or "на" to express the movement with the goal of being inside a specific place or space, as in "идт**и** в шк**о**лу, на п**о**чту, на раб**о**ту" (to go to school, to the post office, and to work).

Use the prepositional case to indicate the location, as in "Я жив**у** в Москв**е**" (I live in Moscow) or "Он встр**е**тил её в те**а**тре" (He met her in the theater).

Chapter Review

Review the material in this chapter and complete the following exercises.

Chapter Quiz

Answer the following questions and check your answers in Appendix A.

1. How many aspects does Russian have?

    _____

2. What is the main function of the verbal aspect?

    _____

3. Can Russian perfective verbs form present tense forms?

    _____

4. What is the most common method of forming perfective verbs?

    _____

5. Which aspect would you use when describing one-time actions in the past tense?

    _____

6. Which aspect would you use when describing habitual actions in the past tense?

    _____

7. What is suffixation?

    _____

8. Which two types of prefixes are common in Russian?

    _____

9. What are two models of forming imperfective verbs from Russian perfective verbs that have prefixes?

    _____

10. Which aspect do you need to use with the Russian adverb "вдруг"?

    _____

11. Name as many Russian verbs of motion as you can.

_____

Translation Exercises

A. Translate the following sentences into English:

1. Она написала книгу.

_____

2. Вдруг он закричал.

_____

3. Моя сестра хорошо рисует.

_____

4. Мы долго говорили и пили чай.

_____

5. Иногда они отдыхали в деревне.

_____

B. Translate the following sentences into Russian:

6. He showed us his school.

_____

7. They usually had breakfast at home.

_____

8. She already did it.

_____

9. My younger brother can read very well.

_____

10. Have you (informal) finished writing this letter?

_____

Translation Practice

A. Translate the following verbs from English into Russian. Make sure that all the Russian verbs are imperfective.

1. to describe _____
2. to copy _____
3. to finish writing _____
4. to write down _____
5. Which suffix is used to mark these verbs as imperfective verbs?

_____

B. Translate the following words from Russian into English or from English into Russian. Indicate whether these words are nouns or adjectives.

6. независимость _____
7. послевоенный _____
8. unscientific _____
9. заграничный _____
10. безопасность _____
11. conversation partner _____
12. международный _____

C. Translate the following mini-dialogues into English.

13. Ты куда идёшь? – На почту.

_____

14. Автобус идёт в центр? – Нет, он идёт к стадиону.

_____

15. Маша ездит на работу на машине или на велосипеде? – Иногда на машине, а иногда на велосипеде.

_____

16. Где **О**ля? – Он**а** пошл**а** к своем**у** бр**а**ту.

_____

D. Translate the following mini-dialogues into Russian.

17. Does this train go to Moscow? – No, it's going to St. Petersburg.

_____

18. Do you (formal) take the train or the bus to work? – The bus.

_____

19. I usually go to my mother's house to have lunch. – Every day? – Yes.

_____

CHAPTER 12

Daily Life and Impersonal Constructions

This chapter introduces impersonal constructions that are often used in Russian to describe various daily occurrences. You will also learn about two forms of the future tense and expand your overall understanding of how grammatical notions of tense and aspect operate in the Russian language. Finally, you'll add several helpful expressions to your lexicon in Russian.

Impersonal Constructions

We express our thoughts in phrases that become complete sentences in writing. A typical sentence usually has a subject and a verb. However, in Russian there are many sentences in which there is no grammatical subject and adverbs are used as predicates (verbs). Such constructions are often referred to as impersonal because the identity of the subject who is performing the described action or instigating a particular state or mood is unclear or irrelevant to the meaning of the sentence. Compare the following sentences in Russian with the corresponding constructions in English:

На **у**лице тепл**о**.	It is warm outside.
Вол**о**де пл**о**хо.	Volodya is feeling sick.

In the first example, the English sentence has a grammatical subject expressed by the pronoun "it," and the predicate consists of the verb "to be" and the adjective "warm." The corresponding Russian sentence does not have a subject, and the adverb alone serves the predicate function. In the second example, the English sentence has a clear subject (Volodya) and a predicate (is feeling sick). The Russian sentence, on the other hand, lacks a grammatical subject, the adverb "пл**о**хо" is used as a predicate, and the dative case "Вол**о**де" of the name "Вол**о**дя" indicates the logical subject of the sentence.

Russian often uses impersonal constructions with adverbs as predicates to describe weather and to refer to a person's immediate physical state or emotional condition, as in:

Сег**о**дня х**о**лодно / тепл**о** / ж**а**рко.
Today it is cold / warm / hot.

Ем**у** пл**о**хо / хорош**о**.
He is feeling bad / sick / well.

Нам в**е**село / ск**у**чно / гр**у**стно.
We are having fun / feeling bored / feeling sad.

Бор**и**су х**о**лодно / ж**а**рко / тепл**о**.
Boris is feeling cold / hot / warm.

На **у**лице **о**чень хорош**о**.
It is very nice outside (literally on the street).

Теб**е** д**у**шно?
Do you feel like it's stuffy?

Russian often relies on impersonal constructions to express needs, permissions, and restrictions. Similarly to the impersonal constructions that we described in the previous section, nouns and pronouns in the dative case express the logical subject of the sentence.

Impersonal constructions with "н**у**жно" and "н**а**до" are used to express needs, as in:

Им н**у**жно **е**хать дом**о**й.	They need to go home.
Ем**у** н**у**жно беж**а**ть в апт**е**ку.	He needs to run to the drugstore.
Теб**е** н**а**до идт**и** в шк**о**лу?	Do you need / must you go to school?

Impersonal constructions with "м**о**жно" express permissions and abilities, as in:

Вам м**о**жно гул**я**ть в п**а**рке?	Are you allowed to walk in the park?

Где м**о**жно куп**и**ть газ**е**ты?	Where can one buy newspapers?
Теб**е** м**о**жно кат**а**ться на конько**а**х?	Are you allowed to skate?
Здесь м**о**жно кур**и**ть?	Is smoking permitted here?

Impersonal constructions with "нельз**я**" are used to express restrictions and prohibitions, as in:

Здесь нельз**я** кур**и**ть.	Smoking is prohibited here.
Мне нельз**я** есть мор**о**женое.	I can't (am not allowed to) eat ice cream.

🅔❗ Alert

Folk remedies for common ailments vary from culture to culture. For example, Russians believe that it is detrimental to your health to eat ice cream when you are suffering from a sore throat. Instead, you are expected to drink hot milk with mixed-in melted butter and eat honey or homemade raspberry jam.

As you can see from the previous examples, Russian impersonal constructions expressing needs, wants, permissions, and restrictions are often used in conjunction with the infinitive of the verb that carries the major semantic meaning. This is similar to English constructions such as "can do," "must read," and "should not cry."

The Future Tense and the Verb Быть

You have already learned how to form the present and past tenses in Russian. In this section, we will look at Russian future tenses. We will begin by looking into the use of the verb "быть" (to be). As you might remember, this verb is always omitted in the present tense, but its present tense conjugation forms are used to express future.

Table 12-1

▼ **THE VERB "БЫТЬ": GROUP I PATTERN 2**

Person	Singular	Plural
I	бу́ду (I will be)	бу́дем (we will be)
II	бу́дешь (you [fam.] will be)	бу́дете (you [plural/formal] will be)
III	бу́дет (he/she/it will be)	бу́дут (they will be)

Compare the following Russian sentences in the present and future tenses. Notice how the verb "быть" is used to express future in Russian impersonal constructions and in Russian sentences that lack the linking verb to be in the present tense.

Сего́дня тепло́.
Today it is warm outside.

За́втра бу́дет тепло́.
Tomorrow it will be warm outside.

Сего́дня ему́ на́до идти́ в шко́лу.
Today he should go to school.

За́втра ему́ на́до бу́дет идти́ в шко́лу.
Tomorrow he will have to go to school.

Мари́на в библиоте́ке.
Marina is at the library.

Мари́на бу́дет в библиоте́ке за́втра.
Marina will be at the library tomorrow.

Remember that the verb "быть" is not omitted in the past tense either, as in "Вчера́ бы́ло тепло́." (Yesterday it was warm outside). In impersonal constructions in the past and future tenses, the verb "быть" is used in the third person singular, respectively as in "бы́ло" (it was) and "бу́дет" (it will be).

Imperfective and Perfective Future Forms

In Russian, there are two forms of the future tense: imperfective and perfective. The major difference between them is that imperfective future expresses unfinished, continuous actions or actions that will be repeated in the future. On the other hand, perfective future describes single, one-time actions that will be completed in the future:

Я куплю газету.
I will buy a newspaper. (Perfective future: a completed action in the future.)

Я буду покупать дом летом.
I will be buying a house in the summer. (Imperfective future: a process in the future.)

Сначала я куплю квартиру, а потом я буду делать в ней ремонт.
First I will buy an apartment, and then I will renovate it. (Perfective future in the first clause: a completed action in the future; imperfective future in the second clause: a process in the future.)

As you can see from these examples, imperfective future forms consist of the conjugated form of the verb "быть" plus the infinitive of the imperfective verb, as in:

Я буду говорить.	I will speak.
Ты будешь говорить.	You (informal) will speak.
Он/она/оно будет говорить.	He/she/it will speak.
Мы будем говорить.	We will speak.
Вы будете говорить.	You (plural/formal) will speak.
Они будут говорить.	They will speak.

To review the definitions of perfective and imperfective verbs, please refer to Chapter 11. In brief, imperfective verbs express actions as continuous processes (e.g. писать – to write), and perfective verbs describe completed actions (e.g. написать – to write, meaning to have written).

Russian imperfective future forms are identical to the simple English future forms "shall/will be." However, in contrast to English, in negative sentences the negative particle "не" (not) is placed in front of the verb "быть", as in the following examples:

Я б**у**ду рисов**а**ть.	I will draw.
Я не б**у**ду рисов**а**ть.	I will not draw.
Ей б**у**дет в**е**село.	It will be fun for her.
Ей не б**у**дет в**е**село.	It will not be fun for her.

Russian perfective future forms only exist for perfective verbs. These forms are produced by conjugating a perfective verb following the rules you studied for Group I and Group II of Russian verbs in the present tense. Look at the following examples to learn the conjugation of the perfective verb "прочит**а**ть" (to read, meaning "to have read)."

Я прочит**а**ю эту кн**и**гу.
I will read this book.

Ты прочит**а**ешь **э**ту стать**ю**.
You (informal) will read this article.

Он/он**а** прочит**а**ет **э**ту инстр**у**кцию.
He/she will read this instruction manual.

Мы прочит**а**ем **э**ту ск**а**зку.
We will read this fairy tale.

Вы прочит**а**ете **э**тот расск**а**з в шк**о**ле.
You (plural/formal) will read this short story at school.

Он**и** прочит**а**ют **э**ту газ**е**ту з**а**втра.
They will read this newspaper tomorrow.

Reading is one of the most beloved Russian pastime activities, so it is good to know the terms for different kinds of reading materials. Study the following list to learn what your Russian friends might be reading.

Table 12-2

▼ **READING MATERIALS IN RUSSIAN**

Russian	English
кн**и**га	book
ром**а**н	novel
п**о**весть	short story

расск**а**з	story
пь**е**са	play
ск**а**зка	fairy tale
б**а**сня	fable
стихотвор**е**ние	poem / poetry
текст	text
газ**е**та	newspaper
журн**а**л	journal/magazine
стать**я**	article (in a magazine/newspaper)
инстр**у**кция	instructions
дневн**и**к	diary/journal

Russian books are different from books in English, not only because they are in a different language, but also because of the way they are put together. For example, don't look for the table of contents at the beginning of a Russian book—it is usually located at the very end of the book.

Tenses and Aspects in Russian

Congratulations! You have now covered the entire system of Russian tenses and aspects. It is one of the most challenging parts of Russian grammar, and it usually requires a lot of practice to get it right. As you continue improving your Russian language skills, always remember the connection between tenses and aspect. See the following table to review what you have learned so far and to solidify your understanding of these important grammatical concepts:

Table 12-3

▼ **CORRELATION OF TENSES AND ASPECT IN RUSSIAN**

Aspect	Infinitive	Present	Past	Future Tense
Imperfective	чит**а**ть	я чит**а**ю	я чит**а**л(а)	я б**у**ду чит**а**ть
In English	to read	I read/am reading	I read/was reading/have been reading	I will read/will be reading

Perfective	прочит**а**ть		я прочит**а**л(а)	я прочит**а**ю
In English	to read/have read		I read/ have read	I will read/will finish reading

Because there is no exact correspondence between Russian and English verbal forms, take a close look at the context in order to choose appropriate verbs. Read the following dialogues to practice recognizing Russian tenses and aspects within a particular conversational context.

Dialogue 1: Conversation about a Daily Routine

Серг**е**й: Влад**и**мир, как ты начин**а**ешь твой день?
Vladimir, how do you begin your day?

Влад**и**мир: Я р**а**но вста**ю**, д**е**лаю заря**д**ку, м**о**ю г**о**лову, ч**и**щу з**у**бы и гот**о**влю з**а**втрак.
I get up early, do exercises, wash my hair, brush my teeth, and make breakfast.

Серг**е**й: А что ты д**е**лаешь днём?
And what do you do in the afternoon?

Влад**и**мир: Днём я раб**о**таю.
In the afternoon, I work.

Серг**е**й: А в**е**чером?
And in the evening?

Влад**и**мир: В**е**чером об**ы**чно я смотр**ю** телев**и**зор и чит**а**ю.
In the evening, I usually watch TV and read.

Серг**е**й: А чем ты заним**а**ешься в субб**о**ту и воскрес**е**нье?
And what do you do on Saturday and Sunday?

Влад**и**мир: По выходн**ы**м я убир**а**ю кварт**и**ру, хож**у** в магаз**и**н и гуля**ю** в п**а**рке.
On weekends I clean my apartment, go to the store, and walk in the park.

Dialogue 2: An Early Morning Dialogue

Mother: В**а**ня, ты уж**е** сд**е**лал заря**д**ку?
Vanya, have you already done your exercises?

Son: Нет, но я уже почистил зубы и вымыл голову.

No, but I already have brushed my teeth and washed my hair.

Mother: Хорошо. Я уже приготовила завтрак. Ты вчера сделал домашнюю работу по математике?

Good. I have already made breakfast. Did you do your math homework yesterday?

Son: Нет, но это не проблема. Урок по математике будет завтра, так что у меня есть время.

No, I didn't, but it's not a problem. The math lesson is tomorrow, so I have time.

In Russian, many of the expressions we use to describe our daily activities contain imperfective or perfective verbs coupled with nouns. Grammatically these nouns are objects, so remember to use the accusative case. The following table provides a brief compilation of phrases for daily activities, both in the imperfective and perfective aspect.

Table 12-4

▼ DAILY ACTIVITIES

Imperfective	Perfective	English
чистить зубы	почистить зубы	to brush one's teeth
мыть голову	вымыть голову	to wash one's hair
принимать душ	принять душ	to take a shower
делать зарядку	сделать зарядку	to exercise / do warm-ups
готовить завтрак	приготовить завтрак	to make breakfast
смотреть телевизор	посмотреть телевизор	to watch television
слушать радио	послушать радио	to listen to the radio
делать домашнюю работу	сделать домашнюю работу	to do homework
убирать квартиру	убрать квартиру	to clean up the apartment
встречать друзей	встретить друзей	to meet friends
выгуливать собаку	выгулять собаку	to walk the dog
мыть посуду	вымыть посуду	to wash dishes
гладить одежду	выгладить одежду	to iron clothes

Multiple Negative Constructions

In English, double negatives are considered grammatically incorrect: Only one negative is permitted. In Russian, multiple negatives are possible. In fact, Russian puts no limit on how many negatives can be included in a sentence. Compare the following sentences in Russian and English:

Я ничего не вижу.
I don't see anything.

Я никого не знаю в этой комнате.
I don't know anyone in this room.

Я никогда здесь не был.
I have never been here.

Он никак не может понять ничего из того, что я говорю.
He can't understand anything that I am saying.

To form a basic negative construction in Russian, use the particle "не" to negate a verb. Use the prefix "ни," as in никто (nobody), ничто (nothing), никогда (never), and никуда (nowhere) to include additional negatives. Pronouns are declined in Russian, but adverbs are not. Following is a table summarizing the declension of the interrogative pronouns кто (who) and что (what). Negative pronouns are declined in a similar fashion.

Table 12-5

▼ **DECLENSION OF INTERROGATIVE PRONOUNS КТО (SOMEBODY) AND ЧТО (NOTHING)**

Case	кто	что
Nominative	кто	что
Accusative	кого	что
Genitive	кого	чего
Prepositional	ком	чём
Dative	кому	чему
Instrumental	кем	чем

Chapter Review

Review the material covered in this chapter and complete the following exercises.

Chapter Quiz

Answer the following questions and check your answers in Appendix A.

1. What is the term for Russian sentences with no clear grammatical subject?

   _____

2. Which case should you use to express a logical subject in impersonal constructions in Russian?

   _____

3. Is the verb "быть" omitted in the future tense?

   _____

4. What are two major differences between perfective and imperfective future forms?

   _____

5. Where will you most likely find a contents page in a Russian book?

   _____

6. Explain why a word-by-word approach will not work when translating verbal forms from English to Russian and vice versa?

   _____

7. How many negatives can be included in a grammatically correct Russian sentence?

   _____

Translation Practice

A. Translate the following sentences into English:

1. Тебе нельзя есть шоколад.

   _____

2. Ему надо идти домой.

   _____

3. Вам можно смотреть телевизор?

   _____

4. Где можно купить коньки?

   _____

5. Мне нужно прочитать эту книгу.

   _____

B. Translate the following sentences into Russian:

6. Is smoking permitted here? – Yes, it is.

   _____

7. Where can one buy a good car? – I don't know.

   _____

8. I need to go to work.

   _____

9. They need to write a letter.

   _____

10. Can you/one play in the park?

    _____

C. Translate the following Russian sentences into English and convert them to the future and past tenses.

11. Ей пло́хо.

_____

12. Здесь нельзя́ игра́ть.

_____

13. Мне мо́жно ката́ться на лы́жах.

_____

14. Вам на́до домо́й.

_____

15. Сего́дня на у́лице хо́лодно.

_____

Conversational Practice

Answer the following questions in Russian to the best of your ability.

1. What do you usually do in the morning?

_____

2. What do you usually do on weekends?

_____

3. What did you do yesterday in the morning?

_____

4. What did you do yesterday in the evening?

_____

5. What daily activities do you usually avoid doing in the morning?

_____

CHAPTER 13

Reflexive Verbs and the Instrumental Case

It's a traveler's worst nightmare: Something breaks or gets lost in an unfamiliar foreign country. Fortunately, if you know how to communicate in the native language, this does not have to be a traumatic experience. This chapter focuses on the reflexive verbs you might need to report different kinds of accidents, losses, and repairs. We will then focus on the basics of the instrumental case, paying special attention to its main functions and forms in nouns and pronouns. Finally, you will learn about two word formation strategies in Russian that will help you expand your vocabulary and see more connections between English and Russian.

Breaking Things and Making Repairs

In Chapter 7, you learned that some Russian verbs are reflexive, or in other words, they express actions that reflect back to the performer. In this chapter, you will learn a new subgroup of reflexive verbs that deal with breaking things and making repairs. In the following table, you will find pairs of perfective verbs that are similar in meaning but different grammatically: The first column contains transitive non-reflexive verbs, and the third column lists reflexive intransitive verbs.

❓ Question

What are the key categories used to describe Russian verbs?
Aspect, transitivity, reflexivity, conjugation type, and tense are the key categories you need to know to use Russian verbs correctly. At this point, it might seem like a daunting task, but the more you practice your Russian, the better you will become at making appropriate choices about verbs and other grammatical and lexical options.

First-person singular forms in the future tense are provided to help you conjugate these verbs. Refer to Chapter 7 for more information about conjugation patterns. All of the verbs except for the verb найти (to find) are regular in the past tense.

Table 13-1

▼ **BREAKING THINGS AND MAKING REPAIRS: VERBS TO REMEMBER**

Transitive Verb	English	Reflexive Intransitive Verb	English
сломать (future: сломаю)	to break	сломаться	to break oneself
разбить (future: разобью/ёшь/ёт/ём/ёте)	to shatter	разбиться	to shatter oneself
разорвать (future: разорву)	to tear up	разорваться	to tear oneself up
потерять (future: потеряю)	to lose	потеряться	to lose oneself
разрушить (future: разрушу)	to destroy	разрушиться	to destroy oneself
починить (future: починю)	to fix	починиться	to fix oneself
построить (future: построю)	to build	построиться	to build oneself
найти (future: найду, past: нашёл, нашла, нашли)	to find	найтись	to find oneself

Remember that not all verbs can be reflexive and not all verbs keep the same meaning if they do become reflexive, as in зашить (future: зашью) - to sew up, зашиться (colloquial) - to be wiped out, and пришить (future: пришью) - to sew onto, пришиться (colloquial) - to bother someone.

What Broke and Who Did It?

The beauty of the reflexive verbs introduced in the previous section is that they allow Russian speakers to report an accident or a problem without necessarily having to acknowledge exactly who the culprit is. Compare the following sentences in English and Russian:

Машина сломалась.	The car broke down.
Моя машина сломалась.	My car broke down. (It is unknown who broke my car.)
У меня сломалась машина.	My car broke down. (Although there is some ambiguity as to who exactly broke the car, it is most likely that I did.)
Ваш сын сломал мою машину.	Your son broke my car. (There is no ambiguity: We know who broke my car.)
Документы потерялись.	The documents got lost.
Их документы потерялись.	Their documents got lost. (It is unknown who lost their documents.)
У них потерялись документы.	Their documents got lost. (Although there is some ambiguity as to who exactly lost the documents, it is most likely that they did.)
Вы потеряли их документы.	You lost their documents. (There is no ambiguity: We know who lost their documents.)

As you can see from these sentences, whenever reflexive verbs are used to report an accident, a loss, or a problem, a certain level of ambiguity is preserved as to who the real culprit or the source of the issue is. It is often said that the two greatest enduring questions of Russian social life and literature have been "Кто виноват?" (Who is to blame?) and "Что делать?" (What is to be done?). Russian grammar allows space for multiple interpretations rather than promoting only one way of seeing things.

In the sentences where the construction with the preposition "у" plus a noun/pronoun in the accusative case is used, the word order is different than in English. Grammatically, these sentences are similar to the impersonal constructions that you studied in Chapter 12; there is no grammatical subject and the logical subject is expressed through a prepositional phrase.

So what else can be broken? Refer to the following list for a variety of things that can be broken and, hopefully, repaired.

Ваза / тарелка / чашка разбилась.
A vase / plate / cup broke.

Машина / компьютер / стиральная машина / пылесос / кофеварка / плита / телевизор / микроволновая печь сломалась / сломался.
A car / computer / washing machine / vacuum cleaner / coffee maker / stove / television set / microwave broke down.

Паспорт / виза / сумка / фотоаппарат / куртка / шапка / ключи потерялся / потерялась / потерялись.
A passport / visa / bag / camera / coat / hat / keys is / are lost.

Дом / здание / дача разрушился / разрушилось / разрушилась.
A house / building / country cottage was destroyed.

The following are three mini-dialogues that illustrate the use of these reflexive verbs and corresponding nouns and pronouns.

Dialogue 1
Катя: Витя, что случилось? Почему ты такой печальный?
What happened? Why are you so sad?

Витя: Ничего страшного. Просто моя любимая книга потерялась.
Nothing terrible. It's just that my favorite book got lost.

Катя: Ты не помнишь куда ты её положил?
Don't you remember where you put it?

Витя: Нет. Да, и моя мама могла положить её куда-нибудь в другое место.
No. But also my mom could have put it somewhere in a different place.

Dialogue 2
Саша: Мария Петровна, ваша хрустальная ваза разбилась.
Maria Petrovna, your crystal vase got broken.

Мария Петровна: Ах, как жалко! Саша, ты её разбила?
Oh, what a pity! Sasha, did you break it?

Саша: Нет, я только нашла осколки на полу на кухне.
No, I only just found the broken pieces on the floor in the kitchen.

Мария Петровна: Наверное, это Вася. Он такой неуклюжий. Ну, что с ним делать? Я просила его быть осторожней.
It was probably Vasya. He is so clumsy. But what can you do with him? I asked him to be more careful.

Dialogue 3

Коля, у меня к тебе просьба. Ты можешь мне помочь?
Kolya, I have a favor to ask. Can you help me?

Конечно, что случилось?
Of course. What happened?

У меня сломался компьютер. Возможно, это вирус. У тебя есть время его проверить?
My computer broke. It's possible it's a virus. Do you have to time to check it?

Да, садись, пожалуйста. Давай посмотрим, что происходит с твоим компьютером.
Yes, sit down please. Let's see what's going on with your computer.

Useful Phrases

Learn the following phrases that are often used to express a feeling of pity, irritation, or embarrassment when something is missing or broken. These phrases consist of the Russian word "как" (how) plus an adverb. Note the difference between English and Russian: Corresponding English phrases use adjectives, not adverbs.

Как жалко!	What a shame!
Как обидно!	How frustrating / insulting!
Как неприятно!	How unpleasant!
Как неудобно!	How inconvenient! / How embarrassing!
Как неожиданно!	How unexpected!

Как оп**а**сно!   How dangerous!
Как стр**а**шно!   How terrifying!
Как уж**а**сно!   How terrible!

Learn the following phrases to ask for help and express your gratitude:

Вы м**о**жете мне пом**о**чь?   Can you (formal/plural) help me?
Как хорош**о**!   How nice/good!
Спас**и**бо за п**о**мощь!   Thank you for your help!
Вы мне так помогл**и**!   You (formal/plural) helped me so much!

If someone asks you for help, remember the following phrases:

Что случ**и**лось?   What happened?
Чем я мог**у** вам/теб**е** пом**о**чь?   How can I help you?

The Basics of the Instrumental Case

The main function of the instrumental case is to indicate the means, manner, or agent of an action, as in the following examples.

Чем ты п**и**шешь? – Я пиш**у** р**у**чкой.
What are you writing with? – I'm writing with a pen.

Чем ты почин**и**шь **э**ту маш**и**ну? – Я д**у**маю, что я почин**ю** её **э**тим инструм**е**нтом.
What are you going to fix this car with? – I think I will fix it with this tool.

Кем ты б**у**дешь, когд**а** в**ы**растешь? – Я б**у**ду врач**о**м, а ты?
What are you going to be when you grow up? – I will be a doctor, and you?

The instrumental case is expressed through specific endings.

- Add the ending -ом/-ем to singular nouns that follow the first declension pattern: masculine nouns ending in a consonant, a soft sign, or "й" as well as neuter nouns ending in -о or -е. For example, хлеб (bread) – хл**е**бом, словарь (dictionary) – словарём, музей (museum) – муз**е**ем, окн**о** (window) – окн**о**м.
- Plural nouns of the first declension pattern take the endings -ами/-ями, as in хлеб**а**ми, словар**я**ми, муз**е**ями, **о**кнами.

- Feminine and masculine nouns ending in -а/-я that belong to the second declension take the endings of –ой/-ей, as in вод**а** (water) – вод**ой**, нед**е**ля (week) – нед**е**лей, п**а**па (dad) – п**а**пой, д**я**дя (uncle) – д**я**дей.
- Plural nouns from the second declension pattern take the endings –ами/ями, as in пап**а**ми and нед**е**лями.
- Feminine nouns ending in a soft sign from the third declension pattern take the ending –ю, as in морк**о**вь (carrot) – морк**о**вью, пл**о**щадь (square) – пл**о**щадью.
- Plural feminine nouns from the third declension pattern take the ending -ями in the instrumental case, as in площад**я**ми.

After ж, ш, щ, ц, write the vowel "о" in stressed singular endings in the instrumental case, and the vowel "e" in unstressed singular endings, as in нож (knife) – нож**о**м, ключ (key) – ключ**о**м, каранд**а**ш (pencil) – карандаш**о**м, госпож**а** (Mrs.) – госпож**о**й, but муж (husband) – м**у**жем, к**а**ша (kasha) – к**а**шей.

Prepositions and the Instrumental Case

The instrumental case is sometimes used with several prepositions. The preposition "c" (with) expresses a joint action, as in Я гул**я**ю в п**а**рке с мо**е**й м**а**мой. (I am walking in the park with my mom.) In addition to the verb "гул**я**ть," the verbs "жить" (to live), "друж**и**ть" (to be friends), and "раб**о**тать" (to work) often express a mutual action (as in to live with, to be friends with, to work with) and are used with the preposition "c" followed by a noun in the instrumental case.

The following prepositions are used in the circumstances outlined here:

- Use the preposition "c" to indicate a combination of two substances, as in the following set expressions: "хлеб с м**а**слом" (bread and butter), "к**о**фе с молок**о**м" (coffee with milk), "пир**о**г с кап**у**стой" (cabbage pie).
- Use the preposition "р**я**дом с" (near to) to indicate proximity, as in the following expressions: "р**я**дом с д**о**мом" (close to home), "р**я**дом со шк**о**лой" (next to school).
- Use the preposition "м**е**жду" (between/among), as in the following expressions: "м**е**жду н**е**бом и земл**ё**й" (between sky and earth; in a suspended, uncertain condition), "м**е**жду людьм**и**" (among people).

- Use the preposition "с" and the pronoun "мы" (we) to indicate either a group of people that includes the speaker or only the speaker and the person expressed by the noun or pronoun in the instrumental case, as in "мы с Ваней" (we and Vanya, word-for-word) and "мы с Ваней" (Vanya and I). The exact meaning is usually clear within the specific communicative context.
- Use the preposition "с" in several set expressions to denote two people, as in "мы с тобой" (you [informal] and I), "мы с вами" (you (formal) and I), "он / она со мной / тобой" (he / she and I / you), "мы с сестрой / братом" (my sister / brother and I), "мы с женой / мужем" (my wife / husband and I).

The instrumental case forms for personal pronouns are grouped with the nominative forms, which were presented in the earlier chapters: я—мной, ты—тобой, он—им (masculine), она—ей (feminine), оно—им (neuter), мы—нами, вы—вами, они—ими. When learning these forms, remember that the third-person singular masculine and neutral forms are identical.

The Instrumental Case: Professions and Family Relations

The instrumental case is also used after the verbs "быть" (to be), "становиться" (to become, imperfective), "стать" (to become, perfective), and "работать" (to work). Compare the following examples in Russian and English:

Ты кем будешь, когда закончишь школу? – Я буду студентом в университете.

What are you going to be when you finish high school? – I will be a student at the university.

Ты не знаешь, кем она работает? – Да, знаю. Она мне сказала, что она работает врачом в больнице.

Do you know what her profession is? – Yes, I do. She told me that she is a doctor at a hospital.

Во время войны он был лётчиком.

During the war, he was a pilot.

Вы не знаете, где работала Анна Михайловна? – После института она долго работала инженером, а потом стала директором завода.

Do you know where Anna Mikhailovna worked? – After the institute (meaning: after graduating from the institute), she worked for a long time as an engineer, and then became the director of a factory.

ⓔ✱ Essential

Note that Russian speakers often use negation in questions for courtesy, as in "Вы не знаете, где здесь кинотеатр?" (You don't know where the movie theater is here, do you?) or "Ты не знаешь, кем он работал в Америке?" (You don't know what his job was in America, do you?)

There are several nouns that form irregular plural endings in the nominative and in the instrumental case. These nouns are often used in sentences with the verbs "быть" (to be) and "становиться" – "стать" (to become).

Table 13-2

▼ **IRREGULAR ENDINGS IN THE INSTRUMENTAL CASE**

Nominative Singular	English	Nominative Plural	Instrumental Singular	Instrumental Plural
брат	brother	братья	братом	братьями
друг	friend	друзья	другом	друзьями
муж	husband	мужья	мужем	мужьями
сын	son	сыновья	сыном	сыновьями
ребёнок	child	дети	ребёнком	детьми
человек	human being	люди	человеком	людьми

Read the following dialogue to practice the use of the instrumental case and learn some new colloquial expressions that Russians often use to share news with each other.

Маша: Ты знаешь новость о Сергее?
Do you know the news about Sergei?

Таня: Нет. А что?
No. What is it?

Маша: Марина мне сказала по секрету, что он скоро станет отцом.
Marina told me in confidence that he'll soon be a father.

Таня: Да ты что! Вот **э**то н**о**вость! Зн**а**чит **О**льга Петр**о**вна б**у**дет б**а**бушкой.

It can't be! Now that's news! That means Olga Petrovna will be a grandmother.

Маша: Да, но б**у**дет ли он**а** р**а**да?

Yes, but will she be happy?

Таня: А почем**у** нет? Он**а** мне мн**о**го раз говор**и**ла, как ей нр**а**вится игр**а**ть с детьм**и**.

Why not? She told me many times she likes to play with children.

Маша: Да, но Мар**и**не и Серг**е**ю н**у**жно б**у**дет помог**а**ть. С детьм**и** всегд**а** мн**о**го хлоп**о**т.

Yes, but Marina and Sergei will need help. There are always many worries with children.

Таня: Это пр**а**вда. Но и мн**о**го р**а**дости. Серг**е**й и Мар**и**на так**и**е молод**ы**е. У них всё пол**у**чится.

That's true. But lots of joy, too. Also, Sergei and Marina are so young. It will all go fine for them.

Common Roots and Loan Words

How can you improve your vocabulary in Russian? One of the techniques is to try to learn frequently used roots and combine these roots with different prefixes and suffixes to form additional words. You might also want to look more carefully into the history of some Russian words to discover their connections to the words that you already know in English or other languages.

Word Building: Recognizing Common Roots

You have probably noticed that several of the verbs included in this chapter have common roots, for example, the verbs "заш**и**ть" (to sew up) and "приш**и**ть" (to sew onto) share the same root "шить" (to sew). The semantic link between these two words is expressed through the use of the same root. This type of word formation is called suffixation, and it is common both in English and Russian. The following are examples of commonly used roots with several words derived from them. It is possible that you already know some of these words, while others might be new to you.

The root крас (red/beauty)

крас**а**	beauty (dated)
кр**а**сный	red
красот**а**	beauty
крас**и**вый	beautiful
крас**а**вец	a handsome man
крас**а**вица	a female beauty
кр**а**ситься	to put on makeup
красов**а**ться	to show off

The root боль (pain)

боль	pain
больн**ой**	an ill/sick person
бол**е**знь	illness/sickness
больн**и**ца	hospital
забол**е**ть	to fall ill
заболев**а**ние	an ailment

The root лекар (cure, treat)

л**е**карь	doctor (dated)
лек**а**рство	medicine, cure
леч**и**ть	to treat medically
леч**е**ние	(medical) treatment
в**ы**лечить	to cure

The root здрав (health)

здр**а**вие	well-being
здор**о**вье	health
здр**а**вствовать	to be well and healthy
здр**а**вствуй(те)	a greeting formula (formal/informal)
в**ы**здороветь	to get better

The root игр (play, game)

игр**а**	game
игр**а**ть	to play
игр**о**к	player
игр**у**шка	toy
в**ы**игрыш	prize, winning
в**ы**играть	to win

пр**о**игрыш	loss, losing
проигр**а**ть	to lose

Etymology is a field of linguistics that deals with the history of words. In addition to scientific etymology based on thorough research, laypeople often create folk etymologies for various words. The best way to learn the etymology of a word is to refer to "этимолог**и**ческий слов**а**рь" (an etymological dictionary).

Loan Words

You already know that languages borrow words from each other. Some borrowings are hard to pinpoint because they are formed with the help of native words. These are called loan words. In Russian there are several loan words from English, for example, "небоскрёб" (from English "skyscraper"), "телохран**и**тель" (from English "bodyguard"), and "карт**и**на" (from English "picture", meaning "movie"). More recent additions to Russian lexicon that have roots in English and are gaining popularity both in Russian press and in everyday conversational language are "делов**а**я ж**е**нщина" (business woman), "говор**я**щая голов**а**" (talking head), "в**о**тум недов**е**рия" (no-confidence vote), and "отмыв**а**ние д**е**нег" (money laundering).

Chapter Review

Review the material covered in this chapter and complete the following exercises.

Chapter Quiz

Answer the following questions and check your answers in Appendix A.

1. What are reflexive verbs?

   _____

2. Can reflexive verbs be transitive?

   _____

3. Give at least three examples of frequently used word roots with several examples illustrating their usage.

   _____

4. What strategies can you employ to expand your vocabulary in Russian?

_____

5. What is the main function of the instrumental case?

_____

Translation Practice

A. Translate the following sentences into Russian and use an appropriate expression of frustration:

1. My computer broke.

_____

2. My keys got lost.

_____

3. Our washing machine is not working.

_____

4. Her new bag got lost.

_____

B. Translate the following dialogue into Russian:

5. What happened?

_____

6. My passport got lost.

_____

7. How can I help?

_____

8. I need to find the American Embassy.

_____

C. Translate the following Russian colloquial expressions into English:

9. По секрету

_____

10. А почему нет?

_____

11. Да ты что!

_____

12. Мы с мужем

_____

13. Между небом и землёй

_____

14. Мы с Мариной

_____

Grammar and Vocabulary Drill

Answer the following questions in Russian to the best of your ability.

1. Вы не знаете где здесь телефон?

_____

2. Мы будем друзьями?

_____

3. Кем ты будешь, когда закончишь школу?

_____

CHAPTER 14

The Genitive Case

In this chapter, you will explore the basics of the genitive case, paying special attention to the system of endings that mark this case in nouns, adjectives, and possessive and demonstrative pronouns. The genitive case is used to express possession, quantity, and negation. To expand your understanding of Russian culture, read about the history and current state of private property and learn more about Russian higher education. Useful vocabulary is introduced and reinforced through dialogues and exercises.

The Basics of the Genitive Case

The main function of the genitive case is to show possession. You already know how to describe possession with the help of possessive pronouns and/or special sentence structures. Compare the following examples:

Это мой брат. Это его машина.
This is my brother. This is his car.

Это мой брат. У него есть машина.
This is my brother. He has a car.

Это машина моего брата.
This is my brother's car.

Это моя сестра. Это её квартира.
This is my sister. This is her apartment.

Это моя сестра. У неё есть квартира.
This is my sister. She has an apartment.

Это кварт**и**ра мо**ей** сестр**ы**.

This is my sister's apartment.

Это маш**и**на моег**о** бр**а**та and Это кварт**и**ра мо**ей** сестр**ы** are examples of the genitive case. As you can see, the genitive case is the most succinct way of describing possessions belonging to people other than the speaker. English, too, has a similar construction, sometimes referred to as the possessive case. However, it is important to note a major difference in the word order: In Russian the word that expresses the owner is always put after the word that stands for the property, as in кварт**и**ра сестр**ы**. In English we use the reverse word order, as in "my sister's apartment."

To remember the correct word order in genitive constructions, it might be useful to consider a similar English construction that we sometimes use to express possession, that is, "an apartment of my sister." In this prepositional phrase, the word order is identical to Russian genitive constructions.

Forming the Genitive Case

As with the other cases, the genitive case is expressed through specific endings.

- Add -а to masculine nouns that end in consonants and neuter nouns that end in -о.

  друг – кварт**и**ра др**у**га   friend – apartment of a friend

  окно – **о**кна

- Add -я to masculine nouns that end in -й and -ь and neuter nouns that end in -е and -ие.

  преподав**а**тель – кн**и**га препод**а**вателя   university instructor – book of a university instructor

  м**о**ре – р**ы**бы м**о**ря   sea – fish of the sea

- Add -и to feminine nouns that end in -я and -ь.

  тетр**а**дь – стран**и**ца тетр**а**ди   notebook – page of a notebook

- Add -ы to feminine nouns that end in -а.

  маш**и**на – вод**и**тель маш**и**ны   car – driver of a car

Remember that some nouns in the accusative case also take the endings -а or -я. The only way to tell which case is being used is to pay attention to the context.

Plural Nouns in the Genitive Case

Plural nouns in the genitive case are used to indicate the quantity or absence of objects. A special note needs to be made about the formation of the genitive case of plural nouns. Plural nouns in the genitive case are rather complex and depend not only on the declension of a particular noun, but also take into consideration whether the noun is hard- or soft-stemmed and what grammatical gender it belongs to.

To make the matter more complex, there are exceptions. The following are several common patterns in the formation of the genitive case for plural nouns.

- Hard-stemmed masculine plural nouns, except for ч, щ, ш, and ж, take the ending of -ов.
  ресторан – рестораны – владелец ресторанов
  restaurant – restaurants – owner of restaurants

- Plural nouns that end in the consonants ч, щ, ш, and ж in the singular nominative case take the ending of -ей in the genitive case.
  мяч – мячи – покупатель мячей
  ball – balls – buyer of balls
  карандаш – карандаши – покупатель карандашей
  pencil – pencils – buyer of pencils

- Soft-stemmed masculine plural nouns take the ending of –ев.
  словарь – словари – владелец словарей
  dictionary – dictionaries – owner of dictionaries

- Hard-stemmed feminine and neuter plural nouns take the zero ending, meaning only the noun's stem is used without the addition of a suffix.
  школа – школы – директор школ   school – schools – principal of schools
  слово – слова – недостаток слов   word – words – lack of words

- Soft-stemmed feminine plural nouns take the ending of –ь or –ей.
  неделя – недели – дни недель   week – weeks – days of weeks

- Feminine plural nouns that already end in -ь take the -ей ending
  тетра́дь – тетра́ди – страни́цы тетра́дей
  notebook – notebooks – pages of notebooks

This may look like an awfully long list of rules, but most masculine nouns in the plural generative case end in –ов, and most feminine nouns in the plural generative case take the zero ending.

Private and Public Property in Russia

During the communist era, all property in Russia was proclaimed to be public. In Soviet lingo, everything belonged to the people. Private property was restricted to a very limited list of necessities, such as one's clothes, furniture, and other very personal necessities. Apartments and houses were leased from the state and were officially under municipal ownership.

All of this changed dramatically after the fall of the Soviet Union, making it possible for people to exercise their rights of ownership unrestrained by the government. A "quick and dirty" and often rigged system of privatization resulted in the concentration of financial and political power in the hands of very few, often referred to in Russian media as олига́рхи (oligarchs). Overall, власть олига́рхов (the power of the oligarchs) has been greatly diminished by the Putin government. The Russian government's technique of digging into the oligarchs' shady past and prosecuting them for illegal activities has been effective in suppressing the oligarchy.

The following is a vocabulary list that will help you discuss private and public property in Russia in Russian.

Table 14-1

▼ **VOCABULARY DEALING WITH PROPERTY**

Russian	English
со́бственность	property
ча́стная со́бственность	private property
обще́ственная со́бственность	public property
пода́рок	gift
завеща́ние	will
владе́лец(а) / владе́льцы	owner (fem.)/ owners

покупать в кредит	to buy using credit
платить наличными деньгами	to pay with cash
продавать/покупать по аукциону	to buy / sell in an auction
недвижимость (fem)	real estate
рынок недвижимости	real estate market
продавец недвижимости	real estate seller
заём	loan
процентная ставка	interest rate
налоги на недвижимость	property taxes
банкротство	bankruptcy

Adjectives and Pronouns in the Genitive Case

As you remember, adjectives and pronouns agree with nouns in number, gender, and case. Generally, masculine and neuter singular nouns take the endings of -ого / -его, while feminine singular nouns in the genitive case end in -ой / -ей, as in "дом известного писателя" (a famous writer's house) and "книга младшей сестры" (a younger sister's book). Remember that the consonant "г" in the endings of the adjectives and pronouns is always pronounced as the Russian consonant "в."

Review the genitive forms and usage of Russian personal pronouns: меня, тебя, его/её/его, нас, вас, их in Chapter 6. Remember that these pronouns are often used with the preposition "у" (by) to indicate either possession (У меня есть кот. - I have a cat.) or close proximity (Я у него. – I [am] at his place.) Now that you know how to form the genitive case of nouns, note that both of these constructions can be applied to animate nouns, as in У врача есть лекарство – The doctor has medicine. or Я живу у дядяи – I live at my uncle's.

The following table summarizes the genitive forms of the possessive and demonstrative pronouns in singular and plural. The first two columns include corresponding masculine forms in the nominative case and the English translation. Note that the pronouns его (his), её (her), and их (their) are not declined and retain their form in the genitive case.

Table 14-2

▼ GENITIVE FORMS OF PERSONAL, POSSESSIVE, AND
DEMONSTRATIVE PRONOUNS

Nominative	English	Masculine	Feminine	Neuter	Plural
мой/твой	my/yours (informal, singular)	моего/ твоего	моей/ твоей	моего/ твоего	моих/ твоих
наш/ваш	our/your (formal, plural)	нашего/ вашего	нашей/ вашей	нашего/ вашего	наших/ ваших
этот/тот	this/that	этого/того	этой/той	этого/того	этих/тех

Some Russian family names in their form are identical to Russian adjectives. For example, think about famous Russian writers (Достоевский, Толстой, and Некрасов) and composers (Чайковский and Мусоргский). These and other grammatically similar names are declined as adjectives: роман Достоевского (Dostoevsky's novel), повесть Толстого (Tolstoy's short story), поэма Некрасова (Nekrasov's poem), балет Чайковского (Tchaikovsky's ballet), опера Мусоргского (Musorgsky's opera).

The Genitive Case in Noun Phrases

The genitive case is also used to modify a noun with another noun or noun phrase, as in the following examples.

Моя сестра – учитель русского языка.
My sister is a Russian language teacher.

Это учебник математики.
This is a math textbook.

This is a useful model, often used to describe academic disciplines, known in Russian as предметы. Consult the following table to learn new vocabulary that will help you discuss your academic interests. Also consider this as a side-note on the Russian system of higher education. All the disciplines mentioned in the following table represent popular majors in Russian universities and colleges.

A college degree in Russia usually means a five-year degree, with the fifth year spent on writing a thesis in the major. Students have to defend their thesis, and if successful are granted a диплом (diploma) that certifies their degree.

In the past, all education was free for qualified candidates; all you needed to do was pass a series of exams held in each institution. Today, there is a complex system in place. There are still many institutions of higher learning that are sponsored by the state and are free for students; however, the competition for admission is extremely high.

On the other hand, there are many private colleges and universities that charge tuition fees. These colleges and universities are less highly regarded. However, if you really want to attend one of the top-notch institutions, you can still do it even if you didn't score too well on the entrance exams. Nearly all of them now admit "paying" students in an effort to improve their financial situation. Another important factor that determines the popularity of higher education is that Russia still has a draft, or призыв, and one of the reasons for delaying service in the armed forces is enrollment in a program of higher learning.

Table 14-3

▼ **ACADEMIC DISCIPLINES: POPULAR MAJORS**

Russian	English
высшее образование	higher education
предмет	subject, discipline
наука	science
биология	biology
медицина	medicine
математика	mathematics
право/юриспруденция	law/jurisprudence
культура	culture
антропология	anthropology
лингвистика	linguistics
архитектура	architecture
искусство	arts
физика	physics
химия	chemistry
литература	literature

ист**о**рия	history
геогр**а**фия	geography
психол**о**гия	psychology
педаг**о**гика	pedagogy

Now that you know the names of several academic disciplines and have a good understanding of the formation of the genitive case, let's explore several standard descriptive phrases related to the academic world. As you will see from the following table, many of the terms used in the academy have Latin and Greek roots in Russian and English.

Table 14-4

▼ **DESCRIBING THE ACADEMIC WORLD**

Lead Noun	Descriptive Noun	Phrase	English
студ**е**нт/ка	п**е**рвый/ втор**о**й/тр**е**тий/ четвёртый/ п**я**тый курс	студ**е**нт/ ка п**е**рвого/ втор**о**го/ тр**е**тьего/ четвёртого/ п**я**того к**у**рса	first-/second-/ third-/fourth-/ fifth-year student
уч**е**бник	ф**и**зика	уч**е**бник ф**и**зики	physics textbook
преподав**а**тель	матем**а**тика	преподав**а**тель матем**а**тики	math instructor
проф**е**ссор	лингв**и**стика	проф**е**ссор лингв**и**стики	linguistics professor
к**а**федра	иностр**а**нные язык**и**	к**а**федра иностр**а**нных язык**о**в	foreign languages department
факульт**е**т	пр**а**во	факульт**е**т пр**а**ва	law school
инстит**у**т	биол**о**гия	инстит**у**т биол**о**гии	biology institute
клуб	междунар**о**дные отнош**е**ния	клуб междунар**о**дных отнош**е**ний	international relations club

The genitive construction is not used with the following nouns: ле́кция (lecture), заня́тие (class), зада́ние (assignment), курсова́я рабо́та (term paper), and дипло́м (diploma). Instead, use the dative case in the prepositional construction with the preposition "по": ле́кция по исто́рии (lecture in history), заня́тие по ру́сскому языку́ (a class in Russian), and дипло́м по фи́зике (diploma/degree in physics).

"Нет" and the Genitive Case

The final use of the genitive case that we will analyze is in negative constructions with the word "нет." Compare the following English and Russian sentences:

В па́рке есть/был/бу́дет фонта́н.
In the park there is/was/will be a fountain.

В па́рке нет/не́ было/не бу́дет фонта́на.
In the park there is no/was not/will not be a fountain.

Он до́ма /он был/бу́дет до́ма.
He is/was/will be at home.

Его́ нет/не́ было/не бу́дет до́ма.
He is not/was not/will not be at home.

У него́ есть/была́/бу́дет кварти́ра.
He has/had/will have an apartment.

У него́ нет/не́ было/не бу́дет кварти́ры.
He doesn't have/didn't have/will not have an apartment.

To express negation, Russian uses a construction with "нет" in the present tense plus a noun in the genitive case. The construction "нет" is transformed into "не́ было" in the past and "не бу́дет" in the future, plus a noun in the genitive case. Note that in the last sentence in the example, the genitive case is used twice: first to express the person who doesn't/didn't/won't have an apartment ("у него́"), and second to indicate what this person is lacking ("кварти́ры").

The negative construction of the past and future tenses of verb "to be" do not seem to be conjugated because the deep structure of such sentences is impersonal, and thus, the linking verb "to be" (which only is physically apparent in the past and future tenses) has to be in the third person singular.

The Genitive Case in Context

Read the following dialogues to practice recognizing and using the genitive case in context. Remember that some of the words and expressions might be new to you. In this case, read the translations and try to memorize them.

Dialogue 1

Оля: Что **э**то у теб**я** в с**у**мке?
What's that in your bag?

Света: **Э**то под**а**рок М**а**ше на день рожд**е**ния. **Э**то кн**и**га.
This is a present for Masha for her birthday. It is a book.

Оля: Кн**и**га?
A book?

Света: Да, **э**то ром**а**н Толст**о**го "Войн**а** и мир." Ты д**у**маешь, ей **э**то понр**а**вится?
Yes, it's Tolstoy's novel *War and Peace*. Do you think she will like it?

Оля: Кон**е**чно. Как**а**я прекр**а**сная ид**е**я! Ты зн**а**ешь, **э**то мо**я** люб**и**мая кн**и**га.
Of course. It is a wonderful idea. You know, that's my favorite book.

Dialogue 2

Юля: Прив**е**т, как дел**а**?
Hi, how's everything?

Ира: Хорош**о**. Я **е**ду на кварт**и**ру моег**о** ст**а**ршего бр**а**та.
Good. I'm going to my older brother's apartment.

Юля: **Э**то далек**о**?
Is it far away?

Ира: Да, но мне н**а**до с ним встр**е**титься и верн**у**ть ег**о** уч**е**бник мат**е**матики.
Yes, but I need to meet with him to return his math textbook.

Юля: Да, а ведь з**а**втра у нас контр**о**льная раб**о**та. Ты гот**о**ва?
Yes, but tomorrow we have a test. Are you ready?

Ира: Не совс**е**м. А ты?
Not completely. And you?

Юля: К сожалению, я тоже. Математика - это так трудно!
Unfortunately, me either. Math is so hard!

Ира: Да, но это любимый предмет моего брата. Он преподаватель математики в институте. Может быть, он сможет нам помочь? У меня так много вопросов! Хочешь поехать со мной?

Yes, but it's my brother's favorite subject. He is a math instructor at an institute. Perhaps he can help us? I have so many questions. Would you like to go with me?

Юля: Это прекрасная идея. Спасибо!
That is a wonderful idea. Thanks!

As you noticed from these dialogues, the genitive case is used quite frequently in everyday conversation.

Chapter Review

Review the material covered in this chapter and complete the following exercises.

Chapter Quiz

Answer the following questions and check your answers in Appendix A.

1. What is the main function of the genitive case?

   _____

2. What are the additional uses of the genitive case?

   _____

3. In addition to nouns, what other parts of speech follow the declension system?

   _____

4. What is the correct pronunciation of the ending -ого / -его?

   _____

5. Why does the form of the verb "to be" in the past and future tenses in negative constructions with the genitive case remain in the third person singular?

   _____

Translation Practice

A. Translate the following expressions into Russian.

1. my sister's car _____
2. his brother's house _____
3. their grandmother's gift _____
4. a writer's notebook _____
5. your (informal; singular) mother's letter_____
6. students' assignment _____
7. an owner of the restaurants _____
8. a buyer of real estate _____
9. a lack of pencils _____
10. a lack of schools _____

B. Translate the following sentences into English.

11. У мен**я** есть брат и сестр**а**.

_____

12. У врач**а** есть лек**а**рство.

_____

13. Я жив**у** у нег**о** в д**о**ме.

_____

14. У мен**я** в к**о**мнате есть компь**ю**тер и телев**и**зор.

_____

15. У них нет кот**а**, но есть соб**а**ка.

_____

16. У мо**е**й сестр**ы** нет дипл**о**ма.

_____

17. Сег**о**дня у нег**о** нет л**е**кции.

_____

18. У неё н**е** было д**о**ма.

_____

19. Марины нет дома.

_____

20. У нас не будет контрольной работы.

_____

Vocabulary Practice

Use these prompts to create phrases describing professions, buildings, and objects found in the academic world.

1. факульт**е**т (international relations)_____
2. преподав**а**тель (anthropology) _____
3. л**е**кция (arts) _____
4. клуб (Russian language) _____
5. зан**я**тие (geography) _____
6. проф**е**ссор (physics) _____
7. уч**е**бник (mathematics) _____
8. студ**е**нт (literature) _____
9. зад**а**ние (chemistry) _____

Comprehension Practice

Answer the following questions by writing down your answers in Russian.

1. If you are a homeowner, in Russia you will be referred to as _____ .
2. When Russian newspapers are writing about the very few who were able to build financial empires during the privatization of public property after the fall of the Soviet Union, they usually refer to _____.
3. You could lose your house if you don't pay _____ to the state.
4. If you would like to ensure that your children inherit your house, you should write a _____.
5. In addition to the quest for knowledge, higher education is so popular among young Russian men because it allows them to avoid _____.

CHAPTER 15

Sentence Structure and the Imperative

In this chapter, you will learn about differences and similarities in English and Russian sentence structure. Now that you've learned the basics of Russian grammar, you can learn how to form complex sentences using several subordinate conjunctions. This chapter will also discuss the notion of grammatical mood and briefly analyze major uses and formation patterns of the imperative mood in Russian. In addition, you'll be able to explore Russian sensibilities about time.

Simple, Compound, and Complex Sentences

Now that you are familiar with major topics in Russian grammar, including cases, verb conjugations, and the system of pronouns, let's examine Russian sentence structure. All Russian sentences can be divided into three major groups: simple, compound, and complex sentences.

Simple Sentences

Simple sentences usually consist of at least a subject and a verb. In addition, depending on the type of the verb used, a sentence can have a direct and/or indirect object as well as various types of modifiers (adjectives, adverbs, prepositional and participle phrases). The structure of Russian simple sentences is similar to that of English sentences with two exceptions: Russian features flexible word order, and some Russian sentences might lack a grammatical subject or verb. Compare the following examples of simple sentences in English and Russian:

Я (subject) рис**у**ю (verb)
I am painting.

Я (subject) рис**у**ю (verb) карт**и**ну (direct object).
I am painting a picture.

Я (subject) рис**у**ю (verb) карт**и**ну (direct object) мо**е**й м**а**ме (indirect object).
I am painting a picture for my mother.

Я (subject) рис**у**ю (verb) хор**о**шую (modifier) карт**и**ну (direct object) мо**е**й дорог**о**й (modifier) м**а**ме (indirect object).
I am painting a good picture for my dear mother.

На **у**лице тепл**о** (the verb "есть" is missing; no grammatical subject).
It is warm outside.

Although Russian is famous for its flexible word order, its preferred word order is the same as in English: subject – verb – object (S-V-O).

Compound Sentences

Simple sentences, both in English and Russian, can combine to form compound sentences. Compound sentences are sentences that consist of two or more simple sentences, also known as clauses, connected by a coordinating conjunction. Clauses in a compound sentence are fully functional and can stand on their own. These clauses are also known as independent clauses.

Simple sentence: Я ид**у** пешк**о**м.
I am walking / going by foot.

Simple sentence: Он **е**дет на трамв**а**е.
He is taking the tram.

Compound sentence: Я ид**у** пешк**о**м, а он **е**дет на трамв**а**е.
I am walking, but he is taking the tram.

The three most commonly used coordinating conjunctions in Russian are: и (and), а (and/but), and но (but). Please refer to Chapter 5 to review the difference between "и" and "а."

Complex Sentences

Complex sentences include two or more simple clauses connected by a subordinating conjunction. In a complex sentence, one of the clauses is independent, and the other is dependent. The independent clause contains key information, while the dependent clause modifies it in some way. The dependent clause cannot stand on its own and must include a subordinating conjunction:

Simple sentence:

Я иду пешком.

I am walking.

Complex sentence:

Когда он едет на трамвае (subordinate clause), я иду пешком (independent clause).

When he is taking the tram, I am walking.

In contrast to English writing conventions, Russian writers prefer longer sentences with multiple clauses, which might be confusing to someone unfamiliar with this style of writing. For example, in *War and Peace*, Tolstoy is said to have written one of the longest sentences in literature; it continues for several pages. What should you do? Just be careful and use your understanding of sentence structure to figure out logical connections between different clauses.

Subordinate Conjunctions

Subordinate conjunctions let us qualify ideas by introducing additional information in dependent clauses. In a way, they are the markers of "fine print"; main ideas are communicated in independent clauses, but the details can only be found in subordinate clauses. What use is it to know that "Мы будем есть" (We will eat) if you don't know the information in the subordinate clause: "когда ты приготовишь завтрак" (when you make breakfast)? Knowledge of major subordinate conjunctions in Russian will allow you to recognize logical hierarchy in the sentences produced by other speakers and to form your own complex sentences. See the following table to learn more subordinate conjunctions in Russian:

Table 15-1

▼ SUBORDINATE CONJUNCTIONS IN RUSSIAN

Russian	English	Example
что	that	Он сказал, что завтра он будет дома. (He said that he will be at home tomorrow.)
когда	when	Лена всегда звонит домой, когда она задерживается на работе. (Lena always calls home when she is delayed at work.)
если	if	Если она любит танцевать, она обязательно придёт на дискотеку. (If she likes to dance, she will surely come to the night club.)
даже если	even if	Мы вас встретим, даже если вы приедете очень поздно. (We will meet you, even if you arrive very late.)
потому, что	because	Я не пойду гулять в парк потому, что на улице очень холодно. (I will not go for a walk in the park because it is very cold outside.)
чтобы	so that / in order to	Мы ждём нашу сестру, чтобы мы вместе поехали на дачу. (We are waiting for our sister so that we all can go to the dacha together.)
хотя	although	Хотя у меня нет твоего телефона, я тебе напишу по Интернету. (Although I don't have your number, I will write to you online.)
после того, как	after	Он пригласит их в гости после того, как он закончит ремонт. (He will invite them to his house after he finishes the renovation.)
перед тем, как	before	Перед тем как вы позавтракаете, вам принесут газету. (Before you have breakfast, they will deliver a newspaper.)
в то время, как	while	Оля слушала музыку в то время, как Настя готовила обед. (Olya listened to the music while Nastya was making dinner.)

The pronoun "того" is pronounced with the Russian consonant "в."

Subordinate conjunctions include clauses that indicate three different situations: cause (I came because you called), purpose (I came in order to talk), and condition (I will come if you call me).

Common Attitudes Toward Time

You probably know that cultures differ in their attitudes toward time. Some value time as a commodity that has to be saved and used wisely, whereas others see it more as a free-flowing river with a current far too strong to control and manipulate. If we were to place Russian and American cultures on a continuum to compare their respective attitudes toward time, they would end up on opposite ends.

In contrast to many Americans, Russians have a very relaxed attitude toward time. Usually being late, or in Russian, "оп**аздывать**" is not considered to be a huge faux pas, and many Russians will wait patiently for their friends for half an hour or so after the agreed-upon time has come and gone. Dinner parties never start on time, and it is better to arrive late than to show up early and catch your host unprepared. If you are traveling by public transportation, you might experience some delays. Exercise your patience in advance; trains and commuter rail rarely arrive on time. The train time schedule, "график прибытия и отбытия поездов" will have signs that read "Поезд задерживается" (the train is delayed) or "Поезд опаздывает" (the train is late).

However, you should know that even in Russia there are several occasions when you are expected to be on time. These include coming to class (even though professors can be five minutes late); boarding a plane; arriving to the theater or a concert; keeping your appointment with a doctor, a lawyer, or a clergy member (they, in turn, might be late); and, alas, arriving for a funeral. The following is a list of verbs, related nouns, and conversational phrases that will help you navigate Russian time sensibilities and explain your own view of time.

Table 15-2

▼ **SUBORDINATE CONJUNCTIONS IN RUSSIAN**

Russian	English
вр**е**мя (neuter)	time
оп**а**здывать (Group I)	to be late (imperfective)
опозд**а**ть (Group I)	to be late (perfective)

опоздание	delay
задерживаться (Group I)	to be late (imperfective)
задержаться (Group I)	to be late (perfective)
задержка	delay
успевать (Group I)	to be on time (imperfective)
успеть (Group I)	to make it/ to be on time (perfective)
объяснять (Group I)	to explain (imperfective)
объяснить (Group II)	to explain (perfective)
объяснение	explanation
извиняться (Group I)	to apologize (imperfective)
извиниться (Group II)	to apologize (perfective)
ждать час/полчаса/двадцать/ пятнадцать/десять минут	to wait for an hour/half hour/ twenty/fifteen/ten minutes
Так получилось.	That's just the way it happened.
Я скоро буду.	I will be in soon.
Не спеши(те).	Don't rush (informal/formal).
Извини(те) меня за задержку/ опоздание.	Forgive me for being late (informal/ formal).
Вовремя	At the proper time; on time.
Ладно.	Okay
Ничего.	It's all right.
На это ушло/уйдёт много времени.	This took/will take a long time.
У нас много/мало времени.	We have a lot of/little time.
У нас ещё есть пять/десять минут/ час, чтобы добраться до . . .	We have five/ten minutes/ an hour to get to . . .
Наконец-то ты/вы здесь! Мы тебя/ вас заждались.	At last you (informal/formal) are here! We've been waiting and waiting for you (informal/formal).

Although time is less valued, Russian culture puts a lot of emphasis on patience, industriousness, and attention to details, as illustrated in the following popular Russian proverbs:

Тише едешь – дальше будешь.
Slow and steady wins the race.

Поспешишь – людей насмешишь.
Literally, "if you rush you'll make people laugh." Similar to "haste makes waste."

Делали наспех, а сделали насмех.
Literally, "they did it in a rush and it turned out to be a joke." Also similar to "haste makes waste."

Играть играй, да дело знай!
Work as hard as you play.

And of course, "Не трать время даром!" (Don't waste time!) translates across cultures and time.

The Grammatical Concept of Mood

When you refer to "mood" in everyday conversation, you describe your attitude toward the events you are experiencing at the moment. The grammatical notion of mood applies to verbs, and it transmits the speakers' attitudes toward what they are saying. In other words, your everyday mood and the grammatical notion of mood are similar in that they express your personal attitude toward what you are describing. In English and Russian, there are three grammatical moods: the indicative, the imperative, and the subjunctive/conditional.

Alert

Instead of using the subjunctive mood, Russian relies exclusively on conditional forms. In this book, we will explain the main functions of the English subjunctive and explore how these forms can be translated into appropriate Russian conditional forms.

So far nearly all of the verbs you have studied in this book have been in the indicative mood. This is because the main function of the indicative mood is to describe facts and events that are occurring now, will happen in the present, or took place in the past. Note in the following conversation that verbs in the indicative mood can be used in statements, questions, and exclamatory remarks with clear tense markers to indicate present, past, and future.

Что ты сейч**а**с д**е**лаешь? – Я чит**а**ю кн**и**гу.
What are you doing now? – I am reading a book.

Что ты д**е**лала вчер**а** в**е**чером? – Снач**а**ла я д**е**лала дом**а**шнюю раб**о**ту, а пот**о**м смотр**е**ла телев**и**зор.
What were you doing yesterday? – First, I did homework and then I watched television.

Что ты б**у**дешь д**е**лать з**а**втра? - Я пойд**у** в библиот**е**ку и б**у**ду гот**о**виться к экз**а**мену по ист**о**рии. – Как**а**я ты трудолюб**и**вая!
What will you do tomorrow? – I will go to the library and prepare for the history exam. – What a hardworking person you are!

The function of the imperative mood in English and in Russian is to express commands. Compare the following examples in Russian and English:

Не крич**и**!   Don't scream!
Ид**и** домой!   Go home!
Пож**а**луйста, говор**и**те громче!   Speak louder, please!

e⊛ Essential

> In Russian the direct object expressed through a personal pronoun in the accusative case (мен**я**, теб**я**, ег**о**/её/ег**о**, нас, вас, их) is often placed before the verb.

The subjunctive mood in English is used to describe hypothetical, unreal events. It is the mood of "wishful thinking" that is often used in conjunction with English conditional forms ("if I had money," and "if he had told me in advance"). Refer to the following examples in English with their Russian translation to get a better understanding of how the subjunctive/conditional forms function in English and how they are rendered in Russian:

If I had money (conditional), I would travel to Brazil (subjunctive).
Если бы у мен**я** б**ы**ли д**е**ньги (conditional), я бы по**е**хал в Браз**и**лию (conditional).

I wish (indicative) you were here (subjunctive).

Мне так хочется (indicative), чтобы вы были здесь (conditional). / Жаль, что вас здесь нет (indicative).

If he had told me about his problem (conditional), I would have helped him (subjunctive). But he didn't (indicative).

Если бы он мне рассказал о его проблеме (conditional), я бы ему помогла (conditional). Но он этого не сделал (indicative).

The Formation and Meaning of the Russian Imperative

The Russian imperative is used to express commands, direct requests, invitations, and warnings. Let's briefly examine three types of imperative forms that are common both in English and Russian.

The imperative is used for commands and warnings directed at "you," as in "Говорите громче!" (Speak louder!). Russian has two "you" forms (informal singular "you" and formal "you," which also overlaps with the plural "you"), so there are two imperative forms.

Formal "you" and plural "you" imperatives end with –айте, -ите, or –ьте. Study the following examples.

читай – читайте	to read
работать – работайте	to work
опаздывать – опаздывайте	to be late
писать – пишите	to write
спешить – спешите	to be in a hurry
идти – идите	to go
готовить – готовьте	to cook/prepare

Informal singular forms end either in –ай, –и, or –ь, as in the following examples.

читай	to read
работай	to work
пиши	to write
спеши	to be in a hurry
иди	to go
готовь	to cook/prepare

Imperatives directed at oneself and groups that include ourselves (e.g., let us), also known as inclusive commands, can be formed with давайте (let us) plus an infinitive, as in "Давайте танцевать" (Let's dance). There are other construction models for this type of command, but they are beyond the scope of this book.

Imperatives that express permission, suggestions, or commands directed at third person singular or plural (let him/her/it/them) are formed by пусть (let) plus the third person singular or plural form of the present tense of imperfective verbs or the future tense of the perfective verbs, as in "Пусть мама отдыхает" (Let Mom take a break) or "Пусть студенты читают" (Let the students read).

✷ Essential

Remember that 'you' imperatives are often used to express warnings. To form negative imperatives, add the negative particle "не" in front of the warning, as in the following examples: Не пей воду из-под крана! (Don't drink the tap water!); Не злись! (Don't be angry!); Не говори глупости! (Don't say silly things!).

It is important to realize that there are major cultural differences in the way Russian and American English speakers use "you" imperatives. In English, imperative forms are often considered to be too direct and can only be interpreted as commands or orders given by the authority or someone trying to assume the authoritative stance. Russians, on the other hand, often use "you" imperatives to form direct requests, which when in combination with пожалуйста (please) are considered culturally appropriate and polite. Also, consider the common expressions that you already know: the greeting Здравствуй(те)! – the imperative from the verb "здравствовать" (to be in good health) and the apology Извини(те)! – the imperative from the verb "извинить" (to excuse).

Chapter Review

Review the material covered in this chapter and complete the following exercises.

Chapter Quiz

Answer the following questions and check your answers in Appendix A.

1. Name three major types of sentences in Russian and English.

    _____

2. What types of conjunctions are used in compound and complex sentences?

    _____

3. Although the structure of a simple Russian sentence is similar to that of an English one, there can be at least two differences. What are they?

    _____

4. Is being on time a big priority for most Russians?

    _____

5. What is the main function of the grammatical notion of mood?

    _____

6. How many moods do Russian verbs have?

    _____

7. What do we express through the imperative?

    _____

Translation Practice

Translate the following commands, requests, suggestions, and warnings. Make sure the imperative forms match the people at whom these statements are directed.

1. Don't rush (informal)!   _____
2. Vera, go home!   _____
3. Excuse me (formal)!   _____
4. Volodya, don't say silly things!   _____
5. Don't drink tap water (informal)!   _____
6. Let the children play.   _____

Comprehension Exercise

Read the following dialogue, then answer the questions in Russian.

Виктор: Привет, Максим! Наконец-то ты здесь! Ты знаешь, я жду тебя уже целых полчаса.

Максим: Виктор, извини. Так получилось. Мне надо было встретиться с моим профессором по биологии, и на это ушло много времени. А потом долго не было автобуса, и мне пришлось идти пешком.

Виктор: Ладно, ничего. У нас ещё есть десять минут, чтобы вовремя добраться до стадиона и найти наши места.

Максим: Хорошо. Хотя у нас есть время, давай поймём такси. Я так хочу увидеть начало матча.

1. Как их зовут?

_____

2. Кто опоздал на встречу?

_____

3. Куда они идут?

_____

4. У них есть время, чтобы туда добраться?

_____

CHAPTER 16

The Conditional Mood and Complex Sentences

This chapter offers more information on the mood system in Russian, with a specific focus on the conditional mood and its formation and semantic functions. In addition, you will learn several new conjunctions that are frequently used in complex sentences, including sentences expressing wishes, regrets, and requests.

Real and Unreal Conditions

When we comment on our surroundings, we often discuss conditions under which certain things are possible or impossible, probable or improbable. In order to be able to do this, we have to be able to differentiate between two types of conditional statements: those that express real conditions that can be met and those that describe improbable conditions. Both types are illustrated in the following examples:

Если у него будут деньги, он купит ей подарок.
If he has the money, he will buy her a present.

Если бы у него были деньги, он бы купил ей подарок.
If he had the money, he would buy her a present. / If he had had money, he would have bought her a present.

The first sentence describes a plausible situation: There is a great certainty that as soon as he gets the money, he will buy her a present. This is why the indicative mood is used. The second sentence, on the other hand, contains a highly hypothetical idea: There is no certainty that he will ever have the money, and thus the situation described is improbable. To describe such improbable situations, English uses the subjunctive mood, and Russian uses the conditional mood.

Be aware of the differences in tense usage in English and Russian to describe real life conditions in the indicative mood. In English, the future tense is not permitted in subordinate conditional clauses, whereas in Russian there is no such limitation and all three tenses, including the future tense, are used depending on the context.

The Subjunctive/Conditional Mood

The functions of the conditional mood in Russian generally correspond to those of the subjunctive in English. However, in contrast to English, the same Russian conditional verbal forms are used both in the main and subordinate conditional clauses, as the following examples illustrate. The conditional mood is formed with the particle "бы" plus the verb in the past tense.

Если бы у него были деньги (conditional), он бы купил ей подарок (conditional).

If he had had the money, he would have bought her a present.

Если бы мы не спешили (conditional), мы бы опоздали (conditional).

If we had not hurried, we would have been late.

In the first example, the implication is that he didn't have the money to buy a present for her, and, thus, no present was bought. In the second example, the implication is that they had to hurry so they would not be late—but they weren't. Thus, both sentences describe hypothetical situations that could have happened but did not.

ⓔ✱ Essential

Wishful thinking is admittedly one of Russia's national vices. It's known in Russia as "маниловщина", which is derived from the "Манилов" character in Nikolai Gogol's "Dead Souls." Манилов idly spends his time fantasizing about doing things and achieving great results, whereas in reality nothing is being done. The name "Манилов" comes from the verb "манить" that can be loosely translated as "to attract, pull toward, magnetize."

The Russian conditional mood does not make references to time, and the past tense forms used to form conditional constructions are not past in their meaning. References to present, past, and future are not achieved through verbal forms but via the context. Also note that negative conditional forms are constructed by adding the particle "не" in front of the verb. At the same time, the place of the particle "бы" that marks the sentence as conditional is relatively flexible; it can either go before the verb or after the verb without any change in the meaning of the sentence. Compare the following sentences in Russian and English:

Table 16-1

▼ **CONDITIONAL FORMS: POSITIVE AND NEGATIVE**

Positive	Negative	English
Он рассказал бы	Он не рассказал бы	He would (not) tell
Он бы рассказал	Он бы не рассказал	He would (not) have told
Он бы вчера рассказал	Он бы вчера не рассказал	He would (not) have told yesterday
Он бы завтра рассказал	Он бы завтра не рассказал	He would (not) tell tomorrow

"Чтобы" Clauses

In Chapter 15, you learned several subordinate conjunctions used in Russian to build subordinate clauses. One of the most commonly used subordinate conjunctions is the conjunction "чтобы," which can be roughly translated as "so that." It is possible to produce at least two types of subordinate clauses with the help of this conjunction. Using the indicative mood, we can create clauses with "чтобы" to express a purpose or a goal; by relying on the conditional mood, we can make clauses that express a desire for someone else to do something that is unreal, improbable, or contrary to fact.

Compare the following examples to see the differences between two types of subordinate clauses formed with the conjunction "чтобы." Notice that subordinate clauses with "чтобы" that express a purpose use the infinitive form of the verb.

Expressing a purpose: Я буду заниматься биологией, чтобы хорошо сдать экзамен

I will study biology so that I pass the exam with a high score.

Expressing a purpose: Я прочитаю эту книгу, чтобы найти ответ на этот вопрос.

I will read this book to find an answer to this question.

Expressing a wish: Я хочу, чтобы ты приготовил мне обед.

I want you to make me dinner. (Literally: "I want that you should make me dinner.")

Expressing a wish: Я хочу, чтобы я была дома.

I wish I were at home.

Examples 1 and 2 illustrate the use of the conjunction "чтобы" followed by the infinitive of the verb to express a purpose or a goal. Examples 3 and 4 show how the same conjunction can be used with the conditional construction to express a command or an unrealistic desire. In both types of constructions, tense references are expressed exclusively through the verb in the main clause, and whenever possible, through context. Verb forms in the subordinate clauses are left unchanged.

 Alert

Sentences that describe hypothetical situations are conditional by definition, and thus should require the presence of the particle "бы." However, because "бы" is already present within the subordinate conjunction "чтобы," no additional "бы" is necessary. Don't forget to use the past tense form of the verb; this marker is consistent with the regular pattern of forming the conditional mood.

"Why" and "Because" Sentences

Now that you know how to use the construction with the conjunction "чтобы" to report on a purpose or goal, let's learn how to ask someone to explain their behavior or give reasons for the choices they made. In this chapter, you look into the construction of "why," "because," "so that," and "in order" statements in Russian:

Почему ты идёшь домой? – Я иду домой потому, что мне надо делать уроки.

Why are you going home? – I am going home because I need to do homework.

Почему ты идёшь домой? – Я иду домой, чтобы делать уроки.

Why are you going home? – I am going home (in order) to do homework.

Почему ты опоздал на лекцию? – Я опоздал на лекцию потому, что мой будильник сломался.

Why were you late for the lecture? – I was late for the lecture because my alarm clock broke.

Examples 1 and 2 illustrate how you can ask someone to explain the goal or purpose of their behavior. Example 3 demonstrates how you can ask someone to explain the underlying reason for their behavior. To form your questions, use the question word "почему" ("why").

When you answer, the most universally used construction, regardless of whether you are reporting on goals or reasons, is "потому, что" ("because") plus a dependent clause. In addition, you may use "чтобы" ("in order to") plus a clause with an infinitive of the verb to explain the goal or purpose, or use "из-за того, что" ("because of") plus a clause to give your reason. Finally, remember you don't have to give a full answer unless, of course, you are practicing your Russian grammar! Just like in English, Russians also often choose brief answers, as in the following examples.

Почему ты идёшь домой? – Потому, что мне надо делать уроки.

Why are you going home? – Because I need to do homework.

Почему ты идёшь домой? – Чтобы делать уроки.

Why are you going home? – (In order) to do homework.

Почему ты опоздал на лекцию? – Мой будильник сломался.

Why were you late for the lecture? – My alarm clock didn't work.

Using Conditional Phrases to Make and Decline Requests

Now it's time to look into some useful vocabulary for making polite requests, expressing your regrets, asking for help, and/or asking for an explanation. In order to achieve all these goals, the most useful verb to remember is мочь (can, be able to, imperfective). It follows Group I conjugation pattern, but has a changing consonant in its root: я мог**у**, ты м**о**жешь, он/он**а**/он**о** м**о**жет, мы м**о**жем, вы м**о**жете, он**и** м**о**гут. Its past tense forms are мог, могл**а**, and могл**и**.

Other verbs and phrases that you should know include:

помог**а**ть	to help (Group I Model 1)
п**о**мощь	(feminine; noun) help
перест**а**ть	to stop (Group I Model 2; there is an additional consonant in the root: я перест**а**ну, ты перест**а**нешь, etc.)
над**е**ется	to hope (Group I Model 1)
над**е**жда	hope (noun)
пл**а**кать	to cry (Group I Model 2; there is a changing consonant in the root: я пл**а**чу, ты плачешь, etc.)
плач	crying, weeping (noun)
в**е**рить	to believe (Group II Model 1)
в**е**ра	faith (noun)

Russians often use imperative forms together with politeness formulas (e.g. "пож**а**луйста," please) to make polite requests. However, conditional forms with "бы" are considered more polite. Examine the following examples to see how the same request can be articulated in two different ways:

Позов**и**те, пож**а**луйста, мо**ю** м**а**му к телеф**о**ну. – Пож**а**луйста, не могл**и** бы вы позв**а**ть мо**ю** м**а**му к телеф**о**ну?
Please call my mom to the telephone. – Could you please call my mom to the telephone?

Пож**а**луйста, помог**и**те мне. – Пож**а**луйста, не могл**и** бы вы мне пом**о**чь?
Please help me. – Could you please help me?

Notice that the second version of this request is structurally more complex. It contains the phrase "не могл**и** бы вы" followed by the infinitive phrase that indicates the actual request. This request model is very formal. In fact, its conditional nature makes it so polite that in some contexts it might border on sarcasm or snobbery. Remember that requests made with the imperative must include the politeness formula "пож**а**луйста," while its inclusion is optional in conditional requests that use "не могл**и** бы вы."

e❗ Alert

Remember to be consistent in your usage of personal pronouns when addressing people. Russians rarely switch from "вы" to "ты," especially in the same conversation. Such a switch could indicate either an intended insult or a profoundly intimate change in the relationship. If neither is your goal, stick with the formal address.

Now imagine that you are unable to fulfill a request. The following are some ways of politely declining requests using conditional phrases:

Я бы с удов**о**льствием, но . . .
It would be a pleasure, but . . .

Я бы с р**а**достью, но . . .
I would be happy to, but . . .

Мне бы хот**е**лось вам/теб**е** пом**о**чь, но я не мог**у**.
I would like to help you (formal/informal), but I can't.

Если бы я мог/могл**а**, я бы вам пом**о**г помогл**а**.
If I could help, I would help /would have helped you.

Кон**е**чно, мне бы хот**е**лось вам/теб**е** пом**о**чь, но к сожал**е**нию я не мог**у**.
Certainly, I would like / would have liked to help you (formal/informal), but unfortunately I can't.

Cultural Notes

Russia has some unique cultural notions that you must know if you are to function well among Russians. Let's begin with an examination of Russian family values. Although things are changing, Russians still put tremendous value on their immediate community, which consists of their extended family and close friends.

Russian Attitudes Toward Family and Community

The community, your sense of where you come from, plays a key role in how you define yourself. A famous Russian proverb declares: "Не им**е**й сто рубл**е**й, а имей сто друзей!" (It's better to have a hundred friends than a hundred rubles!) The notion of "мы и они" (them and us) or "свои и чужие" (ours and theirs) has a tight hold on Russian society, cementing and fragmenting it at the same time.

Family is at the center of one's social circle, and nepotism often becomes an inevitable evil. The frequently heard Russian expressions "по блату" and "по знакомству" refer to getting something not through work or merit, but because of one's connections. Perhaps not exclusively Russian, "блат" is a system of mutual favors that wards off outsiders by distributing power and opportunity within a closely-knit group. The opposite of a meritocracy, "блат" promulgates social injustice, while continuously recreating itself through an ever-extending web of connections and favors.

Personal Space

Everyone knows about tiny Soviet apartments and the lack of privacy in the so-called "коммуналки" (communal apartments). However, what is not widely known outside of Russia is that personal space is culturally of less significance in Russia than in American and Western European cultures. For example, in a conversation Russians have a tendency to lean closer to their counterparts than Americans do, creating a more intimate atmosphere.

Being in closer proximity to your conversation partner in Russia does not have sexual undertones and in most cases is expected as a culturally appropriate communication strategy. If you need more personal space to feel comfortable, make sure to indicate this to your Russian friend. It is almost always better to address the issue directly rather than avoid it. Most likely, you will have to find a balance between protecting your personal space and making your Russian friends comfortable while interacting with you.

Reading Practice: Dialogues

Read the following dialogues to practice recognizing new vocabulary and grammatical notions that you learned in this chapter.

Dialogue A

Лидия: Не могли бы вы мне помочь с моими сумками? Они такие тяжёлые. Could you please help me with my bags? They are so heavy.

Николай : Мне бы хот**е**лось вам пом**о**чь, но я не мог**у**. У мен**я** пробл**е**мы с позвон**о**чником и я не мог**у** поднимать т**я**жести. Но мой брат вам, кон**е**чно, пом**о**жет. Сем**ё**н, помог**и** **э**той ж**е**нщине!

I would like to help you, but I can't. I have problems with my back, and I can't lift heavy things. But my brother, Semyon, will, of course, help. Semyon, help this woman!

Л**и**дия : Огр**о**мное вам спас**и**бо!

Thank you very much!

Dialogue B

Н**и**на: Почем**у** ты пл**а**чешь?

Why are you crying?

С**а**ша : Потом**у**, что я не мог**у** найт**и** мо**ю** люб**и**мую кн**и**гу.

Because I can't find my favorite book.

Н**и**на: Перест**а**нь пл**а**кать и дав**а**й иск**а**ть вм**е**сте.

Stop crying and let's look for it together.

С**а**ша : Я бы с удов**о**льствием, но у мен**я** так бол**и**т голов**а**.

I'd do it with pleasure, but I have such a headache. (My head is hurting so much.)

Н**и**на: Тогд**а** ид**и** отдохн**и**, а я б**у**ду иск**а**ть.

Then go rest, and I will look for it.

С**а**ша: Больш**о**е теб**е** спас**и**бо. Как бы я был**а** без теб**я** – я не зн**а**ю.

Thank you so much. I don't know what I would do without you.

Chapter Review

Review the material covered in this chapter and complete the following exercises.

Chapter Quiz

Answer the following questions and check your answers in Appendix A.

1.   Which mood should you use to describe true-to-life conditions?

_____

2. Which mood should you use to describe hypothetical situations in Russian?

_____

3. Are there any restrictions on tense usage in subordinate conditional clauses in Russian?

_____

4. How are the conditional forms constructed in Russian?

_____

5. Can the conditional forms in Russian refer to present, past, or future tenses?

_____

6. How many and which types of subordinate clauses can be constructed with the conjunction "чтобы"?

_____

7. How do you make tense references in complex sentences containing subordinate clauses with the conjunction "чтобы"?

_____

8. What is "маниловщина"?

_____

9. What is the meaning of the expression "по блату"?

_____

10. What are "коммуналки"?

_____

Translation Practice

Translate the following exchanges from Russian into English.

1. Почему ты сегодня дома? – Потому, что сегодня у нас праздники.

_____

2. Почему вы опоздали на работу? – Потому, что моя машина сломалась.

_____

3. Почему ты кричишь? – Из-за того, что ты меня не понимаешь.

   _____

4. Почему ты идёшь домой? – Я иду домой потому, что мне надо

   поговорить с моими родителями.

   _____

5. Почему вы живёшь в Москве? – Я живу в Москве, чтобы быть рядом с

   моей семьёй.

   _____

Conversational Practice

Use your imagination to create responses to the following statements:

1. Вы не могли бы мне помочь с работой?

   _____

2. Почему ты смеёшься?

   _____

3. Почему ты не в школе?

   _____

APPENDIX A

Answer Key

Chapter 1

Chapter Quiz

1. 33 letters.
2. The Cyrillic alphabet is named after Saint Cyril, a monk from Byzantium.
3. The alphabet was created in order to facilitate the spread of Christianity among the Slavs.
4. Transliteration.
5. 21 letters.
6. One.
7. **А**збука.
8. Russians spell foreign names the way they are pronounced in Russian.

Writing Practice

1. George Washington.
2. Emily Dickinson.
3. Charlie Chaplin.
4. Mark Twain.
5. Kobe Bryant.
6. Nicolas Cage.
7. Detroit.
8. New Orleans.
9. Cincinnati.
10. Boston.
11. California.
12. San Francisco.
13. Seattle.
14. Colorado.
15. Texas.

16. Vicksburg.
17. Oregon.

Chapter 2

Chapter Quiz

1. Four.
2. Vowel reduction.
3. The hard and the soft sign.
4. The soft sign; the vowel sounds Я, Е, Ё, Ю, И signal that the consonant preceding them is soft, and palatalized consonants can make neighboring consonants soft.
5. At the end of words, voiced consonants are pronounced like their voiceless counterparts.
6. Consonant assimilation.
7. Россия.
8. Н**о**вгород, Влад**и**мир, Владивост**о**к, Санкт-Петерб**у**рг.

Pronunciation Practice

1. р
2. л
3. л
4. л
5. с
6. л and д
7. л and т
8. д
9. н
10. с and г
11. г and н

12. с and м
13. к and р
14. с

Practicing Russian Greetings

1. Здравствуйте! Доброе утро!
2. Спокойной ночи! Пока!
3. Добрый день! Здравствуйте!
4. Спокойной ночи!
5. Прощай!

Chapter 3
Chapter Quiz

1. Cognates.
2. Мат.
3. Спаси́бо.
4. Извини́те or Прости́те.
5. Пожа́луйста, говори́те поме́дленней.
6. Повтори́те, пожа́луйста, по-англи́йски.
7. Спаси́бо за ва́шу по́мощь.
8. Где здесь туале́т?
9. Ж stands for Же́нский туале́т and M stand for Мужско́й туале́т.
10. Спаси́бо за приглаше́ние.
11. Entrance is Вход, and Exit is Вы́ход.
12. Сле́дующая ста́нция…
13. Yes is Да, and No is Нет.
14. Осторо́жно.

15. Fire.

Vocabulary Building Exercise

1. Такси́.
2. Оте́ль or Гости́ница.
3. Инспе́кция.
4. Па́спорт.
5. Шко́ла.
6. Университе́т.
7. Ви́за.
8. Рестора́н.
9. Центр (го́рода).
10. Стоп.

Translation Practice

1. Извини́те, где мужско́й туале́т?
2. Извини́те or Прости́те, я не зна́ю.
3. Вы́зовите ско́рую по́мощь
4. Пожа́луйста, подожди́те здесь.
5. Пожа́луйста, приходи́те в го́сти.

Chapter 4
Chapter Quiz

1. Potatoes, wheat, cabbage, and various kinds of meats.
2. By examining their endings.
3. Six.
4. To name and to indicate that the noun is utilized as a subject of the sentence.

5. Masculine, feminine, or neuter.
6. А, Я, Ь.
7. за**в**трак, п**о**лдник, об**ед**, **у**жин.
8. Appetizers; traditionally small dishes served all at once as an accompaniment to a pre-meal shot of vodka or a glass of wine.
9. Answers will vary, but can include блин**ы**, щи, борщ, зак**у**ски, икр**а**, пельм**е**ни, квас.
10. При**я**тного аппет**и**та!
11. **О**чень вк**у**сно!
12. Metaphor for friendship and trust.
13. Gender, number, and case.
14. Adjectives with hard and soft stems have different endings.

Grammar Drill

1. Lunch (masculine).
2. Jam (neuter).
3. Caviar (feminine).
4. Juice (masculine).
5. Bread (masculine).
6. Strawberry (feminine).
7. Potato (masculine).
8. Sausage (feminine).
9. Meat (neuter).
10. Wine (neuter).
11. Restaurant (masculine).
12. Menu (neuter).
13. Bill (masculine).
14. Dessert (masculine).

Translation Drill

1. хор**о**шее вин**о**.
2. н**о**вое мен**ю**.
3. сол**ё**ная колбас**а**.
4. г**о**рький шокол**а**д.
5. вк**у**сный **у**жин.
6. м**я**гкий хлеб.
7. сол**ё**ные огурц**ы**.
8. св**е**жие помид**о**ры.
9. хор**о**ший суп.
10. плох**и**е русские пельмени.

Chapter 5
Chapter Quiz

1. Grandparents.
2. Wrong stress.
3. Conceptualizations of in-law relationships.
4. Mother - м**а**ма, мать; father - от**е**ц, п**а**па.
5. Three: a first name, a patronymic, and a last name.
6. No, all Russian full first names are either masculine or feminine.
7. Ник**и**та or Дан**и**ла.
8. The literal translation of a patronymic name is "the son of" or "the daughter of."
9. To form a patronymic for men use -ович/евич and for women –овна/евна.
10. No, foreigners do not have patronymics.

11. Usually, Russian names have a feminine and a masculine form.
12. Address a Russian doctor or teacher by their first name and patronymic.
13. Ты, вы, вы.
14. By the ending –ть.
15. Answers will vary, but may include the question Кто **э**то? and this is / these are sentences (**Э**то...).

Name Recognition and Vocabulary Drill

1. Мар**ия** Петр**о**вна Серг**е**ева – daughter of of #2, sister of #8, sister of #10 (сестр**а**, дочь).
2. Пётр Никол**а**евич Серг**е**ев – father of #1 and #8, husband of #4 (от**е**ц, муж).
3. Влад**и**мир Серг**е**евич Никан**о**ров – brother of #6, son of #9 (брат, сын).
4. Кс**е**ния Бор**и**совна Серг**е**ева – mother of #1 and #8, wife of #2 (м**а**ма, жен**а**).
5. Никол**а**й Дм**и**триевич Серг**е**ев – father of #2, grandfather of #1 and #8 (от**е**ц, д**е**душка).
6. Станисл**а**в Серг**е**евич Никан**о**ров – brother of #3, son of #9 (брат, сын).
7. Бор**и**с Алекс**е**евич Никан**о**ров – father of #4, father-in-law of #2, grandfather of #1 and #8 (от**е**ц, тесть, д**е**душка).

8. Алекс**а**ндр Петр**о**вич Серг**е**ев – son of #2, brother of #1 (сын, брат).
9. Серг**е**й Матв**е**евич Никан**о**ров – father of #3 (от**е**ц).
10. Нат**а**лья Петр**о**вна Серг**е**ева - daughter of #2, sister of #8, sister of #1 (дочь, сестр**а**).

Grammar Drill

1. Мен**я** зов**у**т Ив**а**н.
2. Как ег**о** зов**у**т?
3. Ег**о** зов**у**т Влад**и**мир. / **Э**то Влад**и**мир.
4. Кто **э**то?
5. **Э**то Мар**и**на. Он**а** – м**а**ма и жен**а**.
6. Как их зов**у**т?
7. Их зов**у**т Алекс**а**ндр и Мар**ия**. / **Э**то Алекс**а**ндр и Мар**ия**.

Chapter 6
Chapter Quiz

1. Russian nouns, adjectives, and pronouns agree in gender, case, and number.
2. Third person singular and plural: ег**о**, её, их.
3. Вы / ваш refers either to second person singular (formal you) or second person plural (you all).
4. Masculine, singular, and in the nominative case.
5. Answers will vary, but may include the following: У теб**я** так**а**я **у**мная

и крас**и**вая сестр**а**! or Как**а**я у теб**я** **у**мная и крас**и**вая сестр**а**!

6. Вы.
7. Господ**и**н / госпож**а** / господ**а**.
8. Есть.
9. By using different intonation: a statement has a falling pitch, and a question has a rising pitch.
10. By adding the particle "не" in front of the word that is being negated.
11. Use the word "нет" (no) for a negative answer and the word "да" or the construction "да, у мен**я** есть…" for a positive answer.
12. No, some have distinctive forms, and others use the masculine form to indicate both females and males.
13. И, а, and но.
14. Not bad; moderately good or acceptable. It's an adjective that expresses modest praise.

Grammar and Vocabulary Drill

1. Тво**я**/в**а**ша крас**и**вая сестр**а**.
2. Ег**о** симпат**и**чный сын.
3. Мо**я** тал**а**нтливая дочь.
4. Ег**о** тёща и тесть.
5. Е**ё** старый д**е**душка.
6. Ваш **у**мный муж.
7. Вы/ты так**а**я крас**и**вая!
8. Вы/ты так**о**й симпат**и**чный!
9. У вас так**о**й хор**о**ший муж!

10. У теб**я**/вас так**а**я тал**а**нтливая и крас**и**вая дочь!
11. **Э**то мо**я** мл**а**дшая сестр**а**. Её зов**у**т Л**е**на. Он**а** – студ**е**нтка.
12. Кто **э**то? – **Э**то мо**я** жен**а**, В**е**ра. Он**а** – тал**а**нтливый учёный и хор**о**ший преподав**а**тель.

Chapter 7
Chapter Quiz

1. Two: Group I (the E Group) and Group II (the И Group).
2. You must remember the present tense stem of the verb. Conjugation endings of the present tense are added to this stem.
3. The particle -сь/-ся at the end of the verb.
4. Three: present, past, and future.
5. No, the вы form should be used.
6. Вы.
7. Check the form of the verb.
8. Д**у**мать: я д**у**маю, ты д**у**маешь, он/он**а** д**у**мает, мы д**у**маем, вы д**у**маете, он**и** д**у**мают.
9. Занима́ться: я занима́юсь, ты занима́ешься, он/он**а** занима́ется, мы занима́емся, вы занима́етесь, он**и** занима́ются.
10. Смотр**е**ть: я смотр**ю**, ты см**о**тришь, он/он**а** см**о**трит, мы см**о**трим, вы см**о**трите, он**и** см**о**трят.

11. Люб**и**ть: я любл**ю**, ты л**ю**бишь, он/он**а** л**ю**бит, мы л**ю**бим, вы л**ю**бите, он**и** л**ю**бят.
12. Л**е**том я любл**ю** пл**а**вать в басс**е**йне.
13. Зим**о**й я любл**ю** кат**а**ться на л**ы**жах и коньк**а**х.
14. Я любл**ю** чит**а**ть кн**и**ги, игр**а**ть на пиан**и**но и заним**а**ться сп**о**ртом.

Writing Dates

1. понед**е**льник, п**е**рвое ноябр**я**.
2. воскрес**е**нье, семн**а**дцатое м**а**я.
3. четв**е**рг, четвёртое сентябр**я**.
4. субб**о**та, седьм**о**е феврал**я**.
5. вт**о**рник, дев**я**тое м**а**рта.
6. сред**а**, од**и**ннадцатое октябр**я**.
7. п**я**тница, дв**а**дцать втор**о**е январ**я**.
8. Answers will vary.

Chapter 8
Chapter Quiz

1. A combination of all possible endings for any particular noun.
2. By considering the noun's final letter in the nominative case and its grammatical gender.
3. To express location.
4. Е, И, and sometimes У.
5. О or Об.
6. No, the kitchen, bathroom, and hallway are not counted toward the total number of rooms in a Russian apartment.

Prepositional Case

1. дом – в д**о**ме.
2. зав**о**д – на зав**о**де.
3. те**а**тр – в те**а**тре.
4. университ**е**т – в университ**е**те.
5. рестор**а**н – в рестор**а**не.
6. Росс**и**я – в Росс**и**и.
7. Санкт-Петерб**у**рг – в Санкт-Петерб**у**рге.

Adjectives and Nouns of Nationality

1. америк**а**нский футб**о**л (American football).
2. яп**о**нский самур**а**й (Japanese samurai).
3. кит**а**йский ч**а**й (Chinese tea).
4. франц**у**зское вин**о** (French wine).
5. нем**е**цкое п**и**во (German beer).
6. англ**и**йский парл**а**мент (English parliament).
7. исп**а**нская принц**е**сса (Spanish princess).
8. мексик**а**нские пирам**и**ды (Mexican pyramids).
9. р**у**сский квас (Russian kvas).
10. К**а**тя Ив**а**нова – р**у**сская. (Katya Ivanova is Russian.)
11. Ху**а**н К**а**рлос и М**а**ркос Гарс**и**я – исп**а**нцы. (Juan Carlos and Marcos Garcia are Spanish.)

12. Франсуа Лерош говорит
    по-французски свободно.
    (Francois Leroch speaks French
    fluently.)
13. Генрих Манн—немецкий
    писатель. (Heinrich Mann is a
    German writer.)
14. Марина Цветаева—русский
    поэт / русская поэтесса. (Marina
    Tsvetaeva is a Russian poet.)

Chapter 9

Chapter Quiz

1. Transitive verbs can take a direct
   object, and intransitive verbs
   cannot.
2. The verb хотеть follows both
   conjugation patterns. It also has
   a consonant variation in the stem
   (т-ч) and a shifting stress pattern.
3. To indicate the direct object.
4. Animate versus inanimate.
5. Ушанка, валенки, and платок.
6. Любить (to like/love) and хотеть
   (to want).
7. Grammatical gender, inanimate/
   animate category, declension
   pattern.

Grammar and Vocabulary Practice

1. Покупать свитер.
2. Ждать друга.

3. Слушать музыку.
4. Читать книгу.
5. Любить Москву.
6. Покупать рубашку.
7. Показывать фильм.
8. Брать книгу.
9. Спрашивать маму.
10. Показывать шубу.
11. I read my newspaper.
12. You listen to their music.
13. She is buying his clothes at GUM.
14. We like your music.
15. He buys groceries / food products.
16. Я покупаю красивый красный
    костюм.
17. Он встречает его хорошего
    друга.

Reading Practice

1. Children's World: toys, clothes,
   shoes, and other products for
   children.
2. Natasha: women's clothes and
   shoes.
3. Milk: Milk and dairy products.
4. GUM: State Universal Store: a big
   department store.
5. Optical Eyewear: glasses, contacts,
   and other eyewear products.
6. Drugstore / Pharmacy: medicine
   and other pharmaceutical
   products.
7. Radio Products: radio-related
   products.

8. Electronics: home electronics and appliances.
9. Books: books, newspapers, and magazines.

Chapter 10
Chapter Quiz

1. To express indirect objects.
2. These and several other verbs are often used with an indirect object, which is always in the dative case.
3. The two verbs have similar meanings, but любить has a more general meaning and describes more intense emotions, whereas нравиться has a more specific meaning focused on a particular object, idea, person. They are also different syntactically.
4. No.
5. Don't look a gift horse in the mouth.
6. Add the –л suffix with the appropriate ending to reflect the gender and number of the subject.
7. There is only one past tense in Russian.
8. The verb быть (to be).

Translation Exercises

1. Помогать Нине.
2. Советовать другу.
3. Предлагать план Елене.
4. Покупать подарок моей маме.
5. Рассказывать историю моей семье.
6. Писать письмо Владимиру.
7. Дать Мише тарелку.
8. Помогать Вере.
9. Мне нравится этот маленький дом.
10. Ей нравится красивая одежда.
11. Ему нравятся эти журналы и газеты.
12. Вам нравятся эти книги?
13. Им не нравится этот университет.
14. Хотеть подарок: я хочу подарок, ты хочешь подарок, он/она хочет подарок, мы хотим подарок, вы хотите подарок, они хотят подарок.
15. Готовить обед: я готовлю обед, ты готовишь обед, он/она готовит обед, мы готовим обед, вы готовите обед, они готовят обед.
16. Я не был / не была дома, но она там была.
17. Она готовила обед, а я была в университете.
18. Мы хотели писать письмо сенатору.
19. Они ждали учителей в классах.
20. Вы говорили Наташе правду.

21. I want to wish you a happy birthday. Я хот**е**л(а) поздр**а**вить теб**я** с днём рожд**е**ния!
22. He does not understand what you were telling him. Он не поним**а**л, **ч**то ты ему говор**и**л(а).
23. Pavel, did you think that this was a good book? П**а**вел, вы д**у**мали, что **э**то был**а** хор**о**шая кн**и**га?
24. Marina likes reading newspapers and magazines. Мар**и**на люб**и**ла чит**а**ть газ**е**ты и журн**а**лы.
25. Do you like the Russian language? Теб**е** нр**а**вится р**у**сский яз**ы**к?

Chapter 11
Chapter Quiz

1. Two: the imperfective and perfective aspects.
2. To express whether the action is in process or completed.
3. No, only imperfective verbs can form present tense forms.
4. Many perfective verbs are formed by adding prefixes to imperfective verbs of similar lexical meaning.
5. Perfective.
6. Imperfective.
7. A word-formation strategy of adding prefixes and suffixes to the root.
8. Grammatical and lexical prefixes.
9. Either drop their prefix, or add an imperfective suffix and retain the prefix.
10. Perfective.
11. Answers will vary, but may include any of these verbs: идти, гулять, ехать, ходить, ездить.

Translation Exercises

1. She has written/wrote a book.
2. Suddenly he screamed.
3. My sister draws well.
4. We spoke and drank tea for a long time.
5. Sometimes they went/used to go on a vacation to the countryside.
6. Он показ**а**л нам сво**ю** шк**о**лу.
7. Об**ы**чно он**и** з**а**втракали д**о**ма.
8. Он**а** уж**е** **э**то сд**е**лала.
9. Мой мл**а**дший брат чит**а**ет **о**чень хорош**о**.
10. Ты уж**е** напис**а**л письм**о**?

Translation Practice

1. Оп**и**сывать.
2. Переп**и**сывать.
3. Доп**и**сывать.
4. Зап**и**сывать.
5. The imperfective suffix -ыва.
6. Independence – noun.
7. Post-war – adjective.
8. Антина**у**чный – adjective.
9. Foreign – adjective.

10. Safety – noun.
11. Собеседник – noun.
12. International – adjective.
13. Where are you going? – To the post office.
14. Does this bus go to the center? – No, it goes toward the stadium.
15. Does Masha go to work by car or by bike? – Sometimes by car, and sometimes by bike.
16. Where is Olya? – She went to her brother.
17. Этот поезд идёт в Москву? – Нет, он идёт в Санкт-Петербург.
18. Вы ездите на работу на поезде или на автобусе? – На автобусе.
19. Обычно я хожу к маме обедать. – Каждый день? – Да.

Chapter 12
Chapter Quiz

1. Impersonal constructions.
2. The dative case.
3. No, it is not.
4. Formation and function/meaning.
5. At the end of the book.
6. There is no complete correspondence between Russian and English verbal forms.
7. There is no limit on the number of negative that are permitted in a Russian sentence.

Translation Practice

1. You are not allowed to eat chocolate.
2. He needs to go home.
3. Are you allowed to watch TV?
4. Where is it possible to buy/can one buy skates?
5. I need to finish reading this book.
6. Здесь можно курить? – Да.
7. Где можно купить хорошую машину? – Я не знаю.
8. Мне нужно идти на работу.
9. Им нужно написать письмо.
10. Тебе можно играть в парке?
11. She is feeling bad. Future: Ей будет плохо. Past: Ей было плохо.
12. Playing is not allowed here. Future: Здесь нельзя будет играть. Past: Здесь было нельзя играть.
13. I am allowed to ski. Future: Мне можно будет кататься на лыжах. Past: Мне можно было кататься на лыжах.
14. You need to go home. Future: Вам надо будет домой. Past: Вам надо было домой.
15. Today, it is cold outside. Future: Завтра на улице будет холодно. Past: Вчера на улице было холодно.

Conversational Practice

1. Answers will vary.
2. Answers will vary.

3. Answers will vary.
4. Answers will vary.
5. Answers will vary.

Chapter 13

Chapter Quiz

1. Reflexive verbs express actions that reflect back to the performer.
2. No, by definition reflexive verbs cannot be transitive.
3. Answers will vary, but may include the following roots: крас-, здрав-, лекар-, боль-.
4. Answers will vary, but may include learning commonly used roots and becoming aware of words with similar histories in English and Russian, such as borrowings and loan words.
5. To indicate the means, manner, or agent of the action.

Translation Practice

1. Мой компьютер сломался. Как неприятно!
2. Мои ключи потерялись. Как неудобно!
3. Наша стиральная машина сломалась. Как неудобно!
4. Её новая сумка потерялась. Как жалко!
5. Что случилось?

6. У меня потерялся паспорт. / Мой паспорт потерялся.
7. Чем я могу помочь?
8. Мне нужно найти американское посольство.
9. In confidence.
10. And why not?
11. That can't be! or What are you saying!
12. My husband and I.
13. Between heaven and earth: in suspension.
14. We (all of us) and Marina, or Marina and I.

Grammar and Vocabulary Drill

1. Answers will vary.
2. Answers will vary.
3. Answers will vary.

Chapter 14

Chapter Quiz

1. To describe possession.
2. In constructions with the preposition "y", to modify a noun with another noun or noun phrase, and in negative constructions with "нет."
3. Adjectives and pronouns.
4. The consonant г in these endings is pronounced as the Russian consonant в.

5. Because sentences of this structure are naturally impersonal.

Translation Practice

1. маш**и**на мо**е**й сестр**ы**.
2. дом ег**о** бр**а**та.
3. под**а**рок их баб**у**шки.
4. тетр**а**дь пис**а**теля.
5. письм**о** тво**е**й м**а**мы.
6. зад**а**ние студ**е**нтов.
7. влад**е**лец рестор**а**нов.
8. покуп**а**тель недв**и**жимости.
9. недост**а**ток карандаш**е**й.
10. недост**а**ток школ.
11. I have a brother and a sister.
12. The doctor has medicine.
13. I live at his house.
14. In my room there is a computer and a television set.
15. They don't have a cat, but they have a dog.
16. My sister has no degree.
17. He doesn't have a lecture today.
18. She didn't have a house.
19. Marina is not at home.
20. We will not have a test.

Vocabulary Practice

1. факульт**е**т междунар**о**дных отнош**е**ний.
2. преподав**а**тель антропол**о**гии.
3. л**е**кция по иск**у**сству.
4. клуб р**у**сского язык**а**.
5. зан**я**тие по геогр**а**фии.
6. проф**е**ссор ф**и**зики.

7. уч**е**бник матем**а**тики.
8. студ**е**нт литерат**у**ры.
9. зад**а**ние по х**и**мии.

Comprehension Practice

1. влад**е**лец/влад**е**лица (д**о**ма).
2. олиг**а**рхи.
3. нал**о**ги на недвиж**и**мость.
4. завещ**а**ние.
5. приз**ы**в.

Chapter 15
Chapter Quiz

1. Simple, compound, and complex.
2. Compound sentences include coordinating conjunctions, whereas complex sentences have subordinating conjunctions.
3. Flexible word order and possible lack of a subject or a verb.
4. In many situations, it is not a priority.
5. To express the attitude of the speakers toward what they are saying.
6. Three: indicative, imperative, and conditional.
7. Commands, orders, permission, direct suggestions, warnings, and invitations.

Translation Practice

1. Не спеш**и**!

2. В**е**ра, ид**и** дом**о**й!
3. Извин**и**те!
4. Вол**о**дя, не говор**и** гл**у**пости!
5. Не пей в**о**ду из-под кр**а**на!
6. Пусть д**е**ти игр**а**ют.

Comprehension Exercise

1. What are their names? В**и**ктор и М**а**ксим.
2. Who was late for the meeting? М**а**ксим.
3. Where are they going? На стади**о**н.
4. Do they have time to get there? Да. / Да, **е**сли он**и** пойм**а**ют такс**и**.

Chapter 16

Chapter Quiz

1. The indicative mood.
2. The conditional mood.
3. No, all tenses can be used.
4. The conditional mood is formed with the particle "бы" plus the verb in the past tense.
5. Russian conditional forms have no references to time.
6. Two types: conditional clauses and clauses that express a purpose or a goal.
7. In these sentences, tense is expressed exclusively through the verb in the main clause and the context.

8. Dreaming about doing things instead of actually doing them.
9. To get something not through work or merit, but because of one's connections.
10. Communal apartments in the Soviet Union where several families shared one apartment.

Translation Practice

1. Why are you at home? – Because today is a holiday.
2. Why are you late for work? – Because my car broke down.
3. Why are you screaming? – Because you don't understand me.
4. Why are you going home? – I am going home because I need to speak with my parents.
5. Why do you live in Moscow? – I live in Moscow to be close to my family.

Conversational Practice

1. Answers will vary.
2. Answers will vary.
3. Answers will vary.

Russian-to-English Glossary

а   and, but
август   August
австралийский   Australian
Австралия   Australia
автобус   bus
агентство   agency
акварель   watercolor
актёр   actor
актриса   actress
алгебра   algebra
алкогольный   alcohol (adj.)
алтарь   altar
американец   American male
американка   American female
американский   American (adj.)
американский футбол   football
английский   English (adj.)
англичанин   Englishman
англичанка   Englishwoman
Англия   England
антигуманитарный   inhumane
антинаучный   unscientific
антропология   anthropology
апельсин   orange (noun)
аппарат   apparatus
аппаратчик   party functionary,
   official or bureaucrat
апрель   April
аптека   pharmacy
артист   performer, artist (male)
артистка   performer, artist (female)
архитектура   architecture
атака   attack
атом   atom
аудитория   lecture hall
аукцион   auction
аэропорт   airport
бабушка   grandmother
балет   ballet

банк   bank
банкротство   bankruptcy
баня   Russian bathhouse
бар   bar
баскетбол   basketball
басня   fable
бассейн   swimming pool
бежать   to run
бежевый   beige
безопасность   safety
безопасный   safe
бейсбол   baseball
белый   white
Берингово море   the Bering Sea
беседа   conversation
библиография   bibliography
библиотека   library
бизнес   business
биология   biology
благодарить   to thank
благодарность   gratitude
бланк   form
блат   connections
близко   close
блин   pancake
блузка   blouse
блюдо   dish
болезнь   illness/sickness
болеть   to be sick, to be ill
болото   swamp
боль   pain
больница   hospital
больной   ill/sick person, patient
большой   big
бор   woods
борщ   borscht (Russian beet soup)
ботинки   boots
Бразилия   Brazil
брат   brother

брать/взять to take
брюки pants
будильник alarm clock
бухгалтер accountant
быт everyday life, daily routine
быть to be
в то время, как while
ваза vase
валенки wool boots
валюта currency
ванная bathroom (usually separate from the toilet)
варенье jam
ваш your (pl., formal)
вдова widow
вдовец widower
вдруг suddenly
вегетарианский vegetarian
великий great
велосипед bicycle
вера faith
верить to believe
весёлый cheerful
весна spring
весь all
ветеринар veterinarian
вечер evening
вечеринка party
вещь thing
вздрагивать/вздрогнуть to shudder
видеть/увидеть to see
видимость visibility
виза visa
вино wine
виноватый guilty
вирус virus
вкусный delicious
владелец owner
влажный humid, damp
власть power
вливать/влить to pour into
вместе together
внук grandson
внучка granddaughter
вода water
водитель driver

военный military serviceman
возвращать/вернуть to return something
возить/привозить to bring something by vehicle
возможно possibly
возраст age
война war
вокзал train station
волейбол volleyball
волосы hair
вопрос question
вор thief
воробей sparrow
воскресенье Sunday
вписывать/вписать to write in
враг enemy
врач doctor
время time
время года season
все everybody
всё everything
всегда always
всего хорошего all the best
всласть to one's heart content
вспоминать/вспомнить to remember
вставать/встать to get up
встреча meeting
встречать/встретить to meet
вторник Tuesday
вход entrance
вчера yesterday
вы you
выгуливать/выгулять to walk the dog
выздоравливать/выздороветь to get better
вызывать/вызвать to summon, to send for
выигрывать/выиграть to win
выигрыш prize, winnings
вылетать/вылететь to fly out (of)
вылечивать/вылечить to cure
выносить/вынести to carry out
выписывать/выписать to write out

вырастать/вырасти To grow up
высший higher
выход exit
газета newspaper
галстук tie
гараж garage
где where
география geography
Германия Germany
гитара guitar
гладить to iron
глаз eye
глупость foolishness
говорить/сказать to say
говядина beef
голова head
голубой light blue
гора mountain
город city
горошек polka dots
горький bitter
горячий hot (to the touch)
господин mister
госпожа madam
гостиная living room
гостиница hotel
гость guest
государственный state
готовить/приготовить to prepare
готовиться/приготовиться to
   prepare oneself, to study
готовый ready
гражданин citizen
гражданство citizenship
граница border
Греция Greece
греческий Greek
гриб mushroom
громкий loud
грустный sad
груша pear
гуляние community celebration
гулять/погулять to walk, to stroll
гуманитарный humane
да yes
давать/дать to give

даже even
далеко far
дань tribute
даром free (at no cost)
дача country house (dacha)
дачник owner of a dacha
дверь door
двоюродная сестра cousin (female)
двоюродный брат cousin (male)
двухкомнатный two-room (adj.)
девочка girl
девушка young woman
дедушка grandfather
декабрь December
делать to do, to make
делать зарядку to do exercises
дело deed, business, affair (noun)
деловой business (adj.)
демократия democracy
демонстрация demonstration
день day
деньги money
деревня village
десерт dessert
десятилетие decade
дети children
дефицит deficit
дешёвый cheap
джинсы jeans
диван couch
диплом diploma
директор director
дискотека dance club, night club
дневник diary, journal
до свидания good-bye
до скорой встречи until
   our next meeting
добираться/добраться to
   get somewhere
доброе утро good morning
доброй ночи have a good night
добрый kind
добрый вечер good evening
добрый день good afternoon
доверять to trust
довоенный pre-war

доиграть   to finish playing
доктор   doctor
документ   document
долг   debt
долгий   long
дом   house
домашний   domestic
доносить/донести   to deliver to
дописывать/дописать   to
   finish writing
дорога   road, way
дорогой   expensive
дочка   daughter
дочь   daughter
друг   friend
другой   different
дружить   to be friends with
думать/подумать   to think
душ   shower
душный   stuffy
дядя   uncle
Египет   Egypt
египетский   Egyptian
еда   food
ездить   to go by vehicle
ёлка   pine tree, Christmas tree
ель   pine tree
ерунда   nonsense
если   if
есть/поесть   to eat
ехать/приехать   to go by
   vehicle/to come by vehicle
жалкий   pitiful
жалоба   complaint
жаркий   hot
ждать   to wait
желание   wish, desire
жёлтый   yellow
жена   wife
жених   groom, fiancé
женский   women's
женщина   woman
живот   stomach
жительство   residence
жить   to live
житьё   life

жук   beetle
журнал   journal, magazine
за   behind, after
забегать/забежать   to run in
заболевание   illness
заболеть   to fall ill
заварка   strong tea
завещание   will
зависимый   dependent
завод   factory, plant
завтра   tomorrow
завтрак   breakfast
завтракать/позавтракать   to
   have breakfast
заговорить   to start a conversation
заграница   abroad (noun)
заграничный   foreign
задание   assignment
задерживаться/
   задержаться   to be late
задержка   delay
заём   loan
заждаться   to get tired of waiting
зайти   to drop in
заказывать/заказать   to order
закрывать/закрыть   to close
закуска   appetizer
заложить   to put, to pawn
замолчать   to go silent, be quiet
занести   to drop off
заниматься   to study,
   to take interest in
занят   busy
занятие   class
запеть   to start singing
записывать/записать   to write down
заполнить   to fill, to fill out
зарплата   wage
засасывать   to suck in
зашить   to sew up
зашиться   to be wiped
   out (colloquial)
заявление   statement,
   application, announcement
звать/позвать   to call
звонить   to call on the phone

здание building
здесь here
здоровье health
здравие well-being
здравствовать to be well and healthy
здравствуйте hello
зелёный green
земля ground, earth, land
зеркало mirror
зима winter
злиться to get angry
знакомство acquaintance
знать to know
зуб tooth
зять son-in-law
и and
игра game
играть/поиграть to play
игрок player
игрушка toy
идея idea
идти/прийти to go/to come
известный famous
извините excuse me/I am sorry
извиняться/извиниться to apologize
из-за because of, from behind of
из-под from beneath of
икона icon
иконостас place where icons are put up
икра caviar
иметь to own
иммиграционная служба immigration service
имя first name
инвалид disabled person
инженер engineer
иногда sometimes
институт institute
инструкция instruction manual
интересный interesting
Интернет the Internet
ирландский Irish
найти to find

искать to look for
искусство art
Испания Spain
испанский Spanish
исполнение fulfillment, performance
история history
Италия Italy
итальянский Italian
июль July
июнь June
к сожалению unfortunately
Кавказ the Caucasus
каждый each
как how
какой which, what
Канада Canada
канадец Canadian male
канадка Canadian female
канадский Canadian (adj.)
капуста cabbage
карандаш pencil
карта map
картина picture, film
картофель potatoes
касса checkout desk
кататься to ride
кафе coffee shop
кафедра university department
кафетерий cafeteria
каша kasha (a dish of cooked grain)
квартира apartment
квас kvas (a traditional Russian soft drink)
киевский Kievan
кино movie, movies
кинотеатр movie theater
Китай China
китайский Chinese
класс school grade
клетчатый checkered
клуб club
клубника strawberry
ключ key
книга book
книжный шкаф bookcase

княгиня   wife of a prince, princess
княжество   principality
княжна   unmarried
   daughter of a prince
князь   prince
ковёр   carpet, rug
когда   when
кожаный   leather (adj.)
Кока-кола   Coca-Cola
коктейль   milkshake
колбаса   sausage
коммуналка   communal apartment
комната   room
компьютер   computer
конечно   of course
консенсус   consensus
консул   consul
консульство   consulate
континент   continent
контрольный   control (adj.)
конфета   candy
концерт   concert
конь   horse
коньки   skates
коричневый   brown
кормить   to feed
костёр   bonfire
костюм   suit, costume
кот   cat (male)
кофе   coffee
кофеварка   coffee machine
конфликт   conflict
кофта   sweater, sweatshirt
кран   tap, faucet
краса   beauty (dated)
красавец   handsome man
красавица   beautiful woman
красивый   beautiful
краситься   to put on makeup
красный   red
красоваться   to show off
красота   beauty
кредит   credit
кресло   armchair
кричать   to shout
кровать   bed

кровотечение   bleeding (noun)
ксерокс   copy machine, Xerox copy
кто   who
культура   culture
купол   dome
курить/закурить   to smoke
курица   chicken
курсовой   course (adj.)
куртка   jacket, coat
кухня   kitchen, cuisine
ладно   okay
лампа   lamp
лежать   to lie
лекарство   medicine
лекарь   doctor (dated)
лекция   lecture
лес   forest
лето   summer
лётчик   pilot
лечение   treatment (medical)
лечить/вылечить   to
   treat (medically)
лингвистика   linguistics
лист   leaf
литература   literature
лицо   face
лишний   extra, superfluous
лодка   boat
лубки   folk pictures
лыжи   skies
любимый   favorite
любить   to love
люди   people
магазин   shop, store
магнитофон   stereo
май   May
мак   poppy seeds
макароны   pasta
маленький   small
мальчик   boy
мама   mom
маниловщина   tendency to
   dream instead of acting
манить   to tempt, pull toward
марка   stamp
март   March

Масленица Maslenitsa, Russia's pre-Lent pancake celebration
масло butter
математика mathematics
материал material
матч match (sports)
мать mother
машина car
мебель furniture
мёд honey
медицина medicine
между between
международный international
межпланетный interplanetary
Мексика Mexico
мексиканский Mexican
менеджер manager
меню menu
место place
месяц month
метро metro
меховой fur (adj.)
микроволновая печь microwave oven
милиция police
минута minute
мир peace, world
младший younger
много many
мобильный телефон cell phone
модель model
модный trendy
может быть maybe
можно allowed, permitted
мой my
молодец Well done! Good job! (literally, fine fellow)
молодой young
молодой человек young man, boyfriend
молоко milk
молчать to be quiet
море sea
морковь carrot
мороженое ice cream
мороз frost

мотоцикл motorcycle
мочь to be able
муж husband
мужской men's
мужчина man
музей museum
музыка music
мы we
мыть to wash
мягкий знак soft sign
мягкий soft
мясо meat
мяч ball
надежда hope (noun)
надеяться to hope
надо need
найти to find
наконец finally
налево to the left
наличные cash
налог tax
нападать to attack
напиток drink
направо to the right
народ people
народный folk
насмешить to make (someone) laugh
наспех in a hurry
настоящий real, genuine
настроение mood
наука science
научный scientific
находиться to be located
национальность nationality
начало beginning
начинать to begin
наш our
Не за что. Don't mention it.
небо sky
небольшой small
небоскрёб skyscraper
невеста bride
невестка daughter-in-law
невкусный not tasty
недвижимость real estate

неделя   week
недешёвый   not cheap
недоверие   mistrust
недоделать   to do incompletely
недоесть   to not finish eating
недорогой   inexpensive
недоспать   to not get enough sleep
независимость   independence
независимый   independent
неинтересный   not interesting
некрасивый   homely, ugly
нельзя   not allowed, prohibited
немаленький   large (not small)
немедленно   at once, immediately
немецкий   German
неожиданный   unexpected
неосторожность   carelessness
неосторожный   careless
неплохой   not bad
неприятный   unpleasant
нервы   nerves
несвежий   not fresh
нестрашный   not scary
нет   no
неудобный   inconvenient,
   embarrassing
неуклюжий   clumsy
нехороший   bad
никак   by no means, in no way
никогда   never
никто   no one, nobody
ничего   nothing, it's all right
   / no big deal (colloquial)
но   but
новость   news (sing.)
новый   new
нож   knife
номер   number
номер рейса   flight number
нора   hole, burrow
ночь   night
ноябрь   November
нравиться   to like
нужно   need
обаятельный   charming
обед   lunch

обедать/пообедать   to have lunch
обида   offence
обидный   offensive
обкрадывать/обокрасть   to rob
обмен   exchange (noun)
образование   education
общежитие   dormitory
общественный   public
объезд   detour
объявление   announcement
объяснение   explanation
объяснять/объяснить   to explain
обычай   custom
обычно   usually
обязательно   by all
   means, necessarily
овощи   vegetables (plural)
огромный   huge
огурец   cucumber
одежда   clothes (sing.)
однокомнатный   one-room
озеро   lake
окно   window
октябрь   October
олигарх   oligarch
он   he
она   she
они   they
оно   it
опаздывать   to be late
опасный   dangerous
опера   opera
описывать/описать   to describe
опоздание   delay
оранжевый   orange
осень   fall, autumn
осколок   broken piece, shard
остановка   stop
осторожно   caution
осторожный   careful
остров   island
ответ   answer
отвечать/ответить   to answer
отдых   rest
отдыхать/отдохнуть   to
   rest, to be on vacation

отель hotel
отец father
открывать/открыть to open
отмывание денег money laundering
отнести to carry away/off
отношение attitude, relation
отойти to walk off
отчество patronymic
отчим stepfather
отъезд departure
офицер officer
официант waiter
официантка waitress
охота hunting
очень very
паб pub
падеж grammatical case
падчерица stepdaughter
пальто coat
папа dad
парк park
паспорт passport
пасынок stepson
певец singer (male)
певица singer (female)
педагогика pedagogy
пельмени Russian
   dumplings, pelmeni
пенсионер a retiree
первый first
перед in front of, before
передумать to change
   one's mind, rethink
перенести to carry over
переписывать/переписать to
   copy down (in writing)
перестать to stop
переход crosswalk
переходить to walk across
перец pepper
перо feather, quill
перчатки gloves
петь to sing
печальный sad
печка oven
печь to bake

пешком on foot
пианино piano
пивная beerhouse
пиджак jacket
пилот pilot
пирог pie
писатель writer (male)
писательница writer (female)
писать to write
письмо letter
пить to drink
плавать to swim
плакать/заплакать to cry
планета planet
платить/заплатить to pay
платок headscarf
платье dress
плач crying, weeping (noun)
племя tribe
племянник nephew
племянница niece
плита stove
плохой bad
площадь square, plaza
повар cook (male)
повариха cook (female)
повесть short story
поворачивать to turn
повторить to repeat
поговорка proverb
погода weather
пограничник border guard
подарить to give as a present
подарок gift
подземелье underground (noun)
подземный underground (adj.)
поднимать to lift, to raise
подписывать/подписать to sign
подпись signature
подсказать to prompt
подъезд entrance to building
поезд train
поездка trip
пожалуйста please,
   you are welcome
пожар fire

позвать   to call, to invite
позволять   to allow
позвоночник   spine
поздний   late
поздравлять   to congratulate
поймать   to catch
пока   bye, while, yet
показывать/показать   to show
покупатель   buyer
покупать/купить   to buy
пол   floor
полдник   light meal between
  lunch and dinner
полка   shelf
положить   to put
полоска   stripe
получать/получить   to get, receive
получиться   to work out
полчаса   half-hour
полюбить   to fall in love with,
  to develop a liking for
померить   to try on
помидор   tomato
помнить   to remember
помогать/помочь   to help
помощь   help (noun)
понедельник   Monday
понимать/понять   to understand
попугай   parrot
послать   to send
после   after
послевоенный   post-war
пословица   saying
посольство   embassy
поспешить   to hurry
Пост   Lent
постоянный   permanent
Строить/построить   to build
посуда   dishes (sing.)
потерять   to lose
потолок   ceiling
потом   then, afterwards
потому, что   because
почему   why
починить   to fix
почта   post office

поэт   poet (male)
поэтесса   poet (female)
правда   truth
право   right, law
православие   Russian Orthodoxy
православный   Russian Orthodox
правый   right
праздник   holiday (noun)
праздничный   holiday (adj.)
прайс-лист   price list
предлагать   to offer, suggest
предмет   subject, discipline
президент   president
прекрасный   wonderful
преподаватель   instructor
  (university/college)
пресный   fresh
привет   hello
приглашать   to invite
приглашение   invitation
придумать   to come up with
примерочная   fitting room
принести   to bring
принимать/ принять   to
  accept, to take
приписывать/приписать   to
  add in writing
прислоняться   to lean
приходить   to come
прихожая   hallway
пришить   to sew
Приятного аппетита!   Bon appetit!
проверять/проверить   to verify
провожать/проводить   to
  see off, accompany
прогноз   forecast
продавец   salesman
продавщица   saleswoman
продукт   product
продуктовый   grocery (adj.)
проиграть   to lose
проигрыш   loss
происходить   to happen
пройти   to walk through
просить/попросить   to ask for
Простите.   Excuse me. / I am sorry.

про́сьба request
профе́ссия occupation
профе́ссор professor
проходи́ть to walk by
проце́нтная ста́вка interest rate
проща́йте farewell
пры́гать/пры́гнуть to jump
пря́мо straight
пря́тки hide-and-seek
психоло́гия psychology
пу́блика public
пусть let it be, let (someone do something)
путеше́ствие travel, trip
путь way
пылесо́с vacuum cleaner
пье́са play
пя́тница Friday
рабо́та work
рабо́тать/порабо́тать to work
рабо́чая manual worker (female)
рабо́чий manual worker (male)
рад glad
ра́дио radio
ра́дость joy
раз time
разби́ть to break
разви́тие development
разгова́ривать to talk, converse
разме́р size
разорва́ть to tear apart
разреши́ть to allow
разру́шить to destroy
ра́нний early
расска́з story
расска́зывать/рассказа́ть to tell
ребёнок child
ребя́та guys
револю́ция revolution
ре́дко rarely
рейс flight
река́ river
ремо́нт repair works, renovation
рестора́н restaurant
рисова́ть to draw
ро́дственник relative

рожде́ние birth
ро́зовый pink
рома́н novel
Росси́йская Федера́ция Russian Federation
Росси́я Russia
россия́нин Russian citizen (male)
россия́нка Russian citizen (female)
рост height
рот mouth
руба́шка shirt
рубль ruble
ру́сский Russian
ру́чка pen
ры́ба fish
ры́нок market
рыть to dig
ря́дом с next to
сад garden, orchard
сади́ться to sit down
сажа́ть to plant
саксофо́н saxophone
сала́т salad
самова́р samovar
санато́рий spa resort
све́жий fresh
свёкр father-in-law on husband's side
свекро́вь mother-in-law on husband's side
светло́ light (adj.)
свини́на pork
сви́стнуть to whistle
сви́тер sweater
свобо́дный free
свой own (pronoun)
свято́й saint
сглаз evil eye
сего́дня today
сейча́с now
секре́т secret
сёмга salmon
семья́ family
сентя́брь September
се́рый grey
сестра́ sister

сидеть   to sit
симпатичный   good-looking
синий   navy blue
сирота   orphan
сказать   to say
сказка   fairy tale
сколько   how much, how many
скорая помощь   ambulance
скоро   soon
скрипка   violin
скучный   boring
сладкий   sweet
следующий   next
словарь   dictionary
слово   word
сломать   to break something
сломаться   to break
случиться   to happen
слушать/послушать   to listen
слышать   to hear
сметана   sour cream
смеяться   to laugh
смотреть   to watch
снег   snow
собака   dog
собеседник   conversation partner
собор   cathedral
собственность   property
советовать   to advise
совсем   thoroughly, at all
сок   juice
солдат   soldier
солёный   salty
солнце   sun
соль   salt
сотрудник   coworker
спальня   bedroom
спасибо   thank you
спектакль   performance
специи   spices
спешить   to hurry
список   list
Спокойной ночи!   Good
  night! (before bed)
спор   debate
спорт   sports

спортсмен   athlete
спрашивать/спросить   to ask
среда   Wednesday
ссора   argument
стадион   stadium
становиться/стать   to become
станция   station
старт   start
старый   old
статья   article
стена   wall
стиральная машина   washing
  machine
стихотворение   poem
стоить   to cost
стол   table
столовая   cafeteria, dining room
стоп   stop
страна   country
страница   page
страшный   terrifying
строитель   builder
студент   student (male)
студентка   student (female)
стул   chair
стюард   flight attendant (male)
стюардесса   flight attendant (female)
суббота   Saturday
субтитры   subtitles
сумасшедший   crazy
сумка   bag, purse
суп   soup
существовать   to exist
Счастливо!   All the best!
счастье   happiness
счёт   bill
считать   to count, to believe
съёмка   film shooting
сын   son
сыр   cheese
сырой   damp
так   so
такси   taxi
талантливый   talented
там   there
таможенная инспекция   customs
  inspection

таможня customs
танцевать to dance
тарелка plate
твёрдый знак hard sign
твёрдый hard
твой your (sing., informal)
театр theater
текст text
телевизор TV set
телефон telephone
тело body
телохранитель bodyguard
тема theme
тёмный dark
температура temperature
теннис tennis
тёплый warm
территория territory
тесть father-in-law on wife's side
тетрадь notebook
тётя aunt
тёща mother-in-law on wife's side
тихий quiet
товар good, commodity, product
товарищ comrade, friend
том tome, volume
торт cake
традиция tradition
трамвай tram
тратить to spend
троллейбус trolleybus
труд work, labor
трудный difficult
трудолюбивый hardworking
туалет bathroom
тумбочка bed stand
турист tourist (male)
туристка tourist (female)
туфли shoes
тухнуть to rot
ты you (sing., informal)
тяжёлый heavy, difficult
тяжесть weight, heaviness
Убирать to tidy up
уверен sure
удобный comfortable

удовольствие pleasure
ужасный terrible
уже already
ужин dinner
ужинать/поужинать to have dinner
улица street
улыбка smile
ультрамодный ultra-trendy
ультраправый ultra-right
ум wit
уметь to be capable of
умный clever
универмаг supermarket
универсальный universal
университет university
Ура! hooray!
Урал the Urals
урок class, lesson
успевать/успеть to be on time
утро morning
учебник textbook
учёный scientist
учитель teacher (male)
учительница teacher (female)
учить to teach
учиться/научиться to learn
ушанка fur hat with ear flaps
факультет college,
    university department
Фамилия last name
фармацевт, аптекарь pharmacist
февраль February
физика physics
Фонтан fountain
Фотоаппарат camera
Фотографировать/
    сфотографировать to photograph
Франция France
Французский French
Фрукты fruits (pl.)
футбол soccer
хвост tail
химия chemistry
хип-хоп hip-hop
хлеб bread
хлопоты worries

хлопчатобумажный cotton (adj.)
хобби hobby
ходить to go
ходьба walking
хоккей hockey
холодильник refrigerator
холодный cold
хороший good
хотеть to want
хотя although
хохот laughter, roar
христианство Christianity
хрустальный crystal
художник painter (male)
художница painter (female)
худой thin, bad
царевич son of a tsar
царевна daughter of a tsar
царица tsarina
царство country ruled by a tsar
царь tsar
цвет color
цветок flower
целый whole
цель goal, purpose
центр center, downtown
центральный central
церковь church
цирк circus
чаевые tip
чаепитие tea drinking
чай tea
частный private
часто often
чашка cup
человек human being, man, person
чемодан suitcase
Чёрное море the Black Sea
Чёрный black
четверг Thursday
число date, number, digit
чистить to clean
читать to read
читать лекцию to read a lecture
что what
чтобы in order to, so that

чужой alien (adj.), strange, other
чуть-чуть a little bit
шаль shawl
шапка hat
шарады charades
шарф scarf
шахматы chess
шёлковый silk (adj.)
шерстяной wool (adj.)
шкаф wardrobe
школа school
школьник pupil
шоколад chocolate (noun)
шоу show
шуба fur coat
шум noise
экзамен exam
экскурсия excursion, tour
электроника electronics
этимологический etymological
этот this
Эфиопия Ethiopia
эфиопский Ethiopian
Юбка skirt
юриспруденция jurisprudence
юрист lawyer
я I
яблоко apple
язык language
язычество paganism
январь January
Япония Japan
японский Japanese
яркий bright
ясли nursery
ясный clear
яхта yacht

English-to-Russian Glossary

a little bit   чуть-чуть
abroad (noun)   заграница
accept   принимать/принять
accountant   бухгалтер
acquaintance   знакомство
  (concept) знакомый (person)
actor   актёр
actress   актриса
add in writing   приписывать/
  приписать
advise   советовать
after   за, после
afterwards   потом
age   возраст
agency   агентство
airport   аэропорт
alarm clock   будильник
algebra   алгебра
all   весь
All the best!   Всего хорошего!
allow   позволять, разрешить
allowed   можно
already   уже
altar   алтарь
although   хотя
always   всегда
ambulance   скорая помощь
American (noun)   американец
  (male)/ американка (female)
American (adj.)   американский
and   и, а
answer (noun)   ответ
answer (verb)   отвечать/ответить
anthropology   антропология
apartment   квартира
apologize   извиняться/извиниться
appetizer   закуска
apple   яблоко
application   заявление

April   апрель
architecture   архитектура
armchair   кресло
art   искусство
article   статья
ask   спрашивать/спросить
ask for   просить/попросить
assignment   задание
at once   немедленно
athlete   спортсмен
atom   атом
attack (noun)   атака
attack (verb)   нападать
attitude   отношение
attract   привлечь, манить
auction   аукцион
August   август
aunt   тётя
Australia   Австралия
Australian   австралийский
bad   плохой, нехороший
bag   сумка
bake   печь
ball   мяч
ballet   балет
bank (noun)   банк
bankruptcy   банкротство
bar   бар
baseball   бейсбол
basketball   баскетбол
bathroom   туалет (public)/
  ванная (private)
be   быть
be able   мочь
be friends with   дружить
be ill   болеть
be late   задерживаться/
  задержаться
be late   опаздывать

be located   находиться
be on time   успевать/успеть
be sick   болеть
be silent   молчать
be well and healthy   здравствовать
be wiped out   зашиться (colloquial)
beautiful   красивый
beautiful woman   красавица
beauty   красота, Краса (dated)
because   потому, что
because of   из-за
become   становиться/стать
bed   кровать
bed stand   тумбочка
bedroom   спальня
beef   говядина
beerhouse   пивная
beetle   жук
before   перед
begin   начинать
beginning   начало
behind   за
beige   бежевый
believe   верить
Bering Sea   Берингово море
between   между
bibliography   библиография
bicycle   велосипед
big   большой
bill (noun)   счёт
biology   биология
birth   рождение
bitter   горький
black   чёрный
Black Sea   Чёрное море
bleeding   кровотечение
blouse   блузка
blue   голубой (light)/синий (dark)
boat   Лодка
body   тело
bodyguard   телохранитель
Bon appetit!   Приятного аппетита!
bonfire   костёр
book   книга
bookcase   книжный шкаф
boots   ботинки

border   граница
border guard   пограничник
boring   скучный
borscht (Russian beet soup)   борщ
boy   мальчик
boyfriend   молодой человек, друг
Brazil   Бразилия
bread   хлеб
break (verb)   разбить, сломаться
break something   сломать
breakfast   завтрак
bride   невеста, fiancée
bright   яркий
bring   принести
bring something by vehicle
   возить/привозить
brother   брат
brown   коричневый
brush (verb)   чистить
build (verb)   строить/построить
builder   строитель
building   здание
burrow   нора
bus   автобус
business (adj.)   деловой
business (noun)   бизнес, дело
busy   занят
but   но, а
butter   масло
buy (verb)   покупать/купить
buyer   покупатель
by no means   никак
bye   пока
cab   такси
cabbage   капуста
cafeteria   кафетерий
cake   торт
call   Звать/позвать
call on the phone   Звонить
camera   Фотоаппарат
Canada   Канада
Canadian (adj.)   Канадский
Canadian female   Канадка
Canadian male   канадец
candy   конфета
car   машина

careful осторожный
careless неосторожный
carelessness неосторожность
carpet ковёр
carrot морковь
carry away отнести
carry out (verb) выносить/вынести
carry over перенести
case (in grammar) падеж
cash наличные
cat (male) кот
catch (verb) поймать
cathedral собор
Caucasus, the Кавказ
caution осторожно
caviar икра
ceiling потолок
celebration гуляние
cell phone мобильный телефон
central центральный
chair стул
change one's mind передумать
charades шарады
charming обаятельный
cheap дешёвый
checkered клетчатый
checkout desk касса
cheerful весёлый
cheese сыр
chemistry химия
chess шахматы
chicken (noun) курица
child ребёнок
children дети
China Китай
Chinese китайский
chocolate (noun) шоколад
Christianity христианство
church (noun) церковь
circus цирк
citizen гражданин
city город
class занятие, урок
clear ясный
clever умный
close близко

close (verb) закрывать/закрыть
clothes одежда (sing.)
club клуб
clumsy неуклюжий
coat пальто
Coca-Cola Кока-кола
coffee кофе
coffee shop кафе
coffee machine кофеварка
cold (adj.) холодный
color цвет
come приходить/прийти
come by vehicle приехать
come up with придумать
comfortable удобный
complaint жалоба
computer компьютер
comrade товарищ
concert концерт
conflict конфликт
congratulate поздравлять
connections блат
consensus консенсус
consul консул
consulate консульство
continent континент
control (adj.) контрольный
conversation беседа
conversation partner собеседник
cook повар (male)/
    повариха (female)
copy down (verb) переписывать/
    переписать
copy machine ксерокс
cost (verb) стоить
cotton (adj.) хлопчатобумажный
couch диван
count (verb) считать
country страна
course (adj.) курсовой
cousin двоюродный брат (male)/
    двоюродная сестра (female)
coworker сотрудник
crazy сумасшедший
credit кредит
crosswalk переход

crying (noun) плач
cry (verb) плакать/заплакать
crystal хрустальный
cucumber огурец
cuisine кухня
culture культура
cup чашка
cure (verb) вылечивать/вылечить
currency валюта
custom обычай
customs таможенная
  инспекция, таможня
dacha дача
dad папа
dance club (noun) ночной
  клуб, дискотека (dated)
dance (verb) танцевать
dangerous опасный
dark тёмный
date (noun) число, дата
daughter дочка, дочь
daughter-in-law невестка
day день
debate спор
debt долг
decade десятилетие
December декабрь
deed дело
deficit дефицит
delay задержка, опоздание
delicious вкусный
deliver доносить/донести
democracy демократия
demonstration демонстрация
department (at a
  university) Факультет
departure отъезд
dependent зависимый
describe описывать/описать
dessert десерт
destroy разрушить
detour объезд
development развитие
diary дневник
dictionary словарь
different другой

difficult Трудный
dig (verb) рыть
dining room столовая
dinner ужин
diploma диплом
director директор
disabled person инвалид
discipline (noun) предмет
dish блюдо
dishes посуда (sing.)
disinterested неинтересный
do делать
do incompletely недоделать
doctor врач, доктор, лекарь (dated)
document документ
dog собака
dome купол
domestic домашний
Don't mention it. Не за что.
door дверь
dormitory общежитие
downtown центр
draw (verb) рисовать
dress (noun) платье
drink (noun) напиток
drink (verb) пить
driver водитель
drop in зайти
drop off занести
dumplings пельмени
each каждый
early ранний
eat есть/поесть
education образование
Egypt Египет
Egyptian египетский
electronics электроника
embassy посольство
enemy враг
engineer инженер
england Англия
English (adj.) английский
Englishman англичанин
Englishwoman англичанка
entrance вход
Ethiopia Эфиопия

Ethiopian эфиопский
etymological этимологический
even даже
evening вечер
everybody все
everyday life быт
everything всё
evil eye сглаз
exam экзамен
exchange (noun) обмен
excursion экскурсия
Excuse me. Извините!, Простите!
exercize делать зарядку
exist существовать
exit выход
expensive дорогой
expensive недешёвый
explain объяснять/объяснить
explanation объяснение
extra лишний
eye глаз
fable басня
face лицо
fairy tale сказка
faith вера
fall (noun) осень
fall ill заболеть
fall in love with something
   полюбить
family семья
famous известный
far далеко
farewell прощайте
father отец
father-in-law on husband's side
   свёкр
father-in-law on wife's side тесть
faucet кран
favorite любимый
feather перо
february февраль
feed (verb) кормить
fiancé жених
fill out заполнить
film shooting съёмка
finally наконец

find (verb) найти
finish playing доиграть
finish writing дописывать/дописать
fire пожар
first первый
first name имя
fish рыба
fitting room примерочная
fix (verb) починить
flight рейс
flight attendant стюард (male)/
   стюардесса (female)
floor пол
flower цветок
fly out вылетать/вылететь
folk (adj.) народный
folk pictures Лубки
food еда
foolishness глупость
football американский футбол
forecast прогноз
foreign заграничный
forest лес
form бланк
fountain фонтан
France Франция
free свободный, даром (at no cost)
French французский
fresh свежий
fresh (water) пресный
Friday пятница
friend друг
from behind из-за
from beneath из-под
frost мороз
fruit фрукты (pl.)
fulfillment исполнение
fur (adj.) меховой
fur coat шуба
fur hat ушанка
furniture мебель
game игра
garage гараж
garden сад
geography география
German немецкий

Germany Германия
get angry злиться
get better (in health) выздоравливать/выздороветь
get silent замолчать
get somewhere добираться/добраться
get tired of waiting for заждаться
get up вставать/встать
gift подарок
girl девочка, девушка
give (verb) давать/дать
give as a present дарить/подарить
glad рад
gloves перчатки
go идти, ходить
go by vehicle ехать, ездить
goal цель
good (adj.) хороший, неплохой
Good afternoon! Добрый день!
Good evening! Добрый вечер!
Good morning! Доброе утро!
Good night! Доброй ночи!, Спокойной ночи! (before bed)
Good-bye! До свидания!
good-looking симпатичный
goods товар (sing.)
grade (in school) класс
granddaughter внучка
grandfather дедушка
grandmother бабушка
grandson внук
gratitude благодарность
great великий
Greece Греция
Greek греческий
green зелёный
grey серый
grocery (adj.) продуктовый
groom жених
ground земля
grow up вырастать/вырасти
guest гость
guilty виноватый
guitar гитара
guys ребята

hair волосы (pl.)
half-hour полчаса
hallway прихожая
handsome man красавец
happen происходить, случиться
happiness счастье
hard твёрдый, трудный
hard sign твёрдый знак
hardworking трудолюбивый
hat шапка
have breakfast завтракать/позавтракать
have lunch обедать/пообедать
have dinner ужинать/поужинать
he он
head (noun) голова
headscarf платок
health здоровье
hear слышать
heaviness тяжесть
heavy тяжёлый
height рост
hello здравствуйте
help (noun) помощь
help (verb) помогать/помочь
here здесь
hi привет
hide-and-seek прятки
higher высший
hip-hop хип-хоп
history история
hobby хобби
hockey хоккей
holiday (adj.) праздничный
holiday (noun) праздник
homely некрасивый
honey мёд
hooray ура
hope (noun) надежда
hope (verb) надеяться
horse конь
hospital больница
hot горячий (to the touch), жаркий (outside), острый (spicy)
hotel отель, гостиница
house дом

how как
how many сколько
how much сколько
huge огромный
human being человек
humane гуманитарный
hunting охота
hurry (verb) спешить/поспешить
husband муж
I я
I am sorry. Извините!, Простите!
ice cream мороженое
icon икона
idea идея
if если
illness болезнь, заболевание
immigration service
    иммиграционная служба
in a hurry наспех
in front of перед
in order to чтобы
inconvenient неудобный
independence независимость
independent независимый
inexpensive недорогой
inhumane антигуманитарный
write in вписывать/вписать
institute институт
instruction manual инструкция
instructor (at university/college)
    преподаватель
interest rate процентная ставка
interesting интересный
international международный
Internet Интернет
interplanetary межпланетный
invitation приглашение
invite (verb) приглашать, позвать
Irish ирландский
iron (verb) гладить
island остров
it оно
Italian итальянский
Italy Италия
jacket пиджак
jacket (knitted) куртка

jam (noun) варенье
January Январь
Japan Япония
Japanese японский
jeans джинсы
joy радость
juice сок
July июль
jump (verb) прыгать/прыгнуть
June июнь
jurisprudence юриспруденция
kasha каша
key ключ
Kievan киевский
kind (adj.) добрый
kitchen кухня
knife нож
know знать
know how (to do something) уметь
kvas квас
lake озеро
lamp лампа
land земля
language язык
large большой, немаленький
last name фамилия
late поздний
laugh (verb) смеяться
laughter хохот
law закон, право
lawyer юрист
leaf лист
lean (verb) прислоняться
learn учиться/научиться
leather (adj.) кожаный
lecture лекция
lecture hall аудитория
lecture in a non-educational
    setting читать нотации
Lent Великий Пост
letter письмо
library библиотека
lie (verb) лежать
life жизнь, житьё
lift (verb) поднимать
light (adj.) светлый

like (verb) нравиться
linguistics лингвистика
list список
listen слушать/послушать
literature литература
live жить
living room гостиная
loan заём
long долгий (time), длинный
  (measurable, i.e. 'long list')
look смотреть
look for искать
lose (verb) потерять, проиграть
loss проигрыш
loud громкий
love (verb) любить
lunch обед
madam госпожа
magazine журнал
make (verb) делать
make laugh насмешить
man мужчина
manager менеджер
manual worker рабочий
many много
map карта
March март
market рынок
Maslenitsa Масленица
match (sports, noun) матч
material материал
mathematics математика
May (noun) май
maybe может быть
meat мясо
medicine лекарство, медицина
meet (verb) встречать/встретить
meeting встреча
men's мужской
menu меню
metro метро
Mexican мексиканский
Mexico Мексика
microwave oven микроволновая
  печь
milk молоко

milkshake коктейль
military serviceman военный
minute минута
mirror зеркало
mister господин
mistrust недоверие
model модель
mom мама
Monday понедельник
money деньги
money laundering отмывание денег
month месяц
mood настроение
morning утро
mother мать
mother-in-law on husband's
  side свекровь
mother-in-law on wife's side тёща
motorcycle мотоцикл
mountain гора
mouth рот
movie кино
movie theater кинотеатр
museum музей
mushroom гриб
music музыка
my мой
nationality национальность
necessarily обязательно
need надо, нужно
nephew племянник
nerves нервы
never никогда
new новый
news новость
newspaper газета
next (adj.) следующий
next to рядом с
niece племянница
night ночь
night club ночной клуб
no нет
no one никто
nobody никто
noise шум
nonsense ерунда

normally обычно
not finish eating недоесть
not get enough sleep недоспать
notebook тетрадь
nothing ничего
novel роман
short story повесть
November ноябрь
now сейчас
number номер
nursery ясли
occupation профессия
October октябрь
of course конечно
offence обида
offensive обидный
offer (verb) предлагать
officer офицер
often часто
okay ладно
old старый
oligarch олигарх
on foot пешком
one-room однокомнатный
open (verb) открывать/открыть
opera опера
orange (adj.) оранжевый
orange (noun) апельсин
order (verb) заказывать/заказать
orphan сирота
our наш
oven печка
own (pronoun) свой
own (verb) иметь
owner владелец
paganism язычество
page страница
pain боль
painter художник
pancake блин
pants брюки
paper бумага
park (noun) парк
parrot попугай
party вечеринка; партия (political)
party functionary
   (Soviet) аппаратчик

passport паспорт
pasta макароны
patient (noun) больной
patronymic отчество
pawn (verb) заложить
pay (verb) платить/заплатить
peace мир
pear груша
pedagogy педагогика
pen ручка
pencil карандаш
people люди, народ
pepper перец
performance спектакль
performer артист (male)/
   артистка (female)
permanent постоянный
pharmacist фармацевт, аптекарь
pharmacy аптека
physics физика
piano пианино
picture картина
pie пирог
pilot лётчик, пилот
pine tree ёлка, ель
pink розовый
pitiful жалкий
place место
planet планета
plant (noun) завод
plant (verb) сажать
plate тарелка
play (noun) пьеса
play (verb) играть/поиграть
player игрок
plaza площадь
please пожалуйста
pleasure удовольствие
poem стихотворение
poet поэт
police милиция
polka dots горошек
pool бассейн
poppy seed мак
pork свинина
possibly возможно
post office почта

post-war послевоенный

potatoes картофель

pour into вливать/влить

power власть

prepare готовить/приготовить

prepare oneself готовиться/
   приготовиться

president президент

pre-war довоенный

price list прайс-лист

prince князь

private частный

prize выигрыш

product продукт

professor профессор

prohibited нельзя

prompt (verb) подсказать

property собственность

proverb поговорка

psychology психология

pub паб

public (adj.) общественный

public (noun) публика

pupil школьник

put положить

put on makeup краситься

quarrel (noun) ссора

question вопрос

quiet тихий

radio радио

raise (verb) поднимать

rarely редко

read (verb) читать

ready готовый

real настоящий

real estate недвижимость

receive получать/получить

red красный

refrigerator холодильник

relative родственник

remember помнить

repairs ремонт

repeat (verb) повторить

request просьба

residence жительство

rest (noun) отдых

rest (verb) отдыхать/отдохнуть

restaurant ресторан

retiree пенсионер

return something возвращать/
   вернуть

revolution революция

ride (verb) кататься

right (adj.) правый

right (noun) право

river река

road дорога

rob обкрадывать/обокрасть

room комната

rot тухнуть

routine быт

ruble рубль

run (verb) бежать

run in забегать/забежать

Russia Россия

Russian русский

Russian bathhouse баня

Russian citizen россиянин
   (male)/ россиянка (female)

Russian Federation Российская
   Федерация

Russian Orthodox православный

Russian Orthodoxy православие

sad грустный, печальный

safe безопасный

safety безопасность

saint святой

salad салат

salesman продавец

saleswoman продавщица

salmon сёмга

salt соль

salty солёный

samovar самовар

Saturday суббота

sausage колбаса

saxophone саксофон

say (verb) говорить/сказать

saying пословица

scarf шарф

school школа

science наука

scientific научный
scientist учёный
sea море
season время года
secret (noun) секрет
see видеть/увидеть
see off провожать/проводить
send послать
send for вызывать/вызвать
September сентябрь
shared apartment коммуналка
shawl шаль
she она
shelf (noun) полка
shirt рубашка
shoes туфли
shop магазин
shout (verb) кричать
show (noun) шоу
show (verb) показывать/показать
show off (verb) красоваться
shower душ
shudder вздрагивать/вздрогнуть
sickness болезнь
sign (verb) подписывать/подписать
signature подпись
silk (adj.) шёлковый
sing петь
singer певец (male)/ певица (female)
sister сестра
sit сидеть
sit down садиться
size (noun) размер
skates коньки
skis лыжи
skirt юбка
sky небо
skyscraper небоскрёб
small маленький, небольшой
smile улыбка
smoke (verb) курить/закурить
snow (noun) снег
so так
soccer футбол
soft мягкий
soft sign мягкий знак
soldier солдат

sometimes иногда
son сын
son-in-law зять
soon скоро
soup суп
sour cream сметана
sew (verb) пришить
sew up зашить
spa resort санаторий
Spain Испания
Spanish испанский
sparrow воробей
spend (verb) тратить
spices специи
spine позвоночник
sports спорт
sports coat куртка
spring (noun) весна
square площадь
stadium стадион
stamp марка
start (noun) старт
start a conversation заговорить
start singing запеть
state (adj.) государственный
station станция
stepdaughter падчерица
stepfather отчим
stepson пасынок
stereo магнитофон
stomach живот
stop (noun) остановка, стоп
stop (verb) перестать
store story рассказ
    магазин
stove плита
straight прямо
strange чужой
strawberry клубника
street улица
stripe полоска
stroll (verb) гулять/погулять
student студент (male)/
    студентка (female)
study (verb) готовиться/
    приготовиться, заниматься
stuffy душный

subtitles субтитры
suck in засасывать
suddenly вдруг
suit костюм
suitcase чемодан
summer лето
summon (verb) вызывать/вызвать
sun солнце
Sunday воскресенье
supermarket универмаг
sure уверен
swamp болото
sweater свитер, кофта
sweet сладкий
swim (verb) плавать
table стол
tail хвост
take (verb) брать/взять
take a photograph
   фотографировать/
   сфотографировать
talented талантливый
talk (verb) разговаривать
tax налог
tea чай
tea drinking чаепитие
teach учить
teacher учитель
tear apart разорвать
telephone телефон
tell рассказывать/рассказать
temperature температура
tennis теннис
terrible ужасный
terrifying страшный
territory территория
text текст
textbook учебник
thank (verb) благодарить
thank you спасибо
theater театр
theme тема
then потом
there там
they они
thief вор

thin худой
thing вещь
think думать/подумать
this этот
thoroughly совсем
Thursday четверг
tidy up убирать
tie галстук
time время, раз
tip чаевые
to the left налево
to the right направо
today сегодня
together вместе
tomato помидор
tome том
tomorrow завтра
tooth зуб
tour экскурсия
tourist турист
toy игрушка
tradition традиция
train (noun) поезд
train station вокзал
tram трамвай
travel (noun) путешествие
treat (medically) (verb) лечить/
   вылечить
treatment (medical) лечение
trendy модный
tribe племя
tribute дань
trip поездка
trolleybus троллейбус
trust (verb) доверять
truth правда
try on померить
tsar царь
Tuesday вторник
turn (verb) поворачивать
TV set телевизор
two-room (adj.) двухкомнатный
ultra-trendy ультрамодный
ultra-right ультраправый
uncle дядя
underground (adj.) подземный

underground (noun) подземелье
understand понимать/понять
unexpected неожиданный
unfortunately к сожалению
universal универсальный
university университет
university department кафедра
unpleasant неприятный
unscientific антинаучный
Urals Урал
vacuum cleaner пылесос
vase ваза
vegetables овощи (plural)
vegetarian (adj.) вегетарианский
verify проверять/проверить
very очень
veterinarian (noun) ветеринар
village деревня
violin скрипка
virus вирус
visa виза
visibility видимость
volleyball волейбол
wage зарплата
wait (verb) ждать
waiter официант
waitress официантка
walk (verb) гулять/погулять
walk across (verb) переходить
walk by проходить
walk off отойти
walk the dog выгуливать/выгулять
walk through пройти
walking ходьба
wall стена
want (verb) хотеть
war война
wardrobe шкаф
warm тёплый
wash (verb) мыть
washing machine стиральная
  машина
watch (verb) смотреть
water вода
watercolor акварель
way путь

we мы
weather погода
Wednesday среда
week неделя
well-being здравие
wet мокрый
what какой, что
when когда
where где
which какой
while в то время, как; пока
whistle (verb) свистнуть
white белый
who кто
whole целый
why почему
widow вдова
widower вдовец
wife жена
will (noun) завещание
win (verb) выигрывать/выиграть
window окно
wine вино
winter зима
wish (noun) желание
wit ум
woman женщина
women's женский
wonderful прекрасный
woods бор
wool (adj.) шерстяной
word (noun) слово
work (noun) работа, труд
work (verb) работать/поработать
work out (verb) получиться
world мир
worries хлопоты
write писать
write down записывать/записать
write out (verb) выписывать/
  выписать
writer писатель (male)/
  писательница (female)
xerox copy ксерокс
yacht яхта
yellow жёлтый

yes   да
yesterday   вчера
yet   пока
you   ты (sing., informal)/
   вы (pl., formal)
you are welcome   пожалуйста
young   молодой
younger   младший
your   твой (sing., informal)/
   ваш (pl., formal)

Index